Using

MICROSOFT®

Word 97

que®

Laurie Ann Ulrich

Using Microsoft® Word 97

Library of Congress Catalog No.: 97-68707

ISBN: 0-7897-1441-8

99 98 97   6 5 4 3 2

Interpretation of the printing code: the rightmost double-digit number is the year of the book's printing; the rightmost single-digit number, the number of the book's printing. For example, a printing code of 97-1 shows that the first printing of the book occurred in 1997.

Screen reproductions in this book were created using Collage Plus from Inner Media, Inc., Hollis, NH.

Contents at a Glance

Table of Contents

IV | Word and The Web

V | Office 97 Integration and Automation

Credits

PRESIDENT
Roland Elgey

SENIOR VICE PRESIDENT/PUBLISHING
Don Fowley

PUBLISHER
Joseph B. Wikert

GENERAL MANAGER
Joe Muldoon

MANAGER OF PUBLISHING OPERATIONS
Linda H. Buehler

PUBLISHING DIRECTOR
Karen Reinisch

EDITORIAL SERVICES DIRECTOR
Carla Hall

MANAGING EDITOR
Thomas F. Hayes

ACQUISITIONS MANAGER
Cheryl D. Willoughby

ACQUISITIONS EDITOR
Don Essig

PRODUCT DIRECTOR
Rick Kughen

PRODUCTION EDITOR
Brian Sweany

EDITORS
Damon Jordan
San Dee Phillips

COORDINATOR OF EDITORIAL SERVICES
Maureen A. McDaniel

WEBMASTER
Thomas H. Bennett

PRODUCT MARKETING MANAGER
Kourtnaye Sturgeon

ASSISTANT PRODUCT MARKETING MANAGER
Gretchen Schlesinger

TECHNICAL EDITORS
Bill Bruns
Curtis Knight
John Purdum
Coletta Witherspoon

SOFTWARE SPECIALIST
David Garratt

ACQUISITIONS COORDINATOR
Michelle R. Newcomb

SOFTWARE RELATIONS COORDINATOR
Susan D. Gallagher

EDITORIAL ASSISTANTS
Jennifer L. Chisholm
Jeff Chandler

BOOK DESIGNER
Ruth Harvey

COVER DESIGNER
Sandra Schroeder

PRODUCTION TEAM
Jennifer Earhart
Bryan Flores
Brian Grossman
Lisa Stumpf

INDEXER
Tim Tate

Composed in *Century Old Style* and *ITC Franklin Gothic* by Que Corporation.

About the Author

Working with computers since 1981, **Laurie Ann Ulrich** has been writing computer reference materials and teaching computer skills to people of all ages and backgrounds since 1990. Currently, she teaches continuing education courses at universities and computer training organizations throughout the PA, NJ, and NY areas. In addition, Laurie is president of Limehat & Company, Inc., a consulting firm in Huntingdon Valley, PA, that specializes in technical documentation, desktop publishing, and electronic presentations. She can be reached at **Limehat@aol.com**.

Acknowledgments

I'd like to thank my acquisitions editor, Don Essig, for giving me the opportunity to write this book. Don's advice and encouragement during the "are we gonna do this book?" and the "you need this done by *when?*" phases of this project kept me from biting my nails right down to the quick. I still look forward to hearing his soothing voice, even if it's only to leave a message in his voicemail.

Thanks also to my development editor, Rick Kughen, for all the 'atta girls and fast responses. Although he was working on several other projects during my book's development, Rick remained a steady and positive force for me. I have thoroughly enjoyed writing this book, and I attribute much of that to Rick and Don. It's wonderful to work with people who respect your abilities and want to help and see you succeed. It really makes all the difference.

My production editor, Brian Sweany, who worked with me during author review, was also a very big help. I moved just after writing this book, and was in the middle of packing and unpacking just as the author review process began. Brian's great work and willingness to accommodate my schedule saved me a lot of stress!

The various technical and copy editors who contributed to this book also did a great job, and I'm not just saying this because I had so little editing to do during author review! I'd be happy to have my writing pass through any of their capable hands in the future.

On a personal basis, I want to thank my mom, Ann Talbot, for being a great friend and accompanying me on many spontaneous excursions when I had to get away from the computer during the writing of this book. My dad, Karl Ulrich, provided much-needed distractions by faxing me blonde jokes and right-wing propaganda, and I will be eternally grateful. Thanks to Nina for checking in so often and sending me positive thoughts. I must also thank my brothers, Joshua and Zachary Ulrich, for phone calls about baseball and swimming and all the things that nine and seven year-olds do. You guys gave me back the month of summer that I missed while writing this book!

Most of all, I want to thank and dedicate this book to my best friend and one true love. Thank you, Robert, for absolutely everything.

We'd Like to Hear from You!

QUE Corporation has a long-standing reputation for high-quality books and products. To ensure your continued satisfaction, we also understand the importance of customer service and support.

Tech Support

If you need assistance with the information in this book or with a CD/disk accompanying the book, please access Macmillan Computer Publishing's online Knowledge Base at **http://www.superlibrary.com/general/support**. If you do not find the answer to your questions on our Web site, you may contact Macmillan Technical Support by phone at **317/581-3833** or via e-mail at **support@mcp.com**.

Also be sure to visit QUE's Web resource center for all the latest information, enhancements, errata, downloads, and more. It's located at **http://www.quecorp.com/**.

Orders, Catalogs, and Customer Service

To order other QUE or Macmillan Computer Publishing books, catalogs, or products, please contact our Customer Service Department at **800/428-5331** or fax us at **800/835-3202** (International Fax: 317/228-4400). Or visit our online bookstore at **http://www.mcp.com/**.

Comments and Suggestions

We want you to let us know what you like or dislike most about this book or other QUE products. Your comments will help us to continue publishing the best books available on computer topics in today's market.

Rick Kughen
Product Director
QUE Corporation
201 West 103rd Street, 4B
Indianapolis, Indiana 46290 USA
Fax: 317/581-4663
E-mail: **rkughen@que.mcp.com**

Please be sure to include the book's title and author as well as your name and phone or fax number. We will carefully review your comments and share them with the author. Please note that due to the high volume of mail we receive, we may not be able to reply to every message.

Thank you for choosing QUE!

Introduction

As a user of Word 97, you can document anything—from your business plan to how you spent your summer vacation. You can share that document with your coworkers down the hall or your best friend across the globe. Word 97 gives you the power to work alone, the ability to work with a team, and the resources to share your work with the world via the Internet.

Word 97 makes it possible to answer Microsoft's question "Where do you want to go today?" with one simple word: Everywhere. ■

Why You Should Use this Book

This book was written by an instructor who has taught hundreds of people to use Microsoft Word. If you want to learn about an effective, vastly improved version of Microsoft's best-selling software program, *Using Microsoft Word 97* was written for you, with your needs and goals dictating its form and content.

This book is aimed at intermediate users, yet the needs of a beginner have not been ignored. Many new users have to get up to speed on a seemingly advanced function, and get there fast. This book was written to give you a simple, direct tool for learning and harnessing the power of Word 97.

Why You Should Use Word

Powerful yet simple, Microsoft Word is the most popular word processor in the world. Word 97 improves upon all previous versions of Word, increasing your productivity and efficiency while at the same time unleashing your creativity and spontaneity with its ease of use.

In addition to improving your productivity, Word 97 can decrease your support costs. Standardizing on Office 97 can bring the same power and simplicity to all of your applications by bringing not only Word, but also Excel, PowerPoint, and Access into your organization. Word 97 (and all the other Office 97 applications) makes it easy for people to learn and remember how to get things done.

Toolbars, menus, and dialog boxes have been improved in Word 97: Accessing Word's powerful functions is faster, easier, and more memorable. Simple but direct terminology, logically-grouped tools and commands, and the ability to customize the Word environment enable every user to transform Word into their own personal desktop application.

Word 97 enables you to share your documents with the world and bring the world into your documents. You can link Internet sites or other applications and files to your documents. You can create a Web page with Word 97 and add your own graphics, animation, and hypertext links.

How this Book Is Organized

Using Microsoft Word 97 is divided into the following parts:

- Part I: Word Processing Power
- Part II: Formatting Documents
- Part III: Special Documents
- Part IV: Word and the Web
- Part V: Integration and Automation

Part I takes you on a tour of the Word 97 window, and covers creating, editing, saving, and printing documents. Use of Word 97's Auto features, Templates, Wizards, and default settings are explained. Section I makes sure you have a strong foundation in the basics of word processing in general, and Word 97 specifically. These topics are covered in Chapters 1 through 5.

Part II covers the methods of customizing and enhancing your documents from an atomic level (character formatting) to an aerial view (page formatting). In Chapters 6 though 12, you'll learn to use features such as columns, tabs, tables, and graphics to turn your Word 97 documents into the polished and professional creations you always knew they could be.

Part III shows you how to work with long documents, generate marketing materials through Mail Merge, and combine your existing Word files into one large Master document. The special concerns of large and complex documents are covered in Chapters 13 through 16, enabling you to control the flow of your documents through the use of sections and chapters. Learn to integrate data into form letters and generate the labels and envelopes that get your document delivered to your target audience.

Part IV describes how Word can be used to easily create sophisticated Web pages for the Internet or your company's intranet. Add visual interest with graphics, scrolling text, and user prompts. Add depth with hypertext links to other Web sites. After reading Chapter 17, you'll be able to accomplish these goals with the Web Page Wizard or start from scratch. In Chapter 18, you'll also learn to share your work quickly and easily with coworkers by adding links to files, applications, and Web sites to your regular documents. Part V demonstrates the uses of the Clipboard and OLE (Object Linking and Embedding) to combine Word and other application files. You'll find these topics in Chapter 19. In Chapter 20, Visual Basic for Applications is covered, showing you how to build a program within your document to insert and format text.

Conventions Used in This Book

Throughout this book the following symbols and text formatting have been used:

- Whenever you see an underlined letter, you're looking at a menu command. File, Save, for example, indicates that the Save command is found in the File menu.
- Names of toolbar buttons and dialog boxes are Capitalized.
- New terms are *italicized*.

N O T E This symbol and the paragraph that accompanies it appear whenever the author wants to give you some supporting information or share an idea to help you get more from Word 97.

 T I P This symbol appears with text that shares a shortcut or suggestion for a quick or more efficient way to perform a given task.

CAUTION

A Caution tells you about possible pitfalls or problems that a given task or feature can present. A Caution also suggests ways to avoid or rectify the problem.

Every effort has been made to make this a book that can be enjoyably read from cover to cover or used as a topic-specific reference. A new and improved Index has been added to make looking up the topic of your choice fast and easy.

Now that you have seen how this book is organized, you should review Word's new features.

What's New In Word 97

With the release of Word 97, Microsoft has achieved two important objectives—the product is more powerful, yet in many ways, it is easier to use. Users of previous versions of Word will notice the visual differences immediately, and after using the product find that the changes and improvements are far more than cosmetic.

Word 97's New Look

The changes that you'll notice immediately are in Word 97's appearance:

- *Toolbars.* The toolbars have a different look, and many have drop-down lists that offer an array of options for the given command. Toolbars are also much easier to customize. You can create your own sets of tools, or edit the existing toolbars. To see a list of all the available toolbars, right-click the toolbar, or choose View, Toolbars from the menu.

  Figure I.1 shows the Standard and Formatting toolbars with the new Font Color drop list displayed. (See Chapter 1, "The Word 97 Window," for more information on customizing your toolbars and menus.)

- *Menus.* A picture of the toolbar button that matches the command accompanies many of the commands on Word 97's menus. The available keyboard shortcuts continue to be listed down the right side of each menu. Word 97 offers two, and sometimes three ways to do most things—from the menu, the toolbar, or the keyboard. Figure I.2 shows the View menu. The submenu displays a list of available toolbars.

FIG. I.1

The buttons on Word 97's toolbars have a flatter, less three-dimensional look, and many have drop-down lists to give you a list of options.

FIG. I.2

Word 97's menus now show the toolbar button for many of the menu commands. This can help you remember which button performs which task.

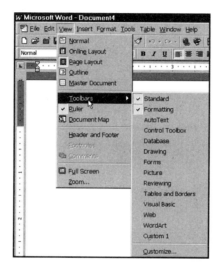

NOTE Don't feel like you're not truly mastering Word if you're not using all the ways to issue a command or perform a given task. The variety of methods exists to support the variety of users. Word 97's incorporation of the toolbar buttons and menus helps to remind you of your alternatives. Pick the method that makes the most sense for you and stick with it. If, for example, you're a 120 word-per-minute typist, you'll probably prefer keyboard shortcuts. ■

Improved Access

Getting what you need and finding it all in one place is a major improvement in Word 97. You'll find new features in several important areas:

■ *Dialog boxes.* More of Word's dialog boxes contain tabs, which enable you to work with a specific task from a variety of perspectives, all in one box. The Apply button allows you to confirm your choices in one tab, and keep the dialog box open to go on and work with the options in another tab. You'll click OK when you want to close the dialog box entirely.

Figure I.3 shows the Font dialog box and its three tabs.

FIG. I.3
Tabbed dialog boxes give you access to more options in one place.

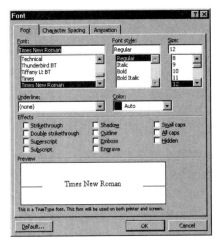

- *Navigation.* Use the Browse button (see Figure I.4) to move from page to page, heading to heading, or to find a particular word, phrase, or graphic in your document.

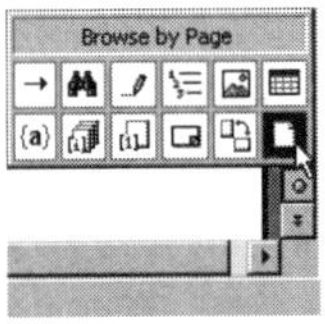

FIG. I.4
The Browse button gives you a large selection of navigation tools to make moving through your document easier.

- *Help.* It's easier and more context-sensitive than before. You'll see a question mark in Word 97's dialog boxes, enabling you to get immediate identification of and help using the various fields and options. The "What's This?" option in the Help menu allows you to get instant help on any item you can click with your mouse. Pop-up windows appear to give you the name and a detailed description of virtually all of Word's on-screen features.

  Figure I.5 shows a Word 97 pop-up help box.

- *Office Assistant.* A friendly little paper clip will pop up in its own window, asking you if you need help. You can type a specific question or choose a topic from a displayed list to tell the Assistant where you need help. You can choose from a series of other Office Assistant characters, such as a bouncing dot, the Power Pup, an Albert Einstein-like Genius, or Scribble the Cat. Figure I.6 shows the Office Assistant offering help with a letter.

FIG. I.5

Click the question mark in any dialog box to get help with the box's options. Choose What's This? from the Help menu to get assistance with any on-screen feature.

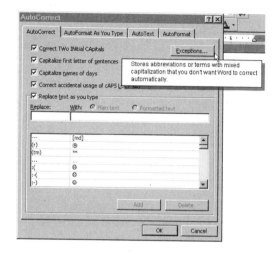

FIG. I.6

The Office Assistant is a cartoon paper clip that offers timely help and context-sensitive assistance as you work in Word 97.

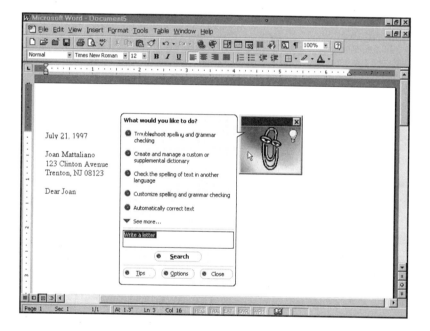

Enhanced Features

Many of your favorite features in previous releases of Word for Windows have been improved:

- *More templates and wizards.* Word 97 gives you many more templates for creating your documents from predesigned formats. Wizards will coach you through the process of building documents from memos to resumes. Create your own templates or enhance the ones Word gives you to suit your particular needs. (Find out more about using templates in Chapter 2, "Creating Documents.")

- *Enhanced AutoCorrect features.* Previous versions of Word had AutoCorrect, AutoText, and AutoFormat. Word 97 has improved all three areas and made them easier to customize.

    Figure I.7 shows the AutoCorrect dialog box, with its four tabs: AutoCorrect, AutoFormat As You Type, AutoText, and AutoFormat. (Many of Word 97's Auto features are covered in Chapter 2, "Creating Documents.")

FIG. I.7
Word 97 has added many new automatic corrections and formats that make reduced errors and consistent documents a reality.

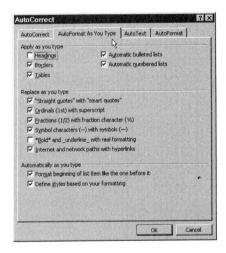

- *Tables and borders.* Word 97 gives you two ways to build a table—you can Draw it with your mouse, and create a customized group of cells, or Insert a table, creating a simple grid of equal columns and rows. Whichever method you choose, you can use the new Tables and Borders toolbar to format your table cells, lines, and text. (See Chapter 10, "Using Tables" for more information.)

- *Graphics and drawing tools.* You can now draw directly on your Word document, and move the drawn item freely. You can also insert clip art and move it in any direction, independently of the surrounding text, without adding the frame that was required in previous versions of Word. Your ability to format pictures is also enhanced, allowing you to crop, scale, size, and wrap text around pictures. You'll find Word's Drawing toolbar easier to use, and the Format, Picture command from the menu opens a very useful and powerful dialog box of tools.

Figure I.8 shows the Format Picture dialog box. (Word 97's drawing tools and use of graphics are covered in Chapter 12, "Using Graphics to Enhance Word Documents.")

FIG. I.8

Change the size, shape, location, and content of your drawn object or inserted clip art—all in one dialog box.

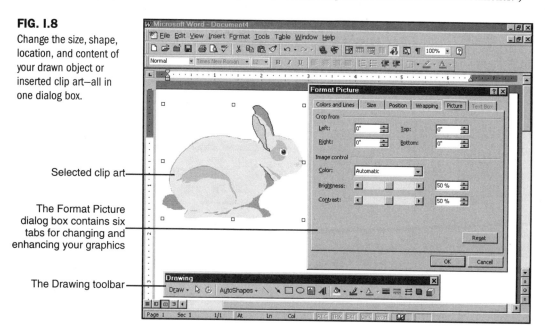

Selected clip art

The Format Picture dialog box contains six tabs for changing and enhancing your graphics

The Drawing toolbar

Powerful New Tools

Word 97 puts powerful tools at your fingertips and gives you a simple interface to work with. The result? You can do more and spend less time learning how:

- *Web publishing*. Word gives you two ways to build your own Web page—through the Web Page Wizard or by building your own content and saving the page as HTML. Creating sophisticated, creative Web pages to publish on the Internet is now a simple procedure, requiring no knowledge of programming.

  Figure I.9 shows the Web Page Wizard's opening dialog box. (For more information about the World Wide Web and how Word 97 can help you make your own Web page a part of it, see Chapter 17, "Creating a Web Page with Word 97.")

- *Visual Basic for Applications*. All of the Office 97 applications now share a common programming language, Visual Basic for Applications. By utilizing this same language for all the products in the Office 97 suite, average users and developers alike can develop automated tools to enhance the applications' functionality and customization. No need to learn the macro language in Excel and then learn another one in Word—consistency shortens the learning curve and strengthens the user's ability to make Office 97 truly his or her own.

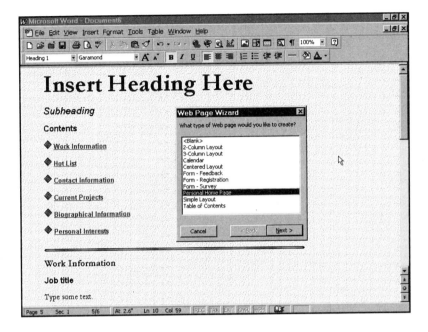

FIG. I.9
Use the Web Page Wizard to create a unique and creative web page. Choose from several layouts and follow the on-screen instructions.

For more information on how to use Visual Basic for Applications with Word 97, see Chapter 20, "Automating Word 97 with Visual Basic for Applications."

■ *Tracking teamwork*. Word 97 supports team development of documents through its Track Changes feature. Each member of the development team (or each hat you wear as the single developer) is represented by a different color text, so that additions and deletions are easily attributed to their contributor. The lead author can then accept or reject them individually or in total, updating the document quickly and easily to reflect the group's input.

For more information on using Word 97's Track Changes feature, see Chapter 3, "Editing Documents."

Word Processing Power

The Word 97 Window

Understanding the menus, toolbars, and other on-screen features of Word 97 will make creating your document easy. In this chapter, you'll learn to use Word's menus and tools to your advantage. ▪

How to use Word's menus and toolbars

For users of Word 7 and any previous versions, there are changes and additions to the menus and toolbars. You'll learn to use Word's menus and toolbars in this chapter.

Viewing your document

The view you use when creating and editing your document can affect the on-screen tools available to you. Use the View menu to select the one that's best for you.

Getting around in your document

Whether you use the scroll bars, keyboard, mouse, or a combination of all three, you'll learn effective methods to navigate in your Word document in this chapter.

Using Menus

When you open a Word document, you might notice items such as a title bar, toolbars, scroll bars, a ruler, and a menu bar (see Figure 1.1).

FIG. 1.1
The Word window provides menus and tools to help you create documents such as this business letter.

Menu bar   Title bar   Toolbars

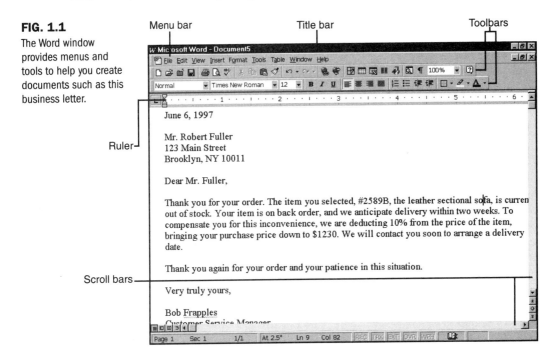

Ruler

Scroll bars

The menu bar contains nine menus across the top of the screen, below the title bar (see Figure 1.2). Each menu name contains an underlined letter (also called a hot key), which you can use to pull down the menu by pressing the Alt key plus that letter. While this menu-access method can be useful if your mouse stops working, the best way to pull down a menu and view its commands is to click the menu name.

T I P   If you click the wrong menu with your mouse, you don't need to deselect it, just point to the menu you wanted. The unwanted menu will close automatically.

FIG. 1.2
Word provides a powerful menu bar with nine available pull-down menus.

File Edit View Insert Format Tools Table Window Help

Menu Features

Each menu contains a list of commands (see Figure 1.3). In Word 97, the menus also contain a picture of the command's corresponding toolbar icon and a keyboard shortcut (if one exists). Here are some other menu features:

- If the menu command is followed by an ellipsis (...), choosing that command will open a dialog box. This is Word's way of saying that it needs more information before it can do what you want.

- If a check mark (✔) precedes the command, the command is in the "on" position. Examples of this are the Toolbars and Ruler commands in the View menu. If the toolbars and ruler are visible on-screen, a check mark appears in front of the command on the menu. To remove the feature from the screen, select its command from the menu. The check mark disappears, signifying that the feature is turned off.

- If a right-pointing triangle (▶) appears to the right of the command, this tells you that another menu containing related options will open when you choose the command.

- If the picture of the corresponding toolbar button appears depressed, the command is already in use.

FIG. 1.3
The figure illustrates a Word 97 menu containing keyboard shortcuts and toolbar icons.

Toolbar icon —

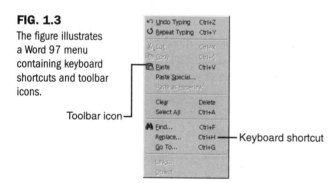

— Keyboard shortcut

Customizing the Menus

You can change the content and appearance of your menus to suit your needs. You can customize Word's existing menus by adding new commands or changing the order of menu items. You can also add new menus and fill them with the commands of your choice.

CAUTION
Keep your changes and additions to the menus to a minimum. Making too many changes can create cluttered, confusing menus. Only add a command to the menu if you use it often, and never remove an original menu command. If someone else uses your computer, make sure you let him know what changes you've made!

Adding Commands to the Menus If there is a Word feature you use often, you can add it to one of the existing Word menus to make it more accessible. To add an item to a menu, perform the following steps:

1. Choose Tools, Customize from the Word 97 menu.
2. Click the Commands tab in the Customize dialog box (see Figure 1.4).
3. Click the menu (on the menu bar) to which you want to add your command. The menu drops down.
4. From the list of Categories in the Customize dialog box, select the one that contains the command you want to add to a menu. If you're not sure which category you need, choose the All Commands category to see every Word command, listed in alphabetical order.

   When you find the command you need, click and drag the command from the Customize dialog box. An I-beam follows your mouse pointer.
5. Drag your command over the spot on the menu where you want to insert the new command. For example, if you're adding the Close All command to the File menu, add it after the existing Close command.

   As soon as you release the mouse, the command is placed. You can add as many other commands as you need to, as long as the Customize dialog box is open.
6. When you finish adding commands, click the Close button.

 T I P Whenever possible, try to place your new commands near similar existing commands. This will make it easier to find them later.

FIG. 1.4
Use the Customize dialog box to change your toolbar commands.

Creating a New Menu A good way to keep from cluttering your existing Word menus with new commands is to create a completely new menu. You can add your new menu at the end of the list of existing menus (after Help), or inserted in between the existing menus. Follow these steps to create a new menu:

1. Choose Tools, Customize.

2. Click the Commands tab.

3. In the Categories list, scroll down until the New Menu category displays. Click New Menu.

4. The words New Menu appear in the Commands list. Drag this text up to the menu bar. As you drag, an I-beam follows your mouse pointer. Release the mouse when the I-beam is where you want to insert your new menu.

The new menu is called New Menu. You may want to call it something else, such as My Menu or Other Commands. To change the menu's name, perform the following steps:

1. Click the Modify Selection button in the Customize dialog box (see Figure 1.5).

2. Select Name from the pop-up menu, and highlight the words New Menu.

3. Type your new menu name, and press Enter. The Modify Selection pop-up menu closes.

4. Add commands to your new menu by selecting them from the Categories list and dragging the commands up to your new menu. Be sure to select your new menu first.

5. After adding all the desired commands to the new menu, click the Close button in the Customize dialog box.

FIG. 1.5

Use the Modify Selection button in the Customize dialog box to name the new menus you've created.

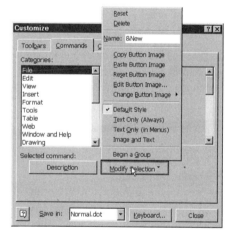

To remove a new menu from the menu bar, open the Customize dialog box (Tools, Customize), and drag the menu off the menu bar, back into the dialog box. Click the Close button to accept your change and close the dialog box.

Changing the Order of Menu Commands   If you want to change the order of Word's menu commands to meet your needs, perform the following steps:

1. Choose Tools, Customize.

2. Click the Commands tab.

3. With the Customize dialog box open, pull down the menu (on the menu bar) that you want to change.

4. To reorder the commands in the menu, click-and-drag them. For example, to move the third command to the first position, click the third command and drag it up, until the mouse pointer is above the current first command.

   Release the mouse when your mouse pointer is pointing to the desired location for your command (see Figure 1.6). The commands are reordered.

5. You can make changes to as many menus and commands as you need. When you finish, click Close in the Customize dialog box.

FIG. 1.6

You can easily change the order of menu items; in this example, the mouse pointer as a menu item is dragged to a new position in the menu.

Removing Menu Commands   You may wish to remove a command that you've added to a menu. While it is not recommended that you remove the default commands from any of Word's standard menus, you may need to shorten a lengthy menu or remove a command from one menu to move it to another.

To remove a menu command, perform the following steps:

1. Choose Tools, Customize from the menu.

2. Click the Commands tab the in the Customize dialog box.

3. On the Word menu bar, click the menu that you wish to edit.

4. With the menu descended, click the command you wish to remove and drag it off the menu.

5. Click Close to save your changes and close the dialog box.

Shortcut Menus

Shortcut menus appear when you click your right mouse button. Depending on where your mouse pointer is when you click the right mouse button, you'll see a different shortcut menu, with menu commands pertaining to the item you're on when you click. To choose a command from the shortcut menu, click the command with either your left or right mouse button.

The following is a list of some of Word's shortcut menus:

- Right-click the selected document text, and the shortcut menu offers choices to Cut, Copy, and Paste the selected text. You can also choose to open the Font, Paragraph, or Bullets and Numbering dialog boxes (see Figure 1.7).

- Right-click any of the toolbars, and a list of other available toolbars appears. (See the following section, "Using the Toolbars," for more information.)

- Right-click Word's title bar, and the shortcut menu will offer you choices to Restore, Move, Size, Maximize, Minimize, or Close Word 97. This is a Windows 95 shortcut menu.

- If any of your document text is underlined in red, you can right-click it to see a Spelling check shortcut menu. If text is underlined in green, right-click it to see the Grammar check shortcut menu.

  ▶ **See** "Using Spell Check," **p. 46**

FIG. 1.7
A shortcut menu appears when you right-click any document text.

Using the Toolbars

Two toolbars appear in your Word 97 window by default. The Standard toolbar is on top, and the Formatting toolbar is below it. The Standard toolbar contains buttons that invoke procedures, such as saving a file, printing a document, or using the Clipboard to Cut, Copy, and Paste. The Formatting toolbar contains options for changing the way your text looks; you can manipulate the font, font size, style, and alignment of your text by using the Formatting buttons. To use a toolbar button, simply click it with your mouse.

Selecting Toolbars

There are several additional toolbars that you can display in addition to the Standard and Formatting toolbars. To see the list of available toolbars and select them for display, follow these steps:

1. Choose View, Toolbars.

2. A submenu appears with the currently displayed toolbars preceded by a check mark (see Figure 1.8). Click the toolbar you want displayed.

3. To turn off (deselect) a checked toolbar, choose it from the menu. This removes the check mark, and the toolbar is no longer displayed.

TIP Some of the toolbar options, such as the Drawing toolbar and the Tables and Borders toolbar, are located on the standard toolbar. Click the Drawing and Tables and Borders buttons on the Standard toolbar to open these menus.

FIG. 1.8

A menu appears when you select View, Toolbars.

Another method of selecting and deselecting toolbars is to choose Tools, Customize. Click the Toolbars tab, and click the box to the left of the toolbar you want displayed. The currently displayed toolbars are already checked (see Figure 1.9). Clicking them again removes the check mark and takes the toolbar out of your Word 97 window. Click the Close button when you finish selecting or deselecting toolbars.

FIG. 1.9

This figure illustrates the toolbars available through the Customize dialog box.

Customizing Toolbars

You can add and remove toolbar buttons on any of the Word toolbars. Most commands already have a designated button face, but if you select a command that doesn't, you can choose from an array of generic pictures to represent your command on the toolbar.

Adding Toolbar Buttons   Using a toolbar button is one of the fastest ways to issue and complete a command. Having the commands you use most often represented by a toolbar button can greatly increase your productivity because it saves you from searching the menus for commands.

To add a button to a toolbar, perform the following steps:

1. Choose Tools, Customize.
2. Click the Commands tab. The same commands you can add to menus can be added to the toolbars.
3. Choose from the Categories on the left, and view the related Commands on the right. Some of the commands have toolbar icons next to them; others appear as text only. To see a list of all of Word's commands, choose the All Commands category.
4. When you find the command you want to add to the toolbar, click-and-drag it out of the Customize dialog box. Drag the button until the I-beam symbol is on the toolbar in the spot where you want to place the button. Release the mouse, and the button is placed on the toolbar.
5. Continue to add buttons as needed, and click Close to accept your additions and close the Customize dialog box.

If a command isn't represented by an icon, text will appear on the toolbar instead. This takes up more room than an icon, and you may find that it makes the toolbar look cluttered. To apply a generic button face and create a picture-only icon, follow these steps:

1. Open the Customize dialog box by choosing Tools, Customize.
2. Click the Commands tab.
3. Select the text button on your toolbar that you want to replace with an icon; click the Modify Selection button.
4. From the pop-up menu, choose Change Button Image. An array of generic button faces appears (see Figure 1.10). Click the picture you want to use on the button. The pop-up menu closes, and the button contains both text and the button face you just selected.

FIG. 1.10

Apply generic button faces to replace text commands on the toolbar.

5. Click the Modify Selection button again to redisplay the pop-up menu. Choose Text Only (in Menus) to remove the text from the button.

6. Continue to add buttons as needed. When you finish, click the Close button. Your additions appear on the toolbar.

Changing the Order of Toolbar Buttons   Whether it's a button you added, or one of the original Word buttons, you can move it to a new location on any of the toolbars. Follow these steps to reorder your toolbar buttons:

1. Choose Tools, Customize. The Customize dialog box opens.

2. Click the Commands tab.

3. On the toolbar, click and drag your toolbar button from its current location to the new location. An I-beam follows your mouse pointer. When the I-beam is in the spot where you want to place your button, release the mouse.

4. Continue to reorder any of your other buttons on any of the displayed toolbars. When you finish, click Close to accept your changes and close the Customize dialog box.

CAUTION

Be careful when repositioning toolbar buttons; it's easy to accidentally place them on a different toolbar than you intended if you drag up or down as you move the button. If you place the button on a toolbar that you don't always display, your button may not be available when you need it.

Removing Toolbar Buttons   The process of removing a toolbar button is very similar to the process of adding or moving one. Open the Customize dialog box by choosing Tools, Customize. Activating the Customize dialog box enables you to remove any of the buttons by dragging them off the toolbar. To remove a button, drag it off the toolbar, and release the mouse as soon as your mouse pointer is below the toolbars. Click the Close button to accept your change and close the Customize dialog box.

Working with Views

Word offers seven views in which you may work. Choosing a view depends on what type of document you want to create, as well your perspective on that document. If, for example, you create an outline, you will want to work in Outline view. When you're concerned with the overall appearance of your document as well as its content, Page Layout view would be a good choice. The following is a list of Word 97 views:

- Normal
- Online Layout
- Page Layout
- Outline
- Master Document
- Document Map
- Full Screen

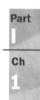

You can switch between these views by choosing them from the View menu (see Figure 1.11), or by clicking the View buttons in the lower left corner of your Word window. The View buttons represent the Normal, Online Layout, Page Layout, and Outline views only.

FIG. 1.11

Use the View button to select the mode in which you want to view your document.

Working with Normal View

Normal view is the default view for new documents. Working in Normal view is best if you aren't concerned with anything other than typing standard paragraph text. If you want to add clip art to your document, Word will prompt you that you must switch to Page Layout view. You should also switch to Page Layout view if you want to work with columns. This isn't to say there isn't any reason to work in Normal view—Normal view provides the least cluttered view of your document and gives you the largest typing area (see Figure 1.12).

FIG 1.12

Use Normal view for typing standard paragraph text.

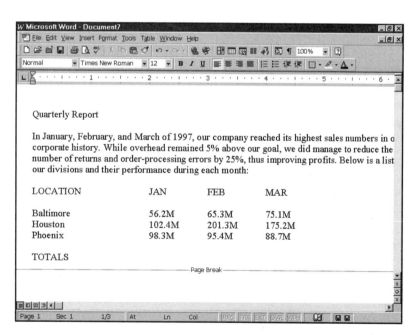

Using Page Layout View

Many Word users prefer Page Layout view for typing, editing, and formatting business documents. When you switch to Page Layout view, a vertical ruler appears, and you see a graphical representation of your page borders and breaks (see Figure 1.13). These features enable you to see a picture of your whole document, which is useful when the overall appearance of your document is as important as its content. Résumés, reports, and marketing documents are examples of documents best developed in Page Layout view.

FIG. 1.13

Use Page Layout view when you want to see your document from a design perspective.

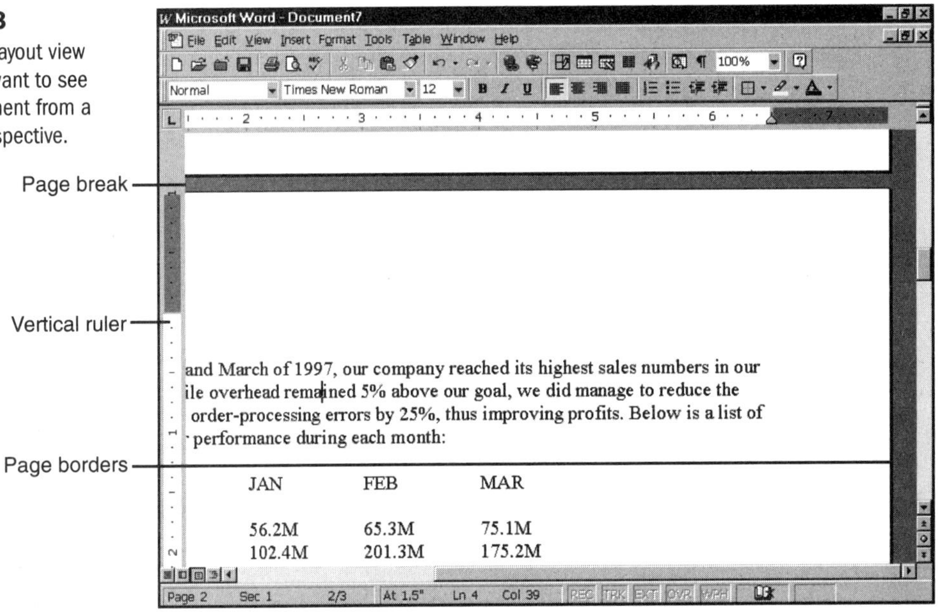

Page break

Vertical ruler

Page borders

Working in Outline View

Creating an outline is an obvious reason to work in Outline view, but it's not the only one. If your document has levels, such as major and minor headings, you can use Outline view to develop the logical order of your topics (see Figure 1.14). Choosing Outline view adds a new toolbar to your window. The tools enable you to promote and demote headings, change the order of your document topics, and expand and collapse your paragraph text.

FIG 1.14
Use Outline View to help develop a logical order for your document topics.

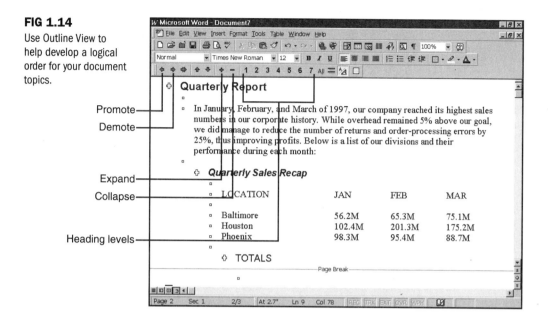

Promote——
Demote——

Expand——
Collapse——

Heading levels——

Using the Document Map

The Document Map is a vertical pane that appears on the left side of your document (see Figure 1.15). This feature is especially useful in very long documents because it shows the overall structure of the document and indicates your cursor's current location.

To view the Document Map for your open document, follow these steps:

1. Choose View, Document Map. You can also click the Document Map button on the Standard toolbar.

2. The Document Map appears on the left side of your window. Click the heading or paragraph text in the Document Map, and your cursor will move to that location in the document.

3. If you've used Heading styles in your document, small plus (+) and (–) symbols appear next to them in your Document Map. You can expand (+) or collapse (–) your paragraph text by clicking these symbols.

4. If your Document Map pane isn't wide enough to read your headings, place your mouse pointer over the border between the Map pane and your document. When your pointer turns to a two-headed arrow, click-and-drag to the right to increase the width of the Document Map pane. You can also decrease the width of the pane by dragging to the left.

Part

I

Ch

1

FIG. 1.15
Use Document Map
view when editing large
documents.

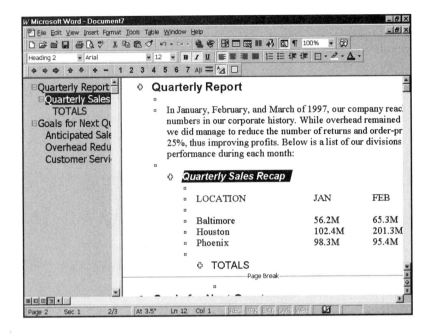

 T I P The Document Map is unlike the other views in that you don't switch to it. Rather, you turn it on and off. The menu command (View, Document Map) and toolbar button both work like toggle switches; one click and the Document Map is on, a second click and it's off.

Using Full Screen View

Choosing View, Full Screen from the menu will remove everything from your Word window except your document and a small floating toolbar (see Figure 1.16). This view is useful when you want to maximize your typing area.

To move the floating toolbar, drag it to the top, bottom, or side of your document. The floating toolbar will adhere to the edge, and become a fixed toolbar. To turn it back to a floating toolbar, drag it away from the edge of the window.

To return to your previous view, press the Esc key or click Close Full Screen in the toolbar.

Navigating Word Documents

You can move from place to place within your document by using your mouse, scroll bars, Browse buttons, and keyboard. Your navigation options range from techniques for moving to the end of a paragraph to moving to a particular footnote or heading on a subsequent page. The longer your document, the greater your navigation requirements.

FIG. 1.16
To maximize your typing
area, use Full Screen
view.

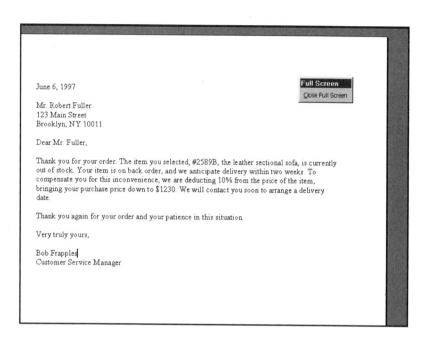

Using Scroll Bars

Your Word window has two scroll bars: a horizontal scroll bar for moving from left to right, and a vertical scroll bar for moving up and down the length of your document. To go to a specific page in your document, drag the vertical scroll bar's elevator box. As you drag it, a yellow pop-up box appears, displaying the page number corresponding to that point in the scroll bar (see Figure 1.17). Release the mouse when the page number you want appears in the pop-up box.

CAUTION

Scrolling from page to page does not reposition your cursor. If, for example, you finish typing on page ten and then scroll up to read page five, your cursor is still on page ten. If you want to start typing on the page you're looking at, you must first click your mouse to place your cursor on that page.

The Browse Buttons

  At the foot of your vertical scroll bar, you see a series of three buttons—Previous, select Browse Object, and Next. These are your Browse buttons. You use these buttons to move page by page, or to browse through your document by searching for document components such as tables and clip art.

FIG. 1.17

Page numbers appear in a pop-up box by the scroll bar as you scroll through the document.

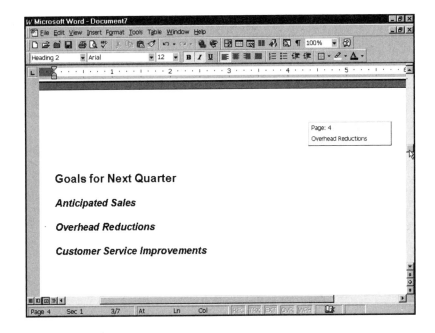

To choose a different Browse setting, click the Select Browse Object button. A toolbox pops up, displaying an array of 12 different Browsing options. Click the Browse option you want to use for navigating your document (see Figure 1.18).

FIG. 1.18

Browse by Page is one of the many options for moving through your document.

The option that works best for you depends on the contents of your document. Table 1.1 describes each of the Browse options.

Table 1.1   The Browse Options Toolbox

Button	Option	Description
→	GoTo	Open the Find and Replace dialog box, with the Go To tab activated. You can go to a particular part of your document, such as a page, section, footnote, or field.

Button	Option	Description
	Find	Search your document for a particular word or phrase.
		The remaining Browse options enable you to move through your document, going from object to object, by clicking the Next and Previous Browse buttons.
	Browse by Edits	If you are editing your document with the Track Changes feature turned on, this option will allow you to move through your document, stopping at each edit.
	Browse by Heading	This option allows you to navigate your document by stopping at each use of a Heading style, such as Heading 1, Heading 2, and so forth.
	Browse by Graphic	Use this option if you have graphics (clipart, photographs, drawings) throughout your document.
	Browse by Table	If you have more than one table within your document, you can quickly move from table to table by using this Browse option.
	Browse by Field	You may wish to check the field codes within your document (for dates, mail merge data, and so forth). This Browse option moves through your document, stopping at each field code.
	Browse by Endnote	Check and edit your endnotes by selecting this Browse option.
	Browse by Footnote	Check and edit your Footnotes by selecting this Browse option.
	Browse by Comment	If you've added comments throughout your document, you can stop at each one by using this option.
	Browse by Section	Move from section to section within your document, stopping at each section break.
	Browse by Page	Enables you to go from page to page in your document.

 TIP The simplest to use and most universally applicable Browse option is Browse by Page.

Keyboard Shortcuts

Table 1.2 lists some useful keyboard shortcuts for moving around in your document. They work in any view. To use any keyboard shortcut, remember to press and hold the first key, and then tap the second key.

Table 1.2 Keyboard Shortcuts

Option	Keyboard Shortcut
Go to the top of the page	Ctrl+Home
Go to the bottom of the page	Ctrl+End
Go to the end of the current line	End
Go to the beginning of the current line	Home
Move one word to the right	Ctrl+right arrow
Move one word to the left	Ctrl+ left arrow
Move up one paragraph	Ctrl+ up arrow
Move down one paragraph	Ctrl+ down arrow
Move up one screen	Page Up
Move down one screen	Page Down

CHAPTER 2

Creating Documents

You start a new, blank document in Word and while it *looks* like a blank document, it isn't. Every blank document you start has preset paper size and margins, as well as font and font size. As you type, your text will be single-spaced, and you have preset tabs at every half-inch mark on the ruler, even if the ruler isn't displayed. These settings enable you to open Word and simply start typing. ∎

Document defaults

Word 97 chooses your fonts, margins, and other format settings for you, and they're ready and waiting when you start a new document.

Templates

Predesigned documents for fax cover sheets, memos, reports, and résumés are available in Word 97. Use and edit these templates that come with the software, or create your own.

Automatic text

Use Word's AutoText and AutoCorrect to speed up your document creation and fix your mistakes.

Understanding Defaults

A document's preset formats are *defaults*. You can change them to suit your requirements, or you can make minor changes to each document you create when the defaults aren't quite what you need. Default settings also apply to Word's tools and features. For example, by default, Word will spell check your text as you type (rather than waiting for you to run Spell Check), and if you choose to bullet any text, the symbol used for the bullet is already selected for you. You can turn these features off or change the settings, but these new settings become the defaults for your next document.

Why have defaults? Because it saves you time. If you take the time to set your margins, choose a font, and turn your favorite Word tools on each time you start a document, it may be several minutes before you can even being typing. The defaults that Microsoft chose for your new blank documents are based on the traditional appearance and content of standard business documents.

Working with a Blank Document

To start a new Word 97 document, you can choose File, New from the menu, or click the New button on the toolbar. If you choose the menu approach, you'll see a large, multitabbed dialog box, from which you can choose the default Blank Document *template* (see Figure 2.1). This template is on the General tab. Even if you start from the New icon, you're still using the Blank Document template.

Figure 2.1 shows the New Document dialog box, with the General tab and Blank Document template.

FIG. 2.1
Choose Blank Document from the General tab to create a new document.

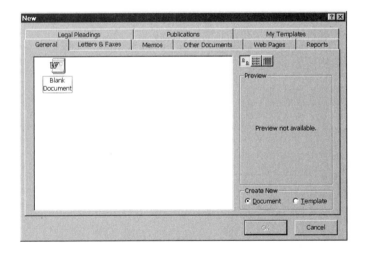

A template is a "cookie cutter" for your document. Just like you stamp out dough with a cookie cutter to determine the shape and size of the cookie, the Blank Document template stamps out a document with the following default settings:

- *Margins* are set to 1" on the top and bottom, 1.25" on the left and right.
- Line *spacing* is set to single.
- Your *Font* is set to Times New Roman, with 10-pt. font size.
- Your paper is set to *Portrait* mode (8.5" × 11").
- Left-aligned *tabs* are set to every half-inch.
- A series of heading *Styles* are already designed for you, such as Heading 1, 2, and 3.
- Your bullet symbol is set to a generic dot (ü), and your numbering style is set to standard Arabic numerals followed by a period, as in 1.

The preceding list contains the settings you'll notice immediately. You'll discover more defaults when you start to work with Word's character and paragraph formatting tools. In short, a default is any setting that's already in effect when you begin to type or when you open a dialog box to format some aspect of your document.

For more information on formatting your document, see Chapter 6, "Enhancing Text with Character Formatting."

Defining the Normal Template

To change the default font for your new documents, select Format, Font. Choose the font, style, size, and color of your text, and click the Default button. You will be prompted to confirm your intention to change the default character formats. If you click Yes, the Blank Document template will be changed, and your current and future blank-based documents will use your new font settings.

If you need to make more extensive changes to the Blank Document Template, follow these information steps:

1. Open the Blank Document template directly by choosing File, Open and going to the Templates folder. The Templates folder is a subfolder of your MSOffice folder.
2. Open the Normal.dot template. This is the actual file name for the Blank Document template.
3. Make your changes to fonts, paragraph formats, paper size, tabs, and styles.
4. Save the Normal.dot file by choosing File, Save or pressing Ctrl+S.
5. Test your changes by opening a new, blank document from the New button on the toolbar. You will see your new formats in effect as soon as you begin to type or use the features to which information you made changes.

See Chapter 7, "Paragraph Formatting," and Chapter 9, "Page Formatting," for more information on paragraph and page formatting.

> **CAUTION**
>
> Do not type any text into the Normal.dot template, or that text will appear on every new document you create (either from the New button or by choosing File, New and selecting Blank Document from the General tab).

N O T E Any changes you make to your defaults should be based on your typical needs. Don't change your defaults to settings you won't need at least 90 percent of the time, or you'll spend too much time reformatting your documents. ▨

Starting with a Template

Aside from the Blank Document template, Word provides an extensive array of document templates for a variety of document types, such as fax cover sheets, memos, reports, résumés, and marketing materials (see Figure 2.2). Some of these templates are accompanied by wizards, which coach you through the process of creating a special document.

FIG. 2.2
Choose a template for your new document or create your new document with the assistance of a wizard.

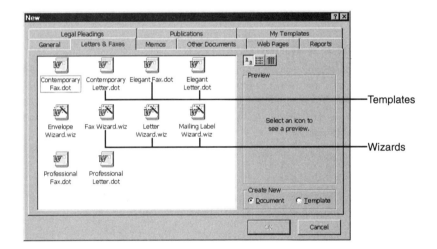

What's a Wizard?

A *wizard* is a program that takes you through the document-creation process by offering a series of dialog boxes that prompt you to make choices and in some cases, enter text that will appear on your document. Wizards are great for a new user or for a more seasoned Word user who is new to a particular type of document. Wizards are provided for the following types of documents:

▨ Fax cover sheets

▨ Letters

- Mailing labels
- Memos
- Résumés
- Web pages
- Newsletters
- Legal pleadings

A Word 97 wizard begins by showing you a list of the steps involved in creating the document and asks you to indicate the step with which you need help first. For example, Figure 2.3 shows the first dialog box of the Fax Wizard, with the Cover Sheet option selected. The wizard is asking you to choose a style for your document, and the standard alternatives are Professional, Contemporary, and Elegant. You may or may not agree with these adjectives, but the wizard will show you samples of each style to help you make your choice. To make your choice and move on, click the style of your choice, and click the Next button.

FIG. 2.3
Use the Cover Sheet dialog box to choose a Fax Cover sheet style.

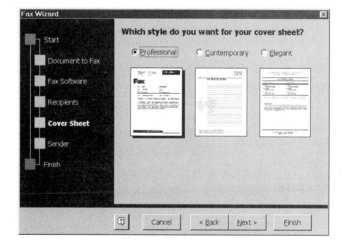

As you proceed with a wizard, you will choose paper orientation and size, select options for different features and components, and insert text that will appear in the document (see Figure 2.4). For example, in the Fax Wizard (Recipients option), you will be asked to enter your recipient's name, address, phone number, and fax number information.

As you use the wizard, you can click Next to move to the next step in your current option or you can click Back to return to a dialog box you've skipped or finished. To go to another option, click the buttons on the left side of the dialog box, such as (in the case of the Fax Wizard) Document to Fax, or Fax Software. You can use the wizard for the options you need and skip the parts you don't need. When you're ready to have the wizard create your document based on your entries, click the Finish button. To abandon a wizard at any point, click Cancel.

FIG. 2.4

A wizard prompts you to enter text that will appear in your document.

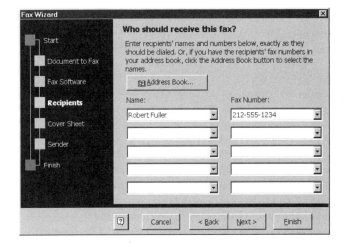

N O T E A template is the foundation for a new document. When you start a document with a template, you aren't opening the template, you're creating a new document based on the template.

Using a Template

Templates that don't require a wizard are simple to use. Instead of giving you dialog boxes to work with, the template creates a document that contains text and prompts that direct you to enter text in the right places (see Figure 2.5).

FIG. 2.5

Read and follow the instructional prompts in the template to insert your text.

Instructional text

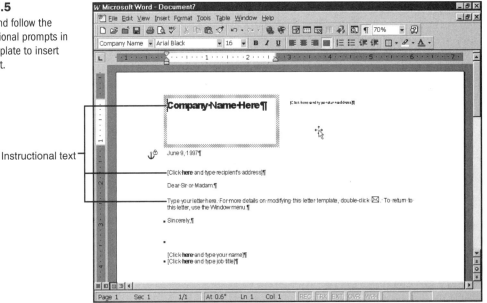

Beyond the process of entering text as prompted by the template's instructional text, you work with a template-based document as you would any other document.

Editing a Template

Imagine that you're using one of Word's templates, and while it serves most of your needs, you find that every time you use it, you end up changing the heading styles or the font, or you reset your margins. To save you the effort of making those changes each time you use the template, you can edit the template, making your typical changes part of the template file. From that point on, each time you use the template, it will be formatted to suit your needs.

Part
I

Ch
2

To edit a template, follow these steps:

1. Choose File, Open or press Ctrl+O.
2. Open the Templates folder, normally found in the MSOffice folder.

 T I P If you don't see your template files in the folders where you expect to, change your Files of Type selection to Document Templates or All Files.

3. Choose the Templates subfolder that matches the tab name that you click when you're starting a document with that template. For example, if you're editing the Elegant Fax Cover template, choose the Letters and Faxes subfolder.
4. Double-click the file name, or click it once and click the Open button, and the template opens. Note that the template's name, followed by a .DOT extension, appears on your title bar.

CAUTION

If you're editing a template or a "regular" document, it can help to know if your system is set to display your files' complete name and extension. If you don't see your file's extension, you can change your Windows 95 settings so that these extensions display on application title bars, dialog boxes, and in Explorer and My Computer.

To display your file extensions, choose View, Options from the My Computer or Explorer menus. In the View tab, click Show All Files, and make sure that the Hide MS DOS File Extensions check box is NOT checked.

 With the template open on-screen, make the changes you need; change the format settings for your text, paragraphs, and pages that will make the documents created with this template more appropriate for your use. When you finish making the changes, save the template file by pressing Ctrl+S or clicking the Save button on the toolbar.

You can also make a new version of your template if you'd like to leave the original version intact. After you've made your changes, choose File, Save As. Give your template a different name, and make sure the Save as Type setting is Document Template.

Creating a Template

Even with all the templates that Word provides, you may still need to create one of your own. If there is a document you create on a consistent basis that looks the same and contains much of the same text each time you create it, that document is a good candidate for a template. Follow these steps to create and save your own template:

1. Choose File, New from the menu, or click the New button on the toolbar. Unless you're basing your new template on an existing template (see the "Editing a Template" section earlier in this chapter), you will start your own template with a blank document.

2. When the new blank document opens, type any text that you want to appear on all documents created with your template.

3. Format your text, paragraphs, and page settings to meet the needs of your template. For example, if the documents you create with your template should have page numbers, insert page numbers on the template.(For more information on templates involving page numbering, see Chapter 13, "Working with Long Documents.")

4. When you finish entering your template's text and setting your various formats, choose File, Save As. In the Save as Type box, choose Document Template (.dot).

5. The Save In box automatically changes to the Templates folder. Choose the subfolder that your template belongs in, such as Letters and Faxes or Reports. Double-click the subfolder name to move it to the Save In box.

N O T E If your new template defies categorization in any of the existing tabs, create your own! Click the Create New Folder button in the Save As dialog box, and type a name for your New Folder (see Figure 2.6). Press Enter or click OK. Double-click the new folder to direct Word to save your new template to that folder. When you go to use your template next time, you'll see a new tab in your New (document) dialog box, with the same name as your new folder.

FIG. 2.6
Create a new template category by creating a new folder that will become a new tab in the Templates dialog box.

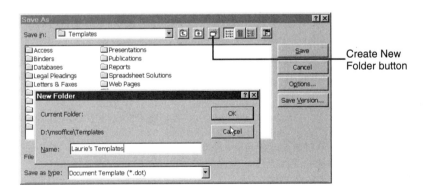

6. Give your template a relevant name, and click Save.

Powerful Tools for Entering Text

Word provides two features for automatically entering text in your documents. *AutoCorrect* contains a list of punctuation marks, misspellings, and abbreviations, and replaces them with symbols, correct spellings, and phrases as you type. *AutoText* allows you to save longer text entries (one or more paragraphs) and graphics that you use often and insert them through the use of an abbreviation "trigger."

Using AutoCorrect

Word provides a list of over 100 common misspellings, abbreviations, and punctuation marks, and their corresponding text and graphic replacements. The replacements are inserted as you type. For example, if you type **adn**, AutoCorrect will replace it with **and** as soon as you press the spacebar or Enter key at the end of the word. You can view the installed AutoCorrect entries by choosing Tools, AutoCorrect, and scrolling through the entries.

Creating AutoCorrect Entries   You can build your own AutoCorrect entries for long company or department names (**hrd** can become **Human Resources Department**), words you tend to misspell, and words or phrases you type often. Throughout the writing of this book, for example, **dialog box** was triggered by typing **db**. To add your own AutoCorrect entry, follow these steps:

1. Choose Tools, AutoCorrect. The AutoCorrect dialog box opens, with the AutoCorrect tab in front (see Figure 2.7).

2. Make sure the Replace Text as You Type check box is selected, and click your mouse in the Replace box. Type the misspelling or abbreviation that you want to serve as your entry's trigger.

3. Press Tab to move to the With box, and type the text that you want to insert whenever your trigger is typed.

4. Click Add, or press Enter.

5. You can continue to add entries, clicking Add after each one. When you finish creating AutoCorrect entries, click OK to save your entries and close the dialog box.

Working with Word's AutoCorrect Features   The AutoCorrect dialog box contains some other automatic entries that Word will make as you type:

- *Correct TWo INitial CApitals.* If you tend to hold the Shift key down too long when capitalizing a word, the second letter of the word often ends up capitalized, too. This feature changes the second letter to lowercase as soon as you press the spacebar or Enter key after typing the word.

- *Capitalize First Letter of Sentences.* This is one feature that you may want to turn off if you type a lot of outlines or bulleted lists in your documents. To turn it off, remove the check mark by clicking the check box.

- *Capitalize Names of Days.* If you tend to forget that the days of the week should be capitalized, you'll find this to be a convenient correction.

FIG. 2.7

Scroll through the list of Word's installed AutoCorrect entries and add your own to the list.

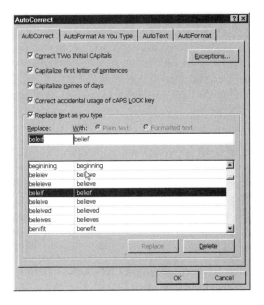

■ *Correct Accidental Use of cAPS LOCK Key.* This feature detects when you've turned on the Caps Lock in error, and turns it off for you. How does it know? If you press the Caps Lock and then press the Shift key as you continue typing, Word assumes that you didn't realize the Caps Lock was on. Word then converts all the characters you've typed since pressing Caps Lock, switching lower- and uppercase letters in your text.

If there are times when you want AutoCorrect to ignore these "mistakes" in your typing, click the Exceptions button and enter the words that you want exempted from the AutoCorrect process (see Figure 2.8). You can enter any words followed by a period that shouldn't be assumed to be the end of a sentence, such as **acct.** and **dept.**. Just because they end with a period, you don't want them to cause the next word to be capitalized. You can also enter any words that should have two initial uppercased letters.

Changing and Deleting AutoCorrect Entries   To change an AutoCorrect entry—either the trigger text or the replacement that Word inserts—or to remove an entry altogether, perform the following steps:

1. Open the AutoCorrect dialog box by choosing Tools, AutoCorrect.

2. Scroll through the list of entries until you see the one you want to change or delete.

3. Click the entry, which places it in the Replace and With boxes at the top of the list.

4. To change either the trigger or the inserted replacement text, select the text with your mouse, and type the new text. Click the Replace button.

5. To remove an entry, click the Delete button while the entry is in the Replace and With boxes.

FIG. 2.8
Customize the way
AutoCorrect works for
you, by entering your
exceptions.

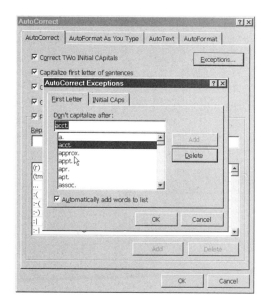

Building a Document with AutoText

The only differences between AutoCorrect and AutoText are the length of the text replacements and the method of insertion. AutoText entries can be one or more paragraphs, even several pages of text. Using an AutoText entry saves you typing and assures consistency each time the entry is used.

To insert an AutoText entry, type the abbreviation trigger, and then press F3. You can also insert AutoText entries using the AutoText submenu, accessed by selecting Insert, AutoText. You can also access the AutoText dialog box (see Figure 2.9) through Tools, AutoCorrect, and by clicking the AutoText tab in the AutoCorrect dialog box.

Word provides a long list of AutoText entries for you to start with, such as "Regards" for a letter closing. You can add your own AutoText entries by performing the following steps:

1. Type the text that you want to store as an AutoText entry. You can also use text that already exists in a document.

    Make sure your text is formatted as you want it to be when it is inserted as AutoText. This includes the font, size, indents, and tab settings.

2. Select the text. If you want your AutoText entry to be preceded or followed by a blank line, select the blank lines above or below it.

3. Choose Insert, AutoText.

4. From the submenu that appears, choose New. A small dialog box opens (see Figure 2.10) asking you to name your AutoText entry.

FIG. 2.9

The AutoText dialog box contains a list of Word's installed entries, plus any that you create.

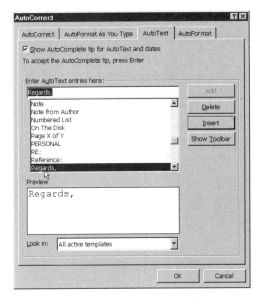

FIG. 2.10

Enter the name of your AutoText entry in the Create AutoText dialog box.

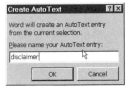

5. Type the abbreviation trigger in the designated box. Choose a name that you'll remember and that clearly indicates the content of the AutoText it represents.

6. Click OK. Your AutoText entry is created and is now available from the AutoText submenu.

N O T E Keep your AutoText abbreviations short. If, for example, your AutoText is a disclaimer paragraph of approximately 50 characters that you use at the end of your proposals or invoices, typing more than 10 characters to trigger it isn't much of a time saving. ▪

Inserting AutoText   You have a variety of insertion methods for AutoText, and you should use the one that's most comfortable for you and easiest to remember. These insertion methods are as follows:

  ▪ Type the AutoText entry name (its trigger) and press F3.

  ▪ Choose your AutoText entry from the Insert, AutoText submenu.

  ▪ Open the AutoText dialog box by choosing Tools, AutoCorrect and clicking the AutoText tab. Choose your entry and click Insert.

TIP You can also access the AutoText dialog box by choosing Insert, AutoText. The AutoCorrect dialog box opens with the AutoText tab in front.

Part

I

Ch

2

CAUTION

Why are there so many different ways to do the same thing? It can be confusing if you keep thinking that you have to use them all! Microsoft (and most other Windows software developers) provides a variety of methods to accommodate a variety of users. Some people like the methodical, step-by-step approach of a menu; others like quick keyboard shortcuts. Pick the method that seems most natural to you.

Editing and Deleting AutoText Entries   You can delete or change your AutoText entries as necessary. Follow these steps to edit an AutoText entry:

1. Insert your AutoText entry in its current state. You can also open a document that already contains the text.
2. Edit the content and/or formatting of the text.
3. Select the text, and choose Insert, AutoText. Click New.
4. Type the existing AutoText name exactly as you named it when this AutoText entry was initially created. Click OK.
5. Word asks you if you want to redefine the AutoText entry associated with that name. Click Yes. Word changes your AutoText entry.

To delete an AutoText entry, choose Insert, AutoText. From the submenu, choose AutoText. The AutoCorrect dialog box opens, with the AutoText tab in front. Scroll through the list of AutoText names, and click the one you want to remove. Click the Delete button. Click OK to close the dialog box.

CHAPTER 3

Editing Documents

Whether you work alone or with a team, any document you create has to be edited for accuracy. If performed manually, this can add hours to the time it takes to create a document. Word 97 has improved its spelling, grammar, content, and collaborative tools, and taken the editing process to a new, more efficient and effective level.

Check your spelling

Word 97 checks your spelling as you type, but you can also run a global spell check after you type. By working with Word's options, you can change Word's settings for when and how a spell check is performed.

Definitions and grammar

Use Word's Thesaurus and Grammar check tools to find out if you're using the right words in the right place.

Seek and you shall find

Word's Find and Replace program will look for text, formats, and special characters, and replace them with the entries of your choice.

Working together

When more than one person works on a document to enter and edit its content, Word's Revision features make it easy for your team to collaborate on a document, coordinating everyone's comments and changes.

Word 97's editing tools include:

- *Spell Check.* As you type, Word compares your words to its internal dictionary. If no match is found, your text is underlined in red.

- *Grammar Check.* Word checks your grammar as you type, underlining any text that defies Word's grammar "rules." Grammar checking can be customized to suit the type of document you're working on, and the level of your audience.

- *Revisions.* If you or someone else will be editing your document, editorial revisions and comments can appear in an alternate color, so that you can tell the original text from the changes. Revisions can be automatically integrated into your original text or removed completely.

- *Find and Replace.* Find and Replace can make checking, changing, removing, and/or inserting text into a document nearly foolproof. No more reading a document over and over to make sure you changed a date or name that has been used throughout the document.

Using Spell Check

By default, Word checks your spelling as you type. As soon as you press the spacebar or Enter key at the end of a word, Word compares it to a list of words in its internal dictionary. If the combination of letters isn't found, the text is underlined in red (see Figure 3.1). This enables you to see, at a glance, how many spelling errors you've made.

FIG. 3.1
A red underline indicates a word that isn't in Word's internal dictionary.

Text underlined in red

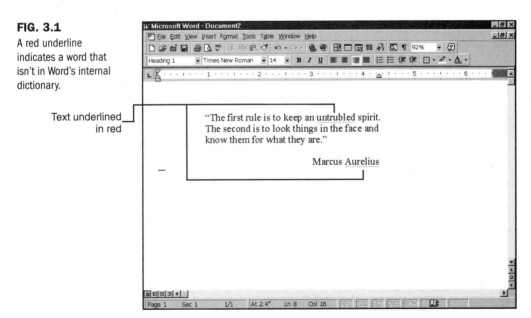

Spelling Shortcut Menus

As the red underlined text appears in your document, you can correct each incident individually by using your right mouse button to open a shortcut menu. Word's shortcut menus are *context sensitive*—the menu you get depends on which item you clicked with your right mouse button. To correct your spelling errors, follow these steps:

1. When a red underline appears, right-click the underlined word. A shortcut menu appears (see Figure 3.2).

FIG. 3.2

From the shortcut menu, choose an alternative spelling, or tell Word to Ignore or Add the word to its dictionary.

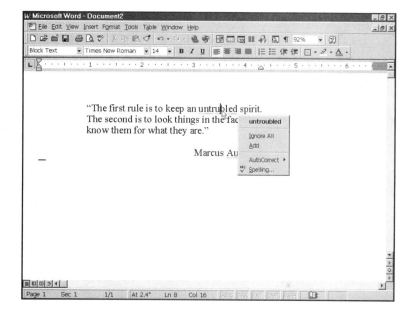

Part

I

Ch

3

2. From the menu, you have the following choices:

   - *Select an alternative spelling.* When Word finds a misspelled word in your text, it looks for similar words in its own dictionary and offers them in bold type at the top of the shortcut menu.

   - *Ignore the misspelling.* For example, if the underlined word is someone's name, a foreign word, or a street or city name, click the Ignore command in the menu. The red underline disappears.

   - *Add the word to the dictionary.* If the underlined word is one that you'll be using a lot in the future, click the Add command.

   - *Edit the word yourself.* If none of the alternatives are correct (or none are offered), and you don't want to ignore or add the word, click the underlined word with your left mouse button. This will close the shortcut menu and position your cursor in the word. Edit the word by using the Delete or Backspace key, or select the text with your mouse and type the correct spelling.

CAUTION

Depending on your system's resources (memory, processing speed), you may want to limit the number of words you add to the dictionary. If you have a great deal of terminology to add, consider using a custom dictionary instead.

Running Spell Check from the Menu or Toolbar

 You can also run a spell check on your entire document, by choosing Tools, Spelling and Grammar from the menu, or clicking the Spelling and Grammar button on the toolbar. The spell-check program will go through your text and stop at each misspelled or questionable word, displaying it in context in the Not in Dictionary box (see Figure 3.3).

FIG. 3.3
View your misspelled word in context in the Spelling and Grammar dialog box.

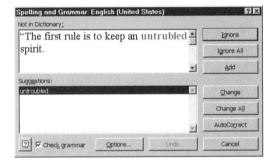

On the right side of the dialog box, a series of buttons offer you the same commands as the shortcut menu, with some exceptions:

- In addition to Ignore, you can choose to Ignore All. Ignore All tells Word to ignore any other occurrences of the word as you've spelled it. This applies to this document only.

- To insert an alternative spelling (from the Suggestions box), choose the alternative and click Change or Change All. Change All will fix any other occurrences of this exact spelling that occur in the document.

- To correct the misspelling (if none of the Suggestions are appropriate), select the word (which appears in red) within the Not in Dictionary box. Type the correct spelling, and click the Change or Change All buttons. Your document is updated with the new correct spelling.

When your spell check is complete, click the Cancel button.

CAUTION

Make sure you act on your last spelling error by changing, ignoring, or adding it *before* you exit the dialog box. If you haven't selected an action, clicking Cancel to close the Spelling and Grammar dialog box will leave your last misspelled word in the document, untouched.

N O T E If you notice that you're making the same spelling mistakes repeatedly, you might want to add the misspelling and its correction to Word's list of AutoCorrect entries. See Chapter 2, "Creating Documents," for more information.

Setting Your Spell Check Options

You can customize the way Word checks your spelling by making some changes to the spell check defaults. To view and change the defaults, choose Tools, Options.

Figure 3.4 shows the Options dialog box.

FIG. 3.4

View and change Word's spell check options.

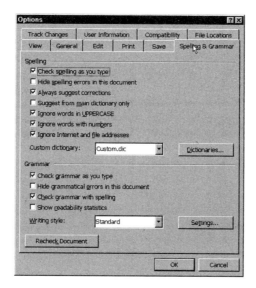

As soon as the Options dialog box opens, click the Spelling & Grammar tab. The top half of the dialog box contains your Spelling settings:

- *Check Spelling as You Type.* Turn this off (it's on by default) if you don't want Word to check your text as you type it.

- *Hide Spelling Errors in This Document.* If you don't want to see the red underlines while you're typing, yet you want Word to be checking your spelling, leave this feature turned off. When you're ready to see your errors and correct them, turn the option on.

- *Always Suggest Corrections.* This option is on by default. If you misspell a word due to a typo, you know how to correct it. If, however, you misspelled it because you didn't know the correct spelling, a list of alternative spellings will be extremely useful. Leave this feature on.

- *Suggest from Main Dictionary Only.* Word has a main dictionary that is an installed part of the Word application. You also have a Custom dictionary that contains the words you add while running spell check. These dictionaries are used together to check your document. This feature is off by default, to enable Word to consult both your Custom dictionary and its own Main Dictionary during spell check.

- *Ignore Words in UPPERCASE.* This feature is on by default. If you type a lot of initials and acronyms (such as RSVP or ASAP), you'll want to leave this feature on.

- *Ignore Words with Numbers.* This is on by default, so that if you type product or serial numbers (which are often a combination of letters and numbers), Word won't see it as a misspelling.

- *Ignore Internet and File Addresses.* Anything preceded by "http://" or that contains forward or backward slashes should be ignored by your spell check, because the words are usually abbreviations or combined words. This feature is on by default.

Working with Custom Dictionaries   Two other buttons in the Spelling and Grammar Options box are the *Custom Dictionary* button and the *Dictionaries* button:

- The Custom Dictionary button shows the name of the supplementary dictionary that Word is using in addition to its own to spell check your documents.

- To create extra custom dictionaries, click the Dictionaries button. This button opens a dialog box that allows you to create and save a custom dictionary that you can add words to later (see Figure 3.5).

FIG.3.5
Click the Dictionaries button to see a list of your custom dictionaries.

Custom dictionaries are useful for people who work with esoteric terminology such as legal and medical jargon. You can add these words to your Custom dictionary, or create separate custom dictionaries for your different sets of jargon.

Creating a New Custom Dictionary   To create a custom dictionary, follow these steps:

1. In the Custom Dictionaries dialog box, click New. In the resulting dialog box, give the custom dictionary a name such as **Medical**. Figure 3.6 shows the Create Custom Dictionary dialog box.

FIG. 3.6

Create a new custom dictionary for your special terminology.

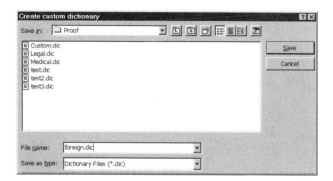

2. Click Save to close the Create Custom Dictionary dialog box.

 TIP If you want Word to use this dictionary in your future spell checks, make sure the box next to it is checked.

3. Click OK to return to the Spelling & Grammar tab in the Options dialog box. Click the Custom Dictionary drop-list button, and you'll see your new dictionary in the list.

N O T E Creating separate custom dictionaries for different terminology groups (such as medical or legal) can make editing the dictionaries easier. If you keep all of your terms in one custom dictionary, you'll have to wade through many words to edit or delete an entry. ▪

Editing and Removing Custom Dictionaries   Custom Dictionaries can be edited and removed by choosing Tools, Options and clicking the Spelling and Grammar tab. Perform the following steps to Edit or Remove a custom dictionary:

1. In the Spelling and Grammar options dialog box, click the Dictionaries button, and select the custom dictionary that you want to edit or remove.

2. If you want to remove a custom dictionary, select it in the list, and click the Remove button.

3. Click OK to save your changes and close the dialog box.

4. If you click Edit, Word opens a document containing a list of the words in that dictionary. Edit the contents as you would edit any document; use Delete or Backspace to remove text, or highlight text with your mouse and type your replacement text.

Part

I

Ch

3

5. Choose File, Save from the menu or press Ctrl+S to save the dictionary. Your custom dictionary is updated.

CAUTION

When removing a custom dictionary, be careful that the one you want to remove is the one that is selected. There is no confirmation prompt.

Using Language Tools

Word gives you several tools for editing and analyzing the content of your document. Tools such as a Grammar check program, Thesaurus, and custom Hyphenation feature allow you to go beyond spell checking to make sure your writing is clear, grammatically correct, and that you aren't overusing any words.

Working with Grammar Check

Grammar check is another proofreading tool that is automatically in effect when you create a document. As you type, if you construct a phrase or sentence that Word feels is in violation of its grammar rules, the text will be underlined in green.

Customizing Grammar Check   To make the best use of Grammar check, it's important to customize the tool so that it fits the way you write. To set your Grammar check options, follow these steps:

1. Choose Tools, Options.

2. A large, multi-tabbed dialog box opens. Click the Spelling and Grammar tab.

3. If you want to make specific changes to your grammatical rules, click the Settings button.

   The Spelling and Grammar dialog box is divided into two sections. The Grammar section (see Figure 3.7) offers the following options:

FIG. 3.7
Make changes to the way Word checks your documents' grammar by selecting Tools, Options and clicking the Spelling and Grammar tab.

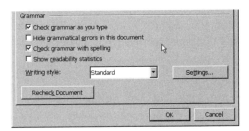

- *Check Grammar as You Type.* This option is on by default. If you don't want to see your grammatical errors as you type, remove the check mark for this option.

- *Hide Grammatical Errors in This Document.* If you don't want to see your errors while you're working, yet want Word to be checking it as you type, click this option to turn it on. When you're ready to see your errors and deal with them, come back to this dialog box and turn the option off.

- *Check Grammar with Spelling.* This option is also in the on position by default and enables you to proofread your document from both a spelling and a grammatical perspective with one command. If this option is left on, Word will check your spelling and grammar when you use the spell checking tool.

- *Show Readability Statistics.* If you aren't sure of your readers' education level, it's best to keep your document's readability set to a lower grade level. This eliminates your risk of speaking "over the head" of your readers. By default, this option is off.

- *Writing Style.* The drop-down list offers Casual, Standard (the default style), Formal, Technical, and Custom options. Each style has its own set of grammatical rules ranging from liberal (Casual) to conservative (Formal).

4. Scroll through the list of Grammar Settings options (see Figure 3.8), turning on those that you want Word to check for, and turning off those that you want Word to overlook. The options are all "toggled" between on and off by clicking the small boxes to the left of the option. If a check mark appears in the box, the option is turned on.

Part

I

Ch

3

FIG. 3.8

Use the Grammar Settings options to select the grammar rules you want to use.

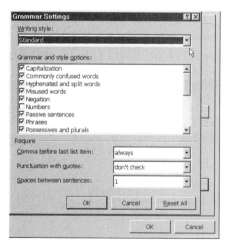

5. Click OK to return to the Spelling and Grammar options dialog box.

 If you changed the Writing Style or settings for your grammar check, you may want to click the Recheck Document button. Word checks your document's grammar again, this time with the new "rules" in effect.

6. Click OK in the Grammar Settings dialog box to accept your changes and close the dialog box.

7. Click OK in the Options dialog box. Your settings will be saved, and the dialog box will close.

 T I P It's easier to Ignore an "error" in an informal document than it is to keep resetting your Grammar style. Unless all of your documents are informal in nature, leave your Grammar style on Standard.

Checking Your Grammar   If you have Word set to check your grammar as you type, each violation of the grammar rules will be underlined in green. To correct or skip the error, right-click the green underlined text. A shortcut menu opens (see Figure 3.9), offering you the following choices:

- One or more alternatives for words or sentence structure will appear in bold at the top of the shortcut menu.

FIG. 3.9

Use the shortcut menu to correct or ignore your grammatical errors.

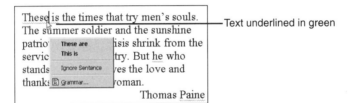

Text underlined in green

- Choosing the Ignore Sentence command will make the green underline disappear.

- The last option, Grammar, will open the Grammar dialog box. You will see the error, in context, and any alternatives or a brief explanation of the error. You can choose to Ignore, Ignore All, or Change the text (see Figure 3.10).

FIG. 3.10

The Spelling and Grammar dialog box gives you more options and information about your grammatical errors.

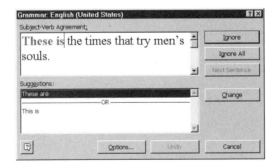

 T I P Use Ignore All sparingly. Ignore All refers to the grammatical rule, not the specific error you're ignoring.

Using the Thesaurus

A thesaurus is a list of words and their *synonyms*. A synonym is a word that means the same thing as another word. For example, a synonym for the word "nice" would be "pleasant."

You can use Word's Thesaurus to find alternatives for words you feel you're overusing, or to determine a word's correct definition by looking at other words meaning the same thing.

Figure 3.11 shows the Thesaurus dialog box.

FIG. 3.11

Use Word's Thesaurus to look for synonyms and definitions by example.

Part

I

Ch

3

To use the Thesaurus to find a synonym for a word in your document, follow these steps:

1. Highlight the word for which you need a synonym.

2. Choose Tools, Language. Choose Thesaurus from the submenu that appears.

3. The Thesaurus dialog box opens. Choose the part of speech that is appropriate for your use of the word from the list in the Meanings box.

4. Based on the part of speech you select, a list of synonyms appears on the right side of the box.

5. Select a word from the list of synonyms, and click Replace. The dialog box closes, and your word is replaced.

To use a word's synonyms to determine its definition, you don't need to start with a word highlighted in your document. You can enter the word you want to look up into the Thesaurus dialog box. Follow these steps to look up a word:

1. With or without a word highlighted in your document, choose Tools, Language. Choose Thesaurus from the submenu.

2. If you didn't highlight the word in your document, type the word you want to look up in the Insert box.

3. Click the Look Up button. The word moves to the left side of the dialog box in the Looked Up box.

4. Choose the part of speech that applies to your use of the word (in the Meanings box), and review the synonyms that display in the Synonyms box.

5. If you were only looking up the word and don't intend to use it in your document, click Cancel to close the Thesaurus. No changes are made to your document.

Working with Hyphenation

By default, Word does not automatically hyphenate your text. As you type, your text stops at the right margin and then flows automatically to the next line. If, at the right margin, an entire word doesn't fit on the line, it is moved to the next line. If you turn on Automatic Hyphenation, Word will break off a word, leaving part of it on one line and continuing it on the next. A hyphen (dash) is appended to the first half of the word. To view and set your hyphenation options, perform the following steps:

1. Choose Tools, Language. Choose Hyphenation from the submenu.
2. In the Hyphenation dialog box (see Figure 3.12), there are two check boxes:
   - *Automatically Hyphenate Document.* This option is off by default.
   - *Hyphenate Words in CAPS.* This option is on by default.

FIG. 3.12
Choose your hyphenation settings from the Hyphenation dialog box.

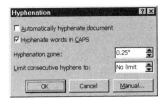

3. If you choose to turn Automatic Hyphenation on, you should also set the Hyphenation Zone, which is the distance from the right margin that a word must be (and not fit) before a hyphen is inserted.
4. Set the number of consecutive hyphens that you'll tolerate in a document. The default is No Limit.

N O T E In general, a No Limit setting for your number of consecutive hyphens doesn't create problems with the appearance or legibility of your document. If, however, you are using a lot of long words, such as medical or legal terminology, you may find that many of your sentences are broken with a hyphen, and your right margin can begin to look "fringed" with these dash symbols. If this occurs, go back to your Hyphenation settings, and choose a number such as 1 or 2 as the acceptable number of consecutive hyphens. Be sure to select your entire document (by pressing Ctrl+A) before you reset, so that your text is rehyphenated according to your new settings. ▓

Document Collaboration

When a team of people work on a document, each person's input is important to the process. Word 97 facilitates this by offering tools that enable you to keep different people's input separate, and to integrate the team members' changes and suggestions into the document without retyping. Through Word's Track Changes feature and User Information options, your teams' edits can be easily coordinated.

Tracking Changes

To turn Word's revision tools on, choose Tools, Track Changes. From the submenu, choose Highlight Changes. Figure 3.13 shows the Highlight Changes dialog box. By default, this feature is turned off, so that additions and deletions to a document's text are not highlighted in any way. Turn revisions on by clicking in the Track Changes While Editing check box.

FIG. 3.13

Use the Highlight changes dialog box to track revisions in your document.

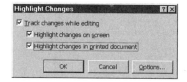

You have two highlighting options, both of which should be turned on in order to effectively track your changes:

- Highlight Changes on Screen
- Highlight Changes in Printed Document

Click OK to accept your settings and close the dialog box.

As soon as you begin editing a document with Track Changes on, you'll notice that whatever text you add is underlined and is a different color. Any text that you delete is crossed out and also is changed to another color.

To view and change your Track Changes settings, choose Tools, Options, and click the Track Changes tab. Figure 3.14 shows the Track Changes dialog box. The dialog box is broken down into four sections, each describing the Mark (style) and Color of changes in the following areas:

- *Inserted Text.* By default, the text appears red and underlined.
- *Deleted Text.* Deleted text also appears red, with a line through it (strikethrough).
- *Changed Formatting.* By default, there is no visual change for formatting changes.
- *Changed Lines.* This option refers to a vertical border that is applied to any text that has been changed. By default, a black border is placed on the left and right sides of the page.

You can change the Mark and Color settings for each of the four options. A preview box to the right of each option shows you how your Mark and Color choices will look. To put your changes into effect and close the dialog box, click OK.

By default, the colors for inserted and deleted text are set to a red/blue combination. This is the best choice for a collaborative editing process because the computer will assign a different color for each user, for a team of up to eight users. A "user" is determined by the User Information stored in your computer. To view or change your User Information, choose Tools, Options, and click the User Information tab.

FIG. 3.14
Use the Track Changes dialog box to view and edit your Track Changes options.

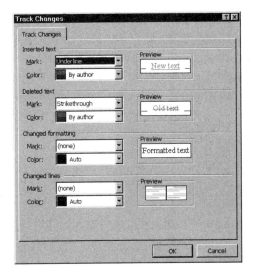

NOTE To edit your own work, you can change the author Name in the User Information dialog box. You can enter a name that defines your editing role, such as "First Draft Editor" or "Final Copy Editor," or merely put a number after your real name to indicate which step in the editing process you're on.

Accepting and Rejecting Changes

When your editing process is complete, you must choose which revisions to accept and which ones to reject. Accepted changes are integrated into the document; rejected changes are removed with no change to the original document.

To review the changes applied by your team, follow these steps:

1. Choose Tools, Track Changes.
2. Click Accept or Reject Changes in the submenu. Figure 3.15 shows the Accept or Reject Changes dialog box.

FIG. 3.15
Use the Accept or Reject Changes submenu to accept or reject changes.

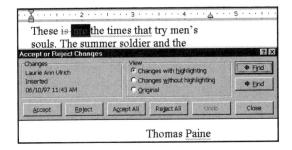

3. In the dialog box, you can use the Find buttons to move forward and backward through your document, viewing each revision one at a time.

4. As the revisions appear on-screen, you will see the name of the user who made the revisions in the Change section of the dialog box.

5. To accept or reject changes, you can choose from the following commands:

- *Accept.* As you're viewing revisions one at a time, click this button when you want the change integrated into the original document.

- *Reject.* The revision will be deleted, leaving the original text intact.

- *Accept All.* If you choose this command, you won't get to see each revision one at a time. Word will integrate all revisions into your document.

- *Reject All.* This option will remove all revisions.

- *Undo.* Use this option if you want to reverse your Accept/Reject action.

- *Close.* Click this button when you finish accepting and rejecting your revisions.

Working with Find and Replace

Word's Find and Replace feature allows you to look for text, formatting, codes (such as tabs or hard returns), and special characters (such as em dashes or spaces) within a document and if desired, replace them with something else. Find and Replace are two separate tools:

- *Find* looks for text or codes and shows you each incident one at a time. You choose how or if to act on each found item. This procedure is often used for proofreading, to check for some consistent feature throughout a document, such as a date or a heading style.

- *Replace* looks for the text, formatting, or code, and at each one found, gives you the opportunity to skip to the next one or replace it with some other predetermined content. Replace is a powerful tool used, for example, to update a document with a current date, or to remove one person's name and replace it with another.

 Find and Replace can be accessed from the Edit menu (Edit, Find or Edit, Replace) or from the Browse buttons at the bottom of your vertical scroll bar by clicking the Find button. However you activate the feature, a three-tabbed dialog box opens (see Figure 3.16) offering you the ability to Find, Replace, or Go To an item in your document.

FIG. 3.16
Use the Find and Replace dialog box to search your document.

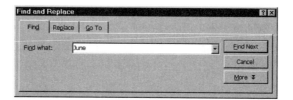

Part
I

Ch
3

Using Find

To Find text, formatting, or a special character in your document, perform the following steps:

1. Choose Edit, Find or click the Find button. The keyboard shortcut to initiate Find is Ctrl+F.

2. In the Find dialog box, enter the text you're looking for in the Find What box. You can enter up to 255 characters, including spaces.

3. To fine-tune your search, click the More button (see Figure 3.17). The dialog box expands to offer the following options:

FIG 3.17

Click More to see options for fine-tuning your search.

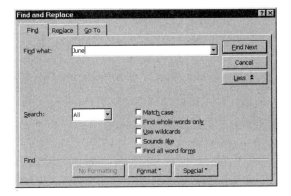

■ *Search.* The Search drop-down list gives you a choice of directions for your search to follow: Up, Down, or All. If, for example, you're in the middle of your document and you want to search only the remaining pages, choose Down. The default and most effective setting is All.

■ *Match Case.* Normally, Find will look for your Find What text regardless of case (upper or lower). Turning on Match Case tells Word to look for the text in the case exactly as you've typed it.

■ *Find Whole Words Only.* Some words occur as whole words on their own, such as "other," yet can also be parts of words such as "mother." Turn this feature on if the word you seek can also be part of another word.

■ *Use Wildcards.* A wild-card character (?) can be inserted into your Find What text to represent any character. If, for example, you type **te?t** into your Find What box, if Use Wildcards is on, Word will find "text," "test," and "tent."

■ *Sounds Like.* This option finds a word's homonym, such as "read" and "reed."

■ *Find All Word Forms.* To search for a word in all of its potential forms, such as "possible" and "possibility," use this option.

■ *Format.* This option allows you to specify which character and paragraph formats have been applied to the text you're looking for (see Figure 3.18). For example, you can fine-tune your search so that it only finds your search text when it is bold,

16 pts, and indented a half-inch from the right margin. Word will ignore any other formatted versions of your Find What text.

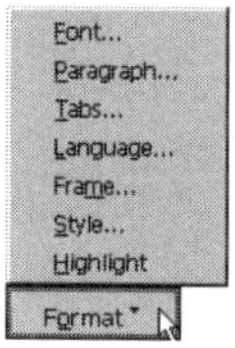

FIG. 3.18
You can include formatting styles to help fine-tune your search.

- *Special.* This option allows you to search for special codes such as tabs, hard returns (paragraph codes), or hyphens (see Figure 3.19). When you choose the characters from the Special list, a series of symbols appears in your Find What box, such as "^P" in a search for hard returns.

FIG. 3.19
You can search for special codes and characters in your document by clicking the Special button.

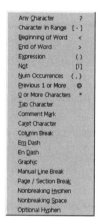

- *No Formatting.* If your last search used formatting and you want to clear it, click this option.

4. Click the Find Next button to initiate the search. As each occurrence of your text, character, or code appears, click Find Next to move to the next occurrence.

5. When your search is complete, click Cancel.

N O T E If you need to edit any of your found text, you can click outside of the Find dialog box and type in your document. The Find dialog box remains open and can be reactivated to continue your search (or start a new one) by clicking the dialog box title bar. ■

Using Replace

Once you find your text or character, it's often useful to replace it with something else. To find and replace an item in your document, perform the following steps:

Part

I

Ch

3

1. Choose Edit, Replace from the menu, or press Ctrl+H. The Find and Replace dialog box opens with the Replace tab in front (see Figure 3.20).

FIG. 3.20

Use Replace to change your found items to something else.

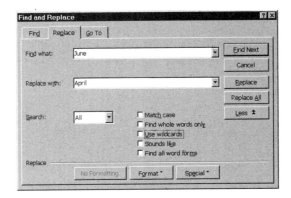

2. Enter the text you're looking for, or choose Special to insert a character or code in your Find What box. Apply your Formatting and other options as necessary.

3. Press Tab or click your mouse in the Replace With box. Type the text or choose Special to insert the character or code that will replace your found items.

4. As necessary, apply formats to your Replace With text by clicking the Format button and selecting the formatting you want to apply.

5. Choose the method of replacement from the buttons on the right side of the dialog box:

   ■ *Find Next.* Starts the process and brings up the first incidence of your Find What item. You can then choose to Replace the item or skip to the next one by pressing Find Next again.

   ■ *Replace All.* Replaces every incidence of your Find What entry with your Replace With content. You will not be able to skip any of them. When the operation is complete, a count of the replacements will display on-screen. Click OK to close the prompt.

6. The Find and Replace dialog box will remain open for a repeated or new search. Click Cancel to close the dialog box.

CHAPTER 4

Managing Word Files

One of your computer's most important jobs is to store your files. Understanding your options for where, when, and how to save them is essential to making Word 97 an effective tool. Adding folders to categorize your files, applying passwords to protect them, and selecting the proper format in which to save your files will enable you to control the documents that you create. ■

Saving tips and tricks

Using Word's tools for saving a file to the correct folder with a name that makes sense will save you time and keep you organized.

File formats

Word gives you a lot of ways to save your files, enabling you to share your work with anyone, using virtually any type of software.

Security

Saving your files with passwords can protect them from prying eyes and accidental changes.

Choosing a File Name and Location

You can save all of your files to the default "My Documents folder," but as you accumulate more and more files, you'll find that saving to subject, author, or date-oriented folders will make finding your files easier and faster.

To keep your files organized, categorize your documents (and other types of files as well) in folders. Name your folders in such a way to clearly indicate the category of files that are stored inside it, such a "First Quarter Reports" or "Letters to Insurance Company." Windows 95 supports up to 255 characters (including spaces) in your file and folder names, which gives you a great deal of flexibility in creating file names. Of course a 255-character folder name would be very cumbersome, but using 20 to 30 characters will clearly describe the contents of your folders.

Word 97 gives you the ability to create a folder at the time you save a file. To create a new folder and save your new file in it, follow these steps:

1. The first time you save your document, choose File, Save; or press Ctrl+S. You can also use File, Save As.
2. In the Save As dialog box, go to the My Documents folder, or another folder that you've been using to store your documents.
3. With that folder displayed in the Save In box, choose the New Folder button. A New Folder dialog box opens (see Figure 4.1).
4. Type the name of your new folder, and choose OK. The folder now appears as a subfolder of your current folder.
5. Double-click the new folder so that it appears in the Save In box.
6. Choose the Save button to store your document in the new folder.

N O T E You can use the Windows Explorer or My Computer to move, copy, delete, or rename your files and folders. You can also use these programs to create new folders to categorize your files. ▪

FIG. 4.1
Create a new folder to store your new document.

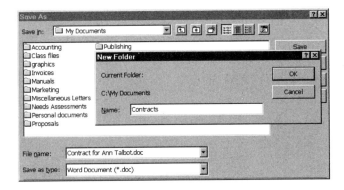

N O T E Remember that the folder you're in when you create a new folder will be the new folder's "parent," and your new folder will be a subfolder, or "child." Understanding this relationship as it applies to folders is essential to effective file management. If you have a parent folder called "Letters," for example, you'll create subfolders within it to categorize your letters. The subfolders could be named "Personal" or "Business" to keep your different types of letters separate.

Saving a New Version

To keep an existing document intact while reusing it as the foundation for a new file, save the existing file with a new name. Word's Save As feature enables you to take one document and create an unlimited number of versions of it.

Perform these steps to create a new version of an existing file:

1. Open the existing saved file and choose File, Save As from the menu.
2. Give the file a new name—you can simply add a **2** or an **A** to the existing file name, or give it an entirely new, descriptive name.
3. Choose a new location for the file, if necessary.
4. Click the Save button. Your original file is automatically closed and is unchanged. Your new version is open on-screen, awaiting your changes.
5. Edit the new version as necessary, and save it by choosing File, Save; or by pressing Ctrl+S.

 Not sure which version is which? File, Open will show you a preview of each of your Word 97 documents that were saved in default Word 97 format. If you saved your document in an older Word format or in a format for another word processor, you will not be able to see a preview.

Word 97 makes it easy to keep track of all your versions of the same file. To save comments pertaining to your new version of a file, perform the following steps:

1. Choose the Save Version button in the Save As dialog box. You can do this the first time you save the document or on any of your update saves, by choosing File, Save As.
2. The Save Version dialog box opens (see Figure 4.2). Type a sentence that describes your file. You can type up to 255 characters of text, including spaces.
3. Click OK to save your comments.

To view information about all versions of any file, open the original file (the file used as the basis for new versions) and choose File, Versions. A list of the files that were created will display. Click the View Comments button to see the comments that were saved about any particular file. To exit the Versions dialog box, click Close.

Figure 4.3 shows the Versions dialog box.

Part
I
Ch
4

FIG. 4.2
Word 97 allows you to save comments about each version of a file as it moves through the editing process.

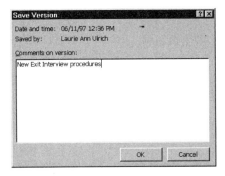

FIG. 4.3
Use View Comments to see a list of all the versions you've created from one original file.

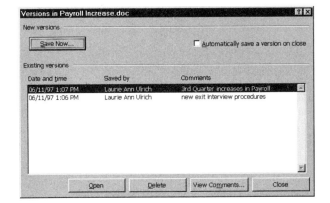

Setting Autosaving Options

It's a good idea to save your work early and often. As soon as you start typing your document, save it by choosing File, Save or pressing Ctrl+S. As you continue to work, save it repeatedly, so your latest changes are always safe from accidental loss.

Don't assume that the AutoRecover that occurs periodically is a substitute for frequent saving. AutoRecover only updates a temporary file that may *possibly* be recovered in the event of a power failure or other unexpected shutdown. To adjust the frequency of your AutoRecover updates, choose Tools, Options from the menu. The default setting is every 10 minutes. You can also turn off AutoRecover by removing the check from the option's check box.

If you can commit the Ctrl+S keyboard shortcut to memory, you'll have a quick, easy way to save your file as you work on it—without taking your hands off the keyboard!

Saving Files in Different Formats

When you save a file in Word 97, the file is saved in Word 97 format. This format cannot be opened by previous versions of Word (6.0 or 7.0) or any other word processing software created prior to the release of Word 97. For this reason, if you're working with people who have older software, you will want to save your file in a different format.

If you've already saved your document in Word 97 for your own use, perform the following steps to resave it in a different format:

1. With your file open, choose File, Save As from the menu.
2. Choose the location for your file, making sure your target folder or drive appears in the Save In box.
3. If you want to keep your Word 97 version of the file separate from this new version, give the new file a different name.

 TIP If you keep the same file name, your Word 97 file will be overwritten in the new format. The next time you open the file in Word 97, it will be converted to Word 97 format.

4. At the bottom of the Save As dialog box, click the Save as Type drop-down list and scroll through the list of available file formats (see Figure 4.4). These formats include:
   - For Word 6.0 and 7.0 users, you should choose Word 6.0/95.
   - For users of any version of WordPerfect (for DOS or Windows), select the matching version from the list of WordPerfect formats.
   - If you don't know what software will be used, and your document contains a lot of graphic content, choose .RTF (Rich Text Format).
   - If you know the person who will be using your file has Windows 3.1, you might choose the .WRI format. They can then use the Windows 3.1 Write accessory to open the file.
   - Other product formats, such as WordStar, Word for DOS, and Works are also found in the list. If your file recipient uses one of these products, choose the matching format.
   - When all else fails, use a .TXT format. Graphic content and any visual formatting (fonts, tabs, indents, and so forth) will be lost, but the text content will be maintained. The user can reformat it in their software. Due to their smaller size (no formatting) text files are often the preferred file format for sending documents over the Internet.
   - You can save your files as HTML (HyperText Markup Language) if you want your document to become a Web page. (For additional details on HTML, see Chapter 17, "Creating Web Pages with Word.")

Part
I

Ch
4

T I P An .RTF format is generally acceptable to document any Windows-based word processor. Since this format also saves your graphic content, it's a good choice when you aren't sure which word processor will be used to open your file.

FIG. 4.4
To share your files with people using different software or older versions of Word, choose a format from the Save as Type drop-down list.

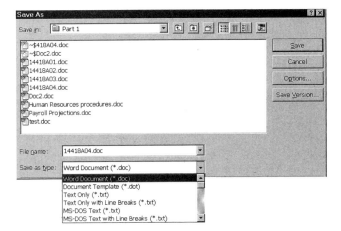

5. Select the appropriate format by clicking it in the list. The format will now display in the Save as Type box.

6. Click the Save button to save your file in the selected format.

N O T E   If you are often saving your documents in formats other than Word 97, you might want to turn off the default Allow Fast Saves in the Save dialog box. A Fast Save quickly updates the file to Word 97 format whenever you click the Save button on the toolbar or press Ctrl+S. To turn this default off, choose Tools, Options, and click the Save tab. Under Save Options, remove the check mark from the Allow Fast Saves check box.

Using Document Passwords

Word allows you to password-protect your document, preventing anyone from opening or changing it without knowing the password.

To password-protect your document, follow these steps:

1. Open the document you want to protect. Choose File, Save As from the menu.

2. Make any desired changes to the file name or location.

3. Click the Options button. The Save dialog box opens (see Figure 4.5).

   In the File Sharing Options section at the bottom of the dialog box, there are two empty boxes:

   • Password to Open

   • Password to Modify

FIG. 4.5

Enter passwords
to protect your
document from being
opened or modified.

4. Type a password into one or both of these boxes. Your typing will appear as asterisks (*).

5. If you want Word to open the file as Read Only, click the Read-Only Recommended check box.

6. Choose OK to save your passwords and close the dialog box.

Part
I

Ch
4

You will be prompted to re-enter your password(s), to make sure you typed them correctly. Click OK after each re-entry. You can now continue to work on your document or close it. The next time you open it, you will be prompted to enter a password before the file opens on-screen.

N O T E   If you choose two different passwords for Open and Modify, you can give other people the ability to look at your document, but not change it. If you choose the Read-Only Recommended option, when someone opens the file (with the Open password), they can choose to open it as Read Only without knowing the Modify password. If they make changes, they will have to save the file with a different name, leaving your original file intact.

   Don't forget your password! If you do, you won't be able to open your file again. Choose a password that others won't be able to figure out, but that you can't forget. Write it down somewhere as a backup.

You can change your password later by choosing Tools, Options while the document is open. Click the Save tab. Highlight either the Open or Modify password and replace it with your new password. Choose OK to close the dialog box and save your changes. You'll be prompted to re-enter the password for verification.

Creating a Backup Copy When You Save

If you want Word to create an automatic backup of the original version of your file each time you save it, you can activate that feature by selecting Tools, Options. Click the Save tab, and place a check mark in the Always Create Backup Copy option (refer to Figure 4.5). A file with a .BAK extension will be created each time you save your file. ●

CHAPTER 5

Printing Documents

During the process of creating a document—and certainly after a document is completed—you will likely want to print it, if only to have a tangible copy for storage. Word 97's printing defaults cover most of your needs for printing letters, reports, and more, but you may want to configure these settings to meet your specific needs. Word offers a variety of tools for customizing your print job, as well as a preview command to allow you to check your document's layout before printing. ■

Print Preview

Save paper by checking out your document before it's printed. View one or several pages at a time and make adjustments to your layout.

Exercise your options

Choose what to print and how to print it. Word's Print dialog box and Print Options contain several tools for eliminating printout surprises.

Previewing a Document Before Printing

 Before you commit your document to paper, it's a good idea to look at a preview by choosing File, Print Preview from the menu. You can also Click the Print Preview button on the toolbar.

> **N O T E** Think of Print Preview as a "thumbnail sketch" of your document. It shows the overall space that your text consumes, and lets you see if you have too much or too little white space. ▄

The Print Preview window contains several tools for viewing and manipulating your document. Figure 5.1 shows the Print Preview window.

FIG. 5.1

You can view one or more pages of your document in Print Preview.

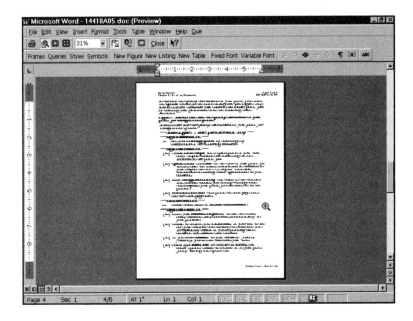

When you open the Print Preview window, you have a new toolbar across the top of the window. Table 5.1 shows each toolbar button and its function.

Table 5.1   Print Preview Toolbar and Command Buttons

Icon	Option	Description
	Print	Sends your document to the printer without opening the Print dialog box. You will get one copy of each page in your document.
	Magnifier	This button is on by default. When you are in Magnify mode, you can click any part of your document and zoom in on it. If you turn this button off (by clicking it), your cursor appears in your

Icon	Option	Description
		document, and you can now actively edit your document in Print Preview.
	One Page	Shows one page of your document at a time.
	Multiple Pages	Click and hold this button to display an array of small white pages. Drag your mouse through the array, selecting the number of pages you wish to see simultaneously. You can expand the array to see a total of 3 rows of 6 pages each, or 18 pages.
100%	Zoom	Click the drop-down list to see magnifications from 500% to 10%. You can also choose Page Width, Whole Page, or Two Pages.
	View Ruler	Places a horizontal and vertical ruler around your document. The ruler will show your margins, in-dents, and any tabs used on the displayed page.
	Shrink to Fit	If just a few words or lines have run onto a new page and you want everything to fit on the previous page, choose this button.
	Full Screen	To view your Preview without the titlebar, menus, or toolbar, choose this button. Press Esc to return to your Print Preview.
Close	Close	Exits Print Preview and returns you to your previous view of the document.
??	Context Sensitive Help	Enables you to select other Preview window features and read a Help article pertaining to them. Choose this button (your mouse gains a question mark [?] appendage) and click the toolbar buttons, rulers, and scrollbars for more information.

For more information on toolbars and command buttons, refer to Chapter 1, "The Word 97 Window."

N O T E Previewing your document allows you to spot layout problems before the document is printed. By turning off the Magnifier tool, you regain cursor control within Print Preview. This enables you to adjust your margins, add or delete blank lines, and insert page breaks.

For more information about Page Setup in any view, see Chapter 8, "Working with Tabs"

T I P While you can zoom in close enough to read and edit your document content while in Print Preview, this feature is best used for visually checking and adjusting your document layout. To edit content, return to Normal or Page Layout view.

Printing Your Document

 For a quick printout of your entire document, click the Print button on the toolbar. Word will print one copy of each page in your document without requiring any further input from you. To customize your print job, open the Print dialog box by choosing File, Print from the menu.

Figure 5.2 shows the Print dialog box.

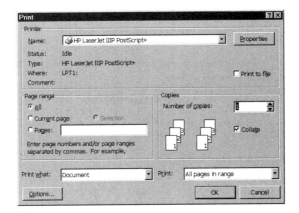

Choosing the Printer

The Print dialog box offers options for selecting the source, scope, and size of your printout:

- *Choose a printer.* If your computer is attached to more than one printer via a network or switching device, you can select one of the available printers for your current print job. The default printer for all your Windows applications is set through the Windows Control Panel.

- *Determine your print range.* You can print All pages (the default) or the Current Page (where your cursor is when you open the Print dialog box). If you have a multi-page document, choose which pages to print. You can enter a range of pages (1-5), a nonconsecutive list of pages (1,3,7), or any combination thereof (1-4, 5,6,9).

- *Choose a number of copies.* The your default is one, but you can enter any number of copies. The number you choose will apply to all pages in your print range. If you're printing more than one copy of multiple pages, leave the Collate feature on.

To control the quality and content of your print job, choose the Options button in the Print dialog box (see Figure 5.3). You can further customize your current and future print jobs by entering your preferences into the following three sections:

FIG. 5.3
You can fine-tune the quality and content of your print job through Print Options.

■ Set your Printing Options by selecting any combination of the following features:

- *Draft Output.* Creates a quick print of your text only. Graphic content and formatting are not included in the print job.

- *Update Fields* and *Update Links.* Ensure that the latest information is included in your output. (See Chapter 19, "Working with Other Office 97 Applications," for more information on linking other applications to your document.)

- *Background Printing.* Enables you to keep working while Word composes your print job and sends it to the printer. It is selected by default.

- *Reverse Print Order.* Prints the last page first and the first page last.

■ Choose which items to Include with Document:

- *Document Properties.* Prints the author name, document size, and modification history in your printout.

- *Field Codes.* Displays how your external data content was inserted. This is especially useful if you're printing out a document that someone else created.

- *Comments.* Reveals any added comments that you may have added to your document by selecting Insert, Comment.

- *Hidden Text.* Normally visible on-screen, but doesn't print. Choose this option to include it in your print job.

- *Drawing Objects.* Prints by default. (For more information on adding drawn objects to your document, see Chapter 12, "Using Graphics to Enhance Word Documents.")

Part
I

Ch
5

■ Use Options for Current Document Only to adjust your active document's output:

* *Print Data Only for Forms.* Simply prints the data and not the form itself. (See Chapter 10, "Using Tables," for more information about creating fill-in forms.)
* *Default Tray.* Is an option only if you have more than one tray on your printer.

 TIP You can also access your Print Options by choosing Tools, Options from the menu, and selecting the Print tab.

Setting Your Printer Properties

The more you know about your printer, the more control you can have over the documents that come out of it. To view and adjust your printer's Properties, choose the Properties button in the Print dialog box. Figure 5.4 shows the Printer Properties dialog box.

FIG. 5.4

View and adjust your printer settings with the Printer Properties dialog box.

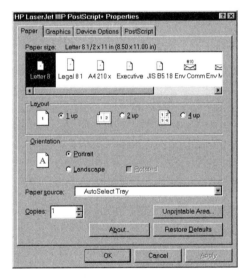

 TIP You can also view your Printer Properties by selecting Settings, Printers from the Start menu. Right-click your printer's icon and choose Properties from the shortcut menu.

The Print Properties dialog box contains four tabs:

■ Paper
■ Graphics
■ Device Options
■ PostScript

Many of these settings are also available through the Print Options dialog box. The content of the four tabs will vary based on what model printer you are using.

CAUTION

Be sure to refer to your Printer documentation for your printer's specifications before making any changes in the Device Options and Postscript tabs.

Part

I

Ch

5

Formatting Documents

Enhancing Text with Character Formatting

Font size and style

Changing the font, size, and style of your text can set the tone of your document and tell the reader what's important.

Color and motion

Bring the impact of color and animation to your documents. You don't have to have a color printer to take advantage of the on-screen effects.

Text characters are the building blocks of your document. Choosing the right font for your text is nearly as important as choosing the right words to convey your message. The fonts you choose can set a mood for your document, as well as direct your reader to what's important. Word 97 gives you simple, yet powerful tools for applying fonts, styles, colors, and even animation to your text, enabling you to add a creative, polished appearance to your documents. ■

Understanding Fonts

Fonts change the appearance of your text. Some fonts are character sets that convert your text to symbols. While there are some rules for combining fonts in a document, choosing the right one for your document is a matter of personal choice.

Fonts (also referred to as *typefaces*) fall into one of three categories:

■ *Serif.* From the Latin word for angels (seraphim), serif fonts have strokes, like wings, at the end of letters.

■ *Sans serif.* "Sans" means without. Sans serif fonts have no strokes at the end of their letters.

■ *Specialty.* Character sets such as Wingdings and highly stylized fonts are considered Specialty fonts.

Figure 6.1 shows a sample of serif, sans serif, and specialty fonts' text and characters.

FIG. 6.1

Fonts and character sets change the appearance of your text and the tone of your document.

Bookman Old Style

Arial

Emelia

Wingdings

TIP   When you install new software (especially word processing and graphics packages), the fonts that are installed are based on your printer's capabilities. Most laser and inkjet printers can accommodate the majority of available fonts.

CAUTION

Windows 95 doesn't tolerate a large group of installed fonts. Try not to install more than 800 fonts—including those that are installed with various software products and any font sets that you purchase separately. When you buy extra font sets, go through them and preview a sample of each font before you install it. Many fonts have different names, but really look alike.

Formatting Text

To apply a new font to your existing text, select the text and choose Format, Font. In the Font dialog box, choose from the list of fonts installed on your computer (see Figure 16.2). You can see how the font will look in the Preview section of the dialog box. When you've found the font you want, click OK and the font is applied to your selected text.

FIG. 6.2

Preview the installed fonts before applying them to your selected text.

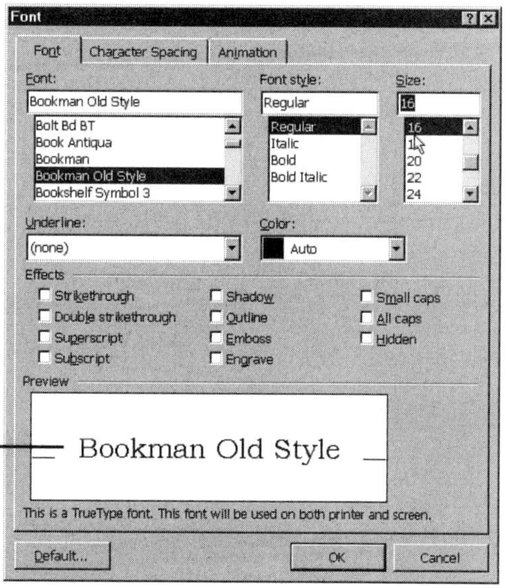

Font preview —————— Bookman Old Style

Font Sizes

Word 97 lists font sizes in *points*, a measurement system developed by typographers for expressing the size of text. There are 72 points in an inch, so 12 point text is 1/6th of an inch.

As you experiment with fonts, you'll find that some of the fancier fonts can be illegible in small point-sizes. While all 12-point fonts are technically the same size, some appear larger or smaller than others, based on the formation of the letters. Figure 1.3 shows 12 pt. Arial text and 12 pt. Times New Roman. You'll see that 12 pt. Arial text appears much larger than the same size text in Times New Roman.

FIG. 6.3
The same size fonts can look bigger or smaller, depending on the formation of the characters.

12 Point text in Times New Roman
12 Point text in Arial

To change the font size of your text, select the text and choose Format, Font from the menu. Choose a font size from the dialog box, and choose OK to apply it to your selected text.

Font Styles

The *style* of your font can be Bold, Italic, or both. Some fonts cannot be made bold or italic, others are bold or italic to begin with. You can apply a font style by clicking the Bold or Italic buttons on the Formatting toolbar.

N O T E   The Font dialog box will show you a preview of the effect that Bold or Italic will have on your text. As you choose different fonts to preview them, the available styles for the selected font appear in the Style list.

Underline Options

To apply a simple single underline to your text, click the Underline button on the Formatting toolbar. To see a list of Underline styles, choose Format, Font, and click the Underline drop-down list in the Font dialog box. Figure 6.4 shows the list of underline styles.

FIG. 6.4
Single, Double, and Dotted are just a few of the many underline styles available in Word.

As you select underline styles, the Preview box will show you how they'll look on your selected text. To apply one to your text, select it from the list and click OK to close the dialog box.

Special Character Effects

The Font dialog box offers some interesting effects that can be applied to your text—several of them new features in Word 97. You can apply one or more of them to your selected text by clicking the check box next to the effect:

■ *Strikethrough.* Applies a line through the center of the text. Although the text is crossed out, it remains legible. This effect is used for marking text for deletion and is applied automatically during the revision process. (See Chapter 3, "Editing Documents," for more information on Word's revision tools.)

- *Double Strikethrough.* Places a double line through your selected text.
- *Superscript.* Raised above the text's *baseline* and shrunken slightly. You can use Superscript for a footnote reference, or to type an exponent, such as 10^3.

 T I P The *baseline* is an invisible line on which your text sits. If you apply Superscript, your text is raised above the baseline. If you apply Subscript, your text is placed below the baseline.

- *Subscript.* Lowered in relation to the baseline and shrunken slightly. The Subscript effect can be applied, for example, to create a chemical formula, such as H_2O.
- *Shadow.* Gives your text a three-dimensional look.
- *Outline.* Creates a border around your characters with no fill inside them. Not all text can be outlined, in which case the option will appear dimmed in the dialog box.
- *Emboss.* Text appears raised, as though the paper were sculpted in the shape of the letters.
- *Engrave.* Produces an indented look, as though the text were carved into the paper.
- *Small Caps.* Creates two levels of capital letters. All the text is in caps, but only the characters that were typed with the Shift key will be a full-height capitals.
- *All Caps.* Changes any selected text to uppercase.
- *Hidden.* Text shows on-screen, but does not print.

Figure 6.5 shows samples of several text effects.

FIG. 6.5
Eleven different effects are available in the Fonts dialog box.

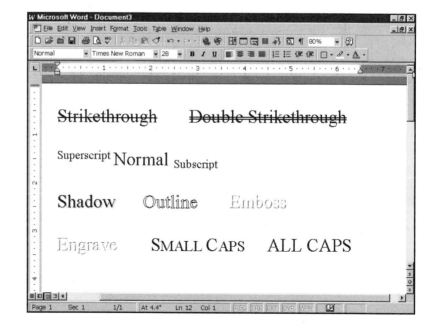

Part

II

Ch

6

Text Spacing

Text spacing is also referred to as *kerning* when it applies to two contiguous letters, and *tracking* when it applies to a string of text. You can adjust the space between letters by choosing Format, Font from the menu, and clicking the Character Spacing tab in the Font dialog box (see Figure 6.6).

FIG. 6.6

Adjust your character spacing in the Font dialog box.

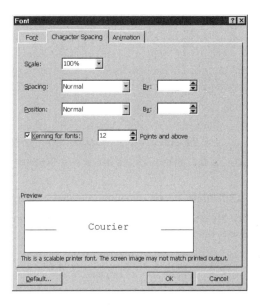

The Character Spacing tab offers the following options:

- *Scale.* Reduces or enlarges your text in proportion to its current size.
- *Spacing.* Gives a choice of Normal, Expanded, or Condensed. Enter the amount of expansion or condensation, measured in points.
- *Position.* Raises or lowers your text in relation to the baseline by the number of points you specify.
- *Kerning for Fonts.* When turned on, applies automatic kerning to any text at or above the point size you choose. The default font size is 12 points.

After you make your adjustments, click OK to save your changes and close the dialog box.

Applying Text Color

Color can enhance your document on-screen, on paper, or both. If you're printing the document on a color printer, the use of color will obviously add visual impact to your document. If you don't need color output, you can still use color to add impact to documents that you share with others on a network or via e-mail. You can apply color to your selected text in either of two ways:

■ Click the Font Color button on the toolbar. An array of colored boxes descends from which you can select the color for your text (see Figure 6.7).

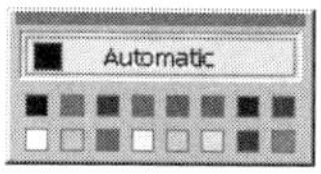

FIG. 6.7
Select a color from the Font Color button on the Formatting toolbar.

■ Choose Format, Font from the menu. Click the Color drop-down list (see Figure 6.8) and select a color for your text.

FIG. 6.8
Select a color for your text from the Color drop-down list.

Using Text Animation

The Font dialog box has three tabs: Font, Character Spacing, and Animation. The ability to animate text is new to Word 97.

To animate your selected text, choose Format, Font from the menu. Click the Animation tab in the Font dialog box. Figure 6.9 shows your animation options.

As you select each of the Animation options, a Preview is shown in the dialog box. When the option you want is displayed, choose OK to apply it to your text and the close the dialog box.

Part
II

Ch
6

FIG. 6.9

Add motion and color to your text with Animation.

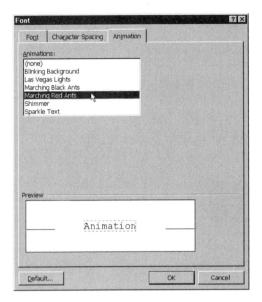

CHAPTER 7

Paragraph Formatting

A complete understanding of Word 97's paragraph formatting options can enhance even the simplest letter you write. By controlling the placement, shape, and relationship between your paragraphs, you can control the overall look and readability of your document. Word 97's paragraph formatting tools and features include indents, bullets and numbers, spacing and flow options, as well as borders and shading applications. Mastering these tools will enable you to create professional-looking documents, quickly and easily. ■

Indents

Set quotes and other special text apart by adjusting the left and right indents from the menu, keyboard, or ruler.

Bullets and numbers

Let Word apply bullets and numbers to your paragraphs and lists automatically. This can save you retyping symbols and numbers if you add or delete items in your list.

Control the flow of text

Keep text where you want it and control the appearance of your document by defining the relationship between paragraphs.

Lines and fills

Enhance the graphic quality of your document by applying borders and shading to your lines and paragraphs.

Formatting Paragraphs

While a paragraph is grammatically defined as a group of sentences about a single topic, Word defines a paragraph as any text followed by a hard return.

To see where your paragraphs are (where you've pressed the Enter key), click the Show/Hide button on the toolbar. Figure 2.1 shows a document in Show/Hide mode.

FIG. 7.1

See your hard returns, tabs, and spaces with Show/Hide.

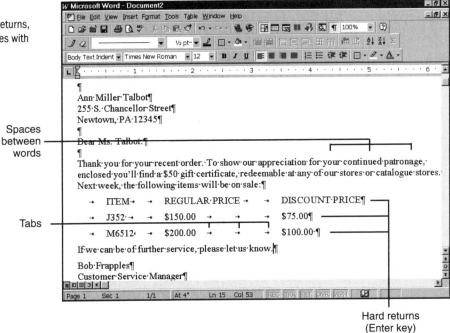

N O T E   The Show/Hide tool allows you to see spaces, tabs, and hard returns. Using Show/Hide can be very helpful when you're working with someone else's document—you can see any errors the user made in their use of spaces instead of tabs, or in pressing Enter unnecessarily.

 If you want to see the non-printing space, tab, and hard return characters in all of your documents, choose Tools, Options from the menu. In the View tab, turn on the non-printing characters you want to see by clicking their check boxes. Choose OK to put your changes into effect.

To view the Paragraph formatting dialog box and make changes to the appearance and function of your paragraphs, choose Format, Paragraph from the menu. Figure 7.2 shows the Paragraph dialog box.

FIG. 7.2

Control your indents, spacing, and flow of paragraph text with the Paragraph Formatting dialog box.

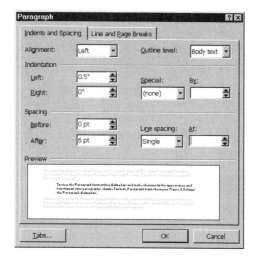

Paragraph Formatting encompasses two areas, each represented by a tab within the Paragraph dialog box:

- *Indents and Spacing.* Set your alignment, indents, and spacing between paragraphs.
- *Line and Page Breaks.* Control the flow of text and the insertion of page breaks between paragraphs.

Paragraph Alignment

To adjust the alignment of your selected text, you have three techniques available to you:

- Choose Format, Paragraph from the menu, and click the Alignment drop list. Choose Left, Centered, Right, or Justified.

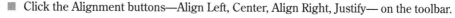
- Click the Alignment buttons—Align Left, Center, Align Right, Justify— on the toolbar.

- Press Ctrl+L for Left alignment, Ctrl+R for Right alignment, Ctrl+E for Centered alignment, or Ctrl+J for Full Justify alignment.

Spacing Between Paragraphs

When typing a document, you can put a horizontal blank space between paragraphs by pressing Enter twice at the end of each paragraph. The downside of this technique, however, is that you end up creating many separate blank paragraphs between your text paragraphs. To avoid creating these extra paragraphs, you can set Space Before or Space After for your paragraphs. With these options set properly, you need only press Enter once at the end of a paragraph to create the appearance of a blank line. To apply these formats, perform the following steps:

Part
II

Ch
7

1. To apply this format to existing text, select the text. If you are imposing the format before typing, make sure your cursor is at the top of the blank document.

2. Choose <u>F</u>ormat, <u>P</u>aragraph from the menu.

3. In the Spacing <u>B</u>efore or Spacing Af<u>t</u>er boxes, enter the amount of space you want to have between your paragraphs. This space is measured in points. To create the illusion of a blank line after each paragraph, set your space in the Spacing Af<u>t</u>er box.

 T I P If you are working with 12-point text, you should set your Spacing Af<u>t</u>er to 12 points so that the space appears to be a full blank line.

4. Click OK to save your formats and close the dialog box.

Figure 7.3 shows paragraphs with Spacing <u>B</u>efore set to 12 points.

FIG. 7.3

Spacing <u>B</u>efore creates the appearance of a blank line between paragraphs.

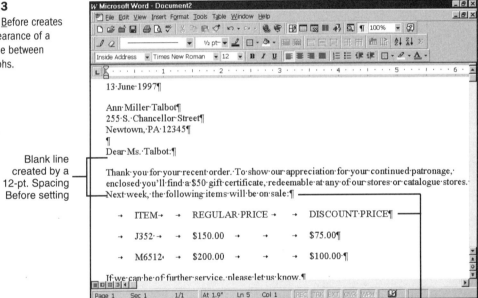

Blank line created by a 12-pt. Spacing Before setting

One hard return at the end of a paragraph

Setting Line Spacing

Your line spacing within paragraphs can also be set from with the Paragraph format dialog box. The default line spacing is Single, but you can choose Double, 1.5 Lines, or a specific number of line-spaces by clicking the Li<u>n</u>e Spacing drop-down list. Choose the spacing you need, and click OK to apply it to your selected text and close the dialog box.

To adjust your line spacing from the keyboard use the following shortcuts:

- Ctrl+1 for single spacing
- Ctrl+2 for double spacing
- Ctrl+5 for 1.5 line spacing

 T I P Use the number keys across the top of your alpha keyboard (not your numeric keypad) for these shortcuts.

Working with Indents

Indenting text moves it closer to the center of the page. You can indent text from either the left or right side of the page, or both. Setting an indent for a particular paragraph can be accomplished using any of the three following methods:

- *Format, Paragraph.* Enter your Left, Right, or Special indent settings in the dialog box. Figure 7.4 shows a variety of indent settings in a document.

FIG. 7.4
Indent your paragraph from the Left, Right, or Special first-line and body indents.

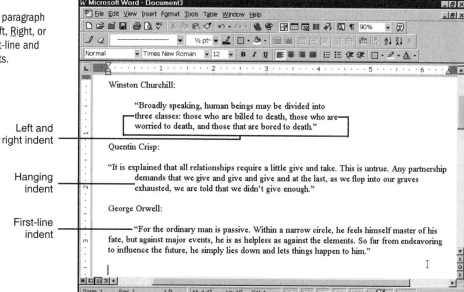

Left and right indent

Hanging indent

First-line indent

Part **II**

Ch **7**

- *The Ruler.* Figure 7.5 shows the indent markers on Word's ruler. Drag them across the ruler to set the indents for your selected text.

FIG. 7.5

Use the Ruler's indent markers to create left, right, first-line, and body indents.

Drag the top triangle to adjust the indent of your paragraph's first line

Drag the box to move both the first line and body in tandem

Drag the bottom triangle to adjust the indent of the paragraph's body lines

The right triangle adjusts the right indent

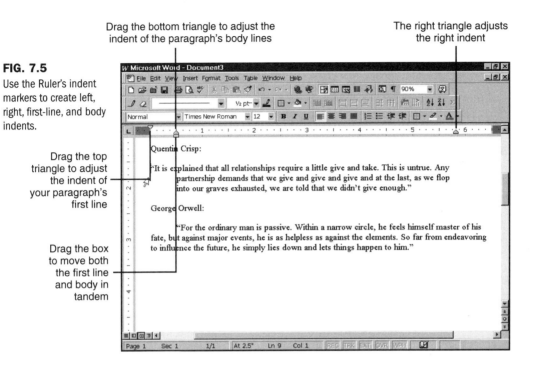

N O T E   When you drag the triangles or box indent markers on your ruler, a dashed vertical line appears to assist you in lining up your text and choosing an indent location.

Dragging the box indent marker will move both the top and bottom triangles together, and they'll keep their relative positions. This enables you to set separate first-line and body indents, and then move the entire paragraph to the right. You'll retain the separate settings for the first line and body of the paragraph.

■ *Keyboard shortcuts.* Use the keyboard shortcuts as described in Table 7.1.

Table 7.1   Paragraph Formatting Shortcuts

Option	Description
Ctrl+M	Indents your text .5" from the left. To increase your left indent in .5" increments, continue to press Ctrl + M until your desired indent is achieved.
Ctrl+T	Creates a hanging indent—the first line of the paragraph remains on the margin, but the body of the paragraph is indented .5".
Ctrl+Q	Removes all indents and paragraph formats.

You can indent your text from the left in .5" increments by clicking the Increase Indent button on the Standard toolbar.

 To reduce your indent, click the Decrease Indent button, also found on the Standard toolbar.

Setting the Text Flow in Your Document

When the text you're typing exceeds the length of the page, a page break is inserted, creating a subsequent page to accept the flow of text. Most of the time, you don't really care where the break occurs—the break can fall in the middle of a paragraph, or between two separate paragraphs. In the event that the flow of text is important to the appearance of your document or the presentation of your topic, you will want to control this process. Page and line breaks can be controlled by setting rules for your general paragraph text and establishing relationships between specific paragraphs.

To view your Paragraph formatting options, choose Format, Paragraph from the menu. Click the Line and Page Breaks tab.

Figure 7.6 shows the Line and Page Breaks tab in the Paragraph format dialog box.

FIG. 7.6

Control the flow of text and relationship between selected paragraphs from the Paragraph format dialog box.

The terms "widow" and "orphan" apply to paragraph text that doesn't fit on the same page with the rest of the paragraph:

- *Widow.* The last line of a paragraph that is pushed to the next page.
- *Orphan.* A line left behind at the bottom of a page when the rest of the paragraph moves on to the next page.

By default, Widow/Orphan Control is on, meaning that if all but one line of a paragraph will not fit on one page, the entire paragraph moves to the next page. Equally, if all but one line fits on a page, the last line is kept with the whole paragraph.

Part

II

Ch

7

Setting Line and Page Breaks

Word sees each of your paragraphs as a separate entity, with no associations between two or more paragraphs. You may need to relate a series of paragraphs in order to control their placement in a document. In addition to Widow/Orphan Control, the Line and Page Breaks tab offers the following options:

- *Keep Lines Together*. This option prevents a page break from occurring within your selected paragraph.
- *Keep with Next*. This option prevents a page break from occurring between your selected paragraph and the paragraph that follows it.
- *Page Break Before*. If your selected paragraph must always be at the top of a page, choose this option to insert a manual page break before the paragraph. The break will remain, no matter what text is added before or after the selected paragraph.

The two remaining options in the Line and Page Breaks tab do not apply to the flow of text, but rather to the appearance of your selected paragraph:

- *Suppress Line Numbers*. If you've been numbering your lines in the document, choose this option to remove the line numbers from your selected paragraph or series of paragraphs. If you aren't using line numbers in your document, this option has no effect.
- *Don't Hyphenate*. If you have any automatic hyphenation settings in place, you can turn them off for a selected paragraph or series of paragraphs.

The Tabs button in the lower left corner of the Line and Page Break tab takes you to the Tabs dialog box. This feature will be discussed in the next chapter of this section.

Using Bullets and Numbers

 Bullets are used for highlighting a list of single lines or paragraphs. Numbers are used to create a series of procedural steps or to prioritize a series of items. The simplest way to bullet or number your text is to select the text and then click the Bullets or Numbering buttons on the toolbar. Using the toolbar buttons will insert the default bullet symbol (a generic black dot) or an Arabic number, followed by a period (1.).

Figure 7.7 shows a bulleted list and a series of numbered paragraphs.

If you want to use another symbol for your bullets, select your bulleted text and choose Format, Bullets and Numbering from the menu. The Bullets and Numbering dialog box opens, with the Bulleted tab in front (see Figure 7.8)

To set the ruler position for your bullet and text, click the Customize button, as shown in Figure 7.9.

FIG. 7.7
Apply bullets or numbers from the toolbar.

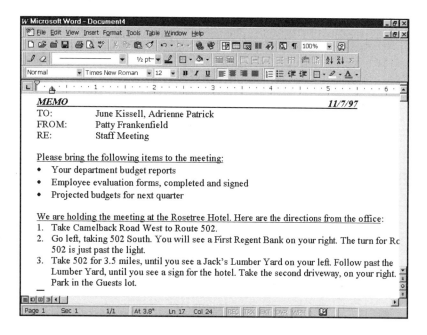

FIG. 7.8
Choose a different bullet symbol from the Bullets and Numbering dialog box.

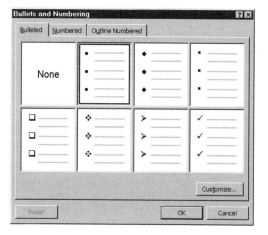

You can adjust your bullet and number placement by moving the indent triangles on the ruler. In the case of bulleted or numbered text, the top triangle represents the bullet or number, and the bottom triangle represents the text.

To change the size and color of your bullet, click the Font button in the Customize Bullet list dialog box. You can change the color and point size of the bullet, and see a preview. Click OK to accept your changes and close the Font dialog box.

Part
II

Ch
7

FIG. 7.9

Select a bullet symbol and determine the placement of your bullets.

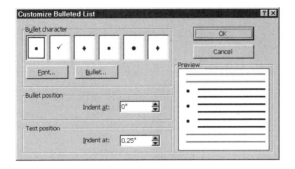

You can also choose a different bullet symbol from another character set by clicking the <u>B</u>ullet button. To change bullet symbols, perform the following steps:

1. In the Symbol dialog box, click the <u>F</u>ont drop-down list, and select a font. The characters for each font are displayed in the grid.

2. To select a particular symbol, click it with your mouse, and click the OK button. You are returned to the Bullets and Numbering dialog box, and your symbol appears selected.

3. Click OK to change to your new selected bullet symbol.

The Wingdings font offers a variety of symbols, such as books, phones, hands, clocks, and checkmarks. Figure 7.10 shows the Wingdings character set.

FIG. 7.10

Choose a Wingdings character for your bullet symbol.

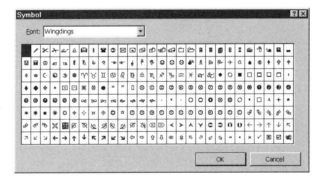

Formatting Numbered Lists

You can automatically number a list of items to prioritize them, or create a set of instructions by numbering a series of paragraphs. Allowing Word to number them for you (as opposed to typing the numbers yourself) enables you to add or delete items from the list and have the numbers update themselves automatically.

 You can number a selected list or group of paragraphs by clicking the Numbering button on the toolbar. The default Arabic numbers with a period will be applied to your list (1.).

To select from other types of number styles, choose Format, Bullets and Numbering from the menu. Click the Numbered tab, as shown in Figure 7.11. Select a numbering style, and choose OK. If you're working with a previously-numbered list, you can renumber it by clicking the Restart Numbering button.

FIG. 7.11
Format your number style by choosing Format, Bullets and Numbering from the menu.

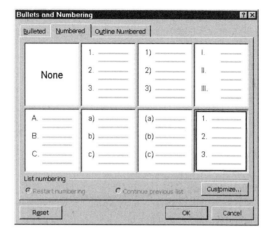

To format the numbers, select a numbering style (Arabic, Roman, upper– and lowercase text) from the Numbered tab, and click the Customize button. The Customize Numbered List dialog box opens (see Figure 7.12), offering the following options:

FIG. 7.12
Format the appearance and placement of your numbers via the Customize Numbered List.

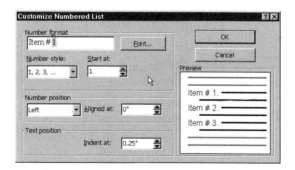

- *Number Format.* Add any text that you want to appear before or after your numbers, such as "Item" or "Step" for a list of directions.
- *Font.* Select a typeface for your numbers and any accompanying text.
- *Number Style.* Click the drop-down list to choose a style, such as upper and lowercase Roman numerals, or letters of the alphabet.
- *Start At.* If your list started on a previous page, continue it on your current page by setting the starting number to be the number that follows your last numbered step.

Part

II

Ch

7

■ *Number Position.* Choose Left, Center, or Right alignment for your numbers.

■ *Text Position.* Enter the distance between your number and your text, such as .25" or .5". You don't need to type the inch marks.

After you enter your formats, click OK to return to the Bullets and Numbering dialog box. Click OK again to return to your document.

After you number your list, you can add or delete items or paragraphs from the list. Word will renumber the list for you.

Using Borders and Shading

Borders can be applied to individual lines or words, and need not be applied to an entire paragraph. Shading, however, is a paragraph format—even if you only select one word within a paragraph, any shading you apply to it will apply to the entire paragraph.

To access your Border and Shading tools, choose View, Toolbars from the menu. Check the box next to Tables and Borders and click OK (see Figure 7.13).

FIG. 7.13

Select Tables and Borders to add shading and border tools to your on-screen toolbars.

The Tables and Borders toolbar will be added to your existing toolbars (see Figure 7.14).

FIG. 7.14

The Tables and Borders toolbar contains buttons for shading and applying a border to your text.

For the purposes of applying shading and borders to paragraph text, you will use the following tools from the toolbar:

Table 7.2 Shading and Border Tools

Icon	Option	Description
	Borders	Displays an array of border options, each representing the sides border. You can place a bottom, top, of a box left, or right border selected text, as well as a on your full border on all sides.
	Shading Color	Lets you choose from a variety of colors. If your text is black, choose a light color or shade of gray, so that you text remains legible.
	Line Style	Offers a variety of lines, such as single, double, triple, and dashed.
½ pt	Line Weight	Enables you to select the thickness of your border line. The line weights are measured in points.
	Border Color	Allows you to choose a color for your border lines.
	Eraser	Removes an existing border. After activating the tool, click and drag briefly along the border line you want to remove.

N O T E   The Border and Shading Color options you choose from the tools' drop-down lists will become the button face for the tools. For example, if you last chose a bottom border, the button will default to a picture of a bottom border until you make another selection from the drop list.

T I P   If you choose black as your shading color, Word automatically changes your text color to white.

Part

II

Ch

7

Working with Tabs

Anyone who has ever used a typewriter is familiar with the Tab key. Word 97 enables you to do more with tabs, however, than just move text across the screen in half-inch increments. You can create tabs at any horizontal ruler position, choose any alignment for the text that will be typed under your tab stops, and add dots, dashes, or lines preceding your tabbed text. Word 97 enables you to add and edit tabs from the ruler or from a dialog box, for use in creating lists and indenting text. ■

Creating Tabs

When you start a new, blank document, there are tabs (also called tab *stops)* already set for you, at every half-inch across the document. The tab stops are all left-aligned, which is suitable for most text. There may be times, however, that you will need to change the alignment of one of these tabs, or to set an entirely customized set of tab stops.

A tab's alignment determines the alignment of the text typed under the tab stop. You can align tab stops in four ways:

- Left
- Right
- Center
- Decimal

Figure 8.1 shows a variety of customized tab settings.

N O T E A decimal tab lines up the tabbed text by any decimal points included in the text. You don't need to align currency with a decimal tab, as there are a fixed number of characters to the right of the decimal. Use a right-aligned tab for currency.

FIG. 8.1
Use different tab settings for different jobs.

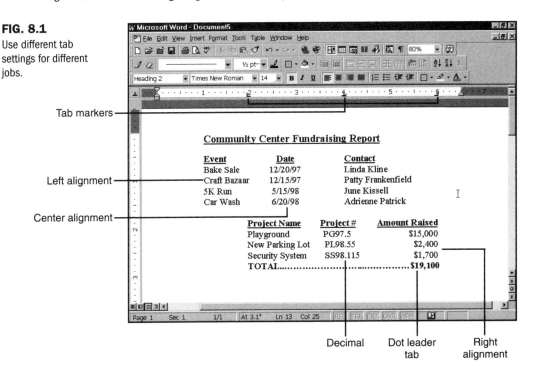

Tab markers

Left alignment

Center alignment

Decimal

Dot leader tab

Right alignment

Setting Tabs from the Menu

Using the Tabs dialog box provides the most control and the greatest number of tab options. To set tabs from the Tabs dialog box (see Figure 8.2), follow these steps:

FIG. 8.2

Create your own tab stops in the Tabs dialog box.

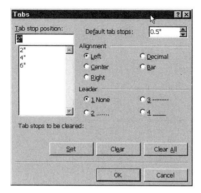

1. Choose Format, Tabs from the menu. This opens the Tabs dialog box.
2. Enter the Tab Stop Position. Type a ruler position such as **2** or **3.5**. You don't need to type any inch marks.
3. Select an Alignment for the text typed under that tab stop.
4. Choose a Leader, if any is required. "None" is the default, but you can choose dots, dashes, or a solid line (series of underscores).
5. Click Set to create the tab stop.
6. You can keep working in the dialog box to set more tabs (clicking Set after each one you create), or click OK to save your tabs and close the dialog box.

N O T E A *leader* is a character, normally a dot, which leads up to the tabbed text. Dot leaders are used in the creation of a table of contents—the dots lead up to the right aligned tab set for the page numbers. ▨

 Dots or other types of leaders cannot be set from the ruler. To set a dot, dash, or underscore leader, you must use the Tabs dialog box.

Setting Tabs from the Ruler

Using the ruler to set tabs is fast and simple. At the far left end of the horizontal ruler, the tab stop indicator button is used to set the alignment of the tabs. Each tab alignment is represented by a symbol, as shown in Figure 8.3.

FIG. 8.3

The horizontal ruler on the Word document screen displays four distinct tab alignment symbols.

Left-aligned tab

Center-aligned tab

Right-aligned tab

Decimal-aligned tab

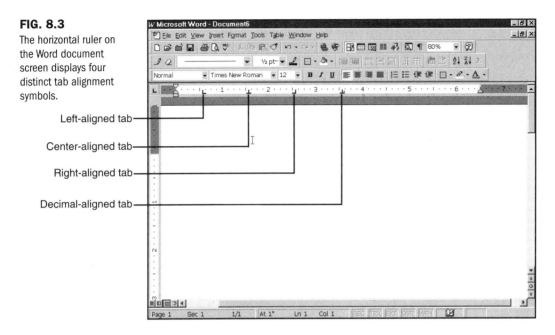

Figure 8.4 shows the ruler's tab stop indicator, and a series of custom tabs.

FIG. 8.4

This figure illustrates how to create tabs on the ruler.

Tab stop indicator

Click below the calibration marks on the ruler to set your tab

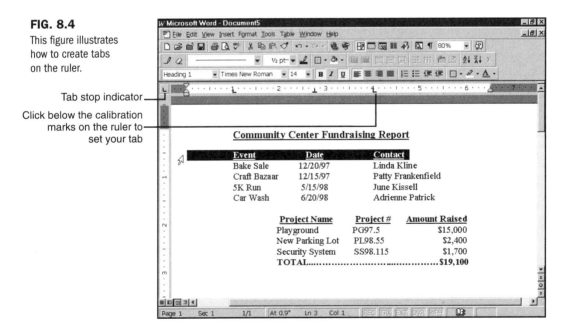

Tab stops are easy to set from the ruler. You can select the alignment of each tab, and place it in your desired location on the ruler. To set your tab alignments from the ruler, follow these steps:

1. For tabs that are Left, Center, Right, or Decimal-aligned, choose the tab-stop indicator button at the far left end of your ruler (refer to Figure 8.4).

 TIP You can cycle through the four available tab alignments by clicking the indicator button repeatedly. If you pass the one you want, keep clicking the button until your desired alignment appears again.

2. Choose a tab stop alignment, then click the ruler to place your tab stop.

3. Continue to reset your tab alignments as necessary, and place as many tab stops as you need on the ruler.

 TIP When clicking the ruler to place a tab stop, be sure to click below the calibration dots and vertical dashes. Clicking the top half of the ruler won't create a tab stop.

NOTE As you build a document, tab stops are in effect from the place your cursor is when you create them until (or unless) new tabs are set. You can, for instance, set tabs for page one, and as you continue to type, set an entirely new group of tabs for page two. You can also have two or more sets of tabs on any single page.

To see which tabs are in effect at any point in your document, position your cursor by clicking your mouse in the document, and view the tab stops on the ruler. If you add tabs to an existing page of text, your tab stops will only affect the selected area. ■

Formatting Tabs

After you've set your tabs, you may want to move, delete, or change the tabs' settings. This can be done from either the Tabs dialog box or the ruler. If you've already typed your tabbed text, any changes or deletions made will affect the text. To control which text is affected, be sure to select the text before making any tab changes or deleting any tab stops.

Changing Tabs

To change or delete individual tab settings from the Tabs dialog box, perform the following steps:

1. Position your cursor in the document where the tabs you wish to change or delete are in effect. If there is any text typed under these tab stops, be sure to select the text.

2. Choose Format, Tabs from the ruler to open the Tabs dialog box.

3. In the Tab Stop Position box, click the tab setting you wish to change or remove.

4. To change the position of the tab setting, type a new ruler position. This will replace the selected location. Click Set.

5. Click OK to accept your changes and close the dialog box.

N O T E You can make as many changes as needed in the dialog box before clicking OK to close it. You can, however, only change or delete tab stops that are in effect where your cursor is at the time that you open the Tabs dialog box. To change tabs set elsewhere in your document, you must reposition your cursor where those tabs are in effect, and then open the Tabs dialog box again.

To change tabs by using the ruler, follow these steps:

1. Position your cursor where the tabs you want to change or delete are in effect. If any text has been typed under the tab stops, select it before making any changes or deletions.

2. To change a tab setting from one point on the ruler to another, drag the existing tab stop down and off the ruler. The tab marker disappears, and any selected text will lose its tab alignment.

3. Choose your new alignment if necessary, and click the ruler to set the new tab position. Any selected text will "snap to" the new tab setting.

N O T E You can't set or change a leader tab from the ruler, so if the tab you wish to reposition has a leader, you must use the Tabs dialog box to change it. You can, however, delete a leader tab by using the ruler.

Deleting Tabs

To remove all existing tab stops from your document or from a selected section of text, select the text (Ctrl+A to select the entire document) and choose Format, Tabs from the menu. Click the Clear All button in the dialog box, and click OK. All tabs are removed.

Individual tab stops can be removed by using the ruler or the Tabs dialog box. Be sure that any text that was typed using the tab stops you want to delete is selected before you employ either method:

■ To remove a tab stop directly from the ruler, simply click the tab marker, and drag it down and off the ruler.

■ To remove a tab stop by using the Tabs dialog box, choose Format, Tabs from the menu. In the Tabs dialog box, click the tab position you want to remove, and click the Clear button. Choose OK to close the dialog box.

CHAPTER 9

Page Formatting

Word 97 gives you a complete set of tools for controlling the layout of your document. Your page formatting options include adjusting the size of your page and your margins within it, changing your page orientation, and controlling the flow and appearance of text by adding sections to your document. Word 97 has also added a tool that allows you to change the background color of your pages, so now you can see how your text will look on colored paper before you print it! ■

Set your margins

Determine how much white space you need around the edges of your document by setting top, bottom, left, and right margins.

Portrait or landscape?

Choose the size and orientation for one page or your entire document.

Layout options

Design the overall look of your document by controlling section breaks and inserting line numbers.

Setting Margins

Margins confine your typing area. As you type, your text automatically flows to the next line as soon as you come to the right margin. When your text reaches the bottom margin, a new page is created, and your text flows onto it.

When you open a new, blank document, your default margins are already set for you. Your top and bottom margins are set to 1", and your left and right margins are set to 1.25". These are the traditional settings for a business document.

To change these default margins to meet the needs of a particular document, you can use the Page Setup dialog box or set them on-screen from the horizontal and vertical rulers.

Setting Margins with Page Setup

Some documents will require larger or smaller margins than those set by default. To change your margins, choose File, Page Setup from the menu (see Figure 9.1).

FIG. 9.1

Set your Margins by choosing File, Page Setup from the menu.

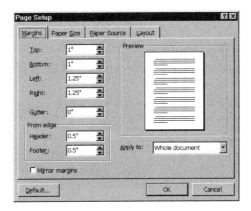

Click the Margins tab and view the following options:

- *Margins.* You can increase or decrease the current margin settings by clicking the increment and decrement triangles next to each margin box (Top, Bottom, Left and Right), or by selecting the existing setting and typing the new measurement.
- *Gutter.* Your gutter is an edge you can add to your margin width, increasing the unprintable frame around your document. The default setting of 0" is fine for most documents. If your document is a book that will be bound, you can increase the gutter to allow for the binding.
- *From Edge.* The default space for headers and footers is .5". Increasing the space will leave more white space above your header and below your footer. (Discover more about headers and footers in Chapter 13, "Working with Long Documents.")

- *Mirror Margins.* Use this setting if your document will be printed on both sides of the paper, and bound. If your odd-numbered pages, for example, will have a wider left margin (to accommodate the binding), mirroring your margins will automatically create a wide right margin on your even-numbered pages.

- *Apply To.* Allows you to specify the portion of your document that these changes will effect. The default is Whole Document. You can also choose to apply your changes From This Point Forward (from where your cursor was when you opened the dialog box), or to Selected Text (if you had text selected when you opened the dialog box).

- *Preview.* This area uses a sample document to show you the effect your changes will have.

Part

II

Ch

9

 TIP Press the Tab key to move through the boxes in this dialog box. Pressing Tab to move to a box also highlights the contents of the box, making it easier to type a replacement setting.

After you make your changes, click the OK button to save your settings and close the dialog box.

Setting Margins from the Ruler

To set your margins "by eye" using the horizontal and vertical rulers, perform the following steps:

1. Select the text for which you wish to change the margins. If you want the change to apply to the entire document, press Ctrl+Home to move to the top of the document, and be sure no text is selected.

2. Make sure your ruler is visible. If it's not showing, choose View, Ruler from the menu. This displays your horizontal ruler, from which you can adjust your left and right margins.

3. From the View menu, choose Page Layout. This will add a vertical ruler to your screen, enabling you to change your top and bottom margins.

4. To adjust margins, place your mouse on the edge where the gray ruler area (representing your current margin) and the white ruler meet. Your mouse will turn to a two-headed arrow (see Figure 9.2).

   - To increase your margin, drag toward the center of the ruler. Watch your ruler calibrations to determine the exact margin measurement.

   - To decrease your margin, drag toward the end of the ruler, away from the center.

 TIP To assure you that you have the appropriate mouse pointer for adjusting your margins, Word provides a ToolTip that appears with the two-headed arrow.

FIG. 9.2

Adjust your Top, Bottom, Left, and Right margins from the rulers.

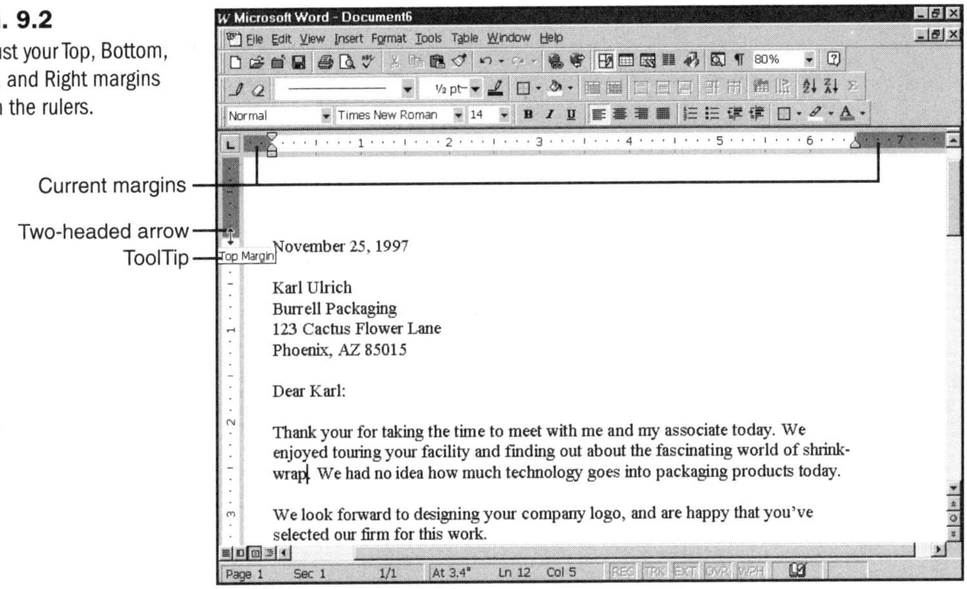

Current margins —

Two-headed arrow —

ToolTip —

5. When your margins are adjusted as you desire, release the mouse.

 T I P

41% ▼

To see your entire page as you adjust the margins, reduce your document zoom to Whole Page. You'll be able to see all four sides of the document, which can make adjusting your margins easier. To set a different Zoom, choose View, Zoom from the menu, or click the Zoom drop-down button on the toolbar.

N O T E Adjusting your margins from the ruler isn't always an exact method. You may find that instead of a 2" margin, you have a 1.98" margin instead. In most cases, this doesn't matter, but if it does, you can increase your Zoom to 200% (or higher), or check your ruler-created margins by choosing File, Page Setup. Click the Margins tab and make any exacting adjustments there. ▪

Working with Page Size and Orientation

Page size refers to the dimensions of the paper. Orientation refers to how the paper is "turned." The following describes the two separate orientations:

- ▪ *Portrait* orientation is taller than it is wide.
- ▪ *Landscape* orientation is wider than it is tall.

Word's default orientation is Portrait. In addition to the appearance of your document, your page orientation determines how your printer creates your document. If your paper is set to Landscape, the paper will feed through the printer in the same way as it would for Portrait documents, but the image will print sideways.

You can set your paper size and orientation by choosing File, Page Setup from the menu. A four-tabbed dialog box opens. To set your page dimensions and orientation, click the Paper Size tab (see Figure 9.3).

FIG. 9.3
Set your Paper Size and orientation by choosing File, Page Setup.

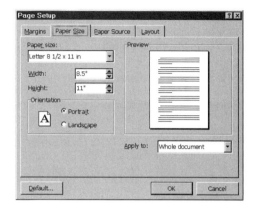

The Page Size tab offers the following options:

- *Paper Size*. Click the drop-down list to choose from Letter (8.5" × 11"), Legal (8.5" × 14"), various envelope sizes, and Custom. When you choose a size, the dimensions for that size appear in the Width and Height boxes.

- *Portrait* or *Landscape*. Click the button next to your desired orientation.

- *Apply To*. Your choices are Whole Document or This Point Forward (from where your cursor was positioned when you opened the dialog box). If you have any text selected prior to opening the dialog box, Selected Text will be an option.

- *Preview*. See the effect your size and orientation choices will have on a sample document.

N O T E   If you choose a Custom paper size, you will need to enter the dimensions of your paper in the Width and Height boxes. Be sure you know the exact measurement of your custom paper before entering your dimensions, as your other Page formatting options (such as your margins) will depend on the accuracy of your entries. ■

 When you make a change to the paper size or orientation of a portion of your document, click the Page Layout tab before exiting the Page Setup dialog box. You'll want to tell Word how to insert the section break that results from your changes. See the next section in this chapter, "Controlling Page Layout" for more information.

Controlling Page Layout

When you change your paper size and orientation, you are also affecting your document's layout. Applying these changes to individual pages or selected text within your document creates a new *section* in your document. The Layout tab in the Page Setup dialog box allows you to control when and how these sections will be applied in your document. To access your Layout options, choose File, Page Setup from the menu, and click the Layout tab.

N O T E   A *section* is a break that is inserted into your document whenever you make a change in your document's layout. You can insert section breaks manually, or allow them to occur automatically as you make changes to the margins and orientation in portions of your document. ▨

Figure 9.4 shows the Layout tab in the Page Setup dialog box.

FIG. 9.4

Click the Layout tab in the Page Setup dialog box to control your document's sections.

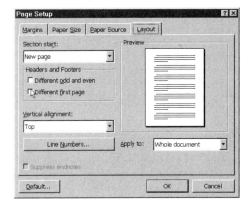

The Layout tab offers the following options:

- ▨ *Section Start.* Choose from Continuous, New Column, New Page, Even Page, or Odd Page. New Page is the default, resulting in a simultaneous section and page break being inserted into your document.

- ▨ *Vertical Alignment.* Choose Top, Center, or Justified to set the alignment of your document (or a section thereof) from top to bottom.

- ▨ *Headers and Footers.* If you want to have different headers and footers for your odd and even pages, click the Different Odd and Even box. To create a section break after your document's first page, click the Different First Page box. This will allow you to format your first page differently from the rest of your document. You can choose either or both of these options.

- ▨ *Line Numbers.* Click this button to open the Line Numbers dialog box (see Figure 9.5). Set a starting number, distance from the text, and numbering increments (Count By). Choose OK to return to the Page Setup dialog box.

FIG. 9.5

Use the Page Layout tab to insert line numbers in your document.

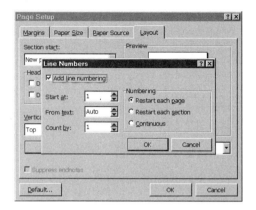

■ *Preview.* As you change your settings, Preview displays a sample document, showing the effect your changes will have.

To apply your changes and close the Page Setup dialog box, choose OK.

Setting Page Defaults

Most traditional business documents require Word's Page defaults—standard margins, letter-size paper, and Portrait orientation. If your "typical" documents are not traditional, however, you may want to reset some of these defaults.

To reset your Page Setup defaults for all new documents, perform the following steps:

1. Open an existing or new document. Page Setup will not be available from the File menu unless there is a document open on-screen.

 If you have an existing document that is already set to the Page Setup options you want to use as your defaults, open that document.

2. Press Ctrl+Home to be sure you're at the top of the document with no text selected.
3. Choose File, Page Setup from the menu.
4. Set or confirm your existing custom settings by checking the four tabs—Margins, Paper Size, Paper Source, and Layout.
5. Click the Default button in the lower-left corner of the Page Setup dialog box.
6. A prompt appears, asking you to confirm your intention to reset your defaults to the current settings. Click Yes to reset.
7. Click OK in the Page Setup dialog box.

N O T E Be sure that the defaults you set will be appropriate for the majority of your documents. If they're not, you'll be wasting a lot of time resetting them for individual documents that require different settings. ■

CHAPTER 10

Using Tables

Word 97's Table feature may be the most powerful tool you have for creating and enhancing documents. Tables can be used to create columns, lists, forms, as well as control the placement of text and graphics. You can calculate numbers in a table, and table content can be used and manipulated as data. The table tools you've used in previous versions of Word are still here in Word 97, with many added and simplified features for creating and formatting your tables. For example, you can now draw a table with a mouse tool that creates random-width columns and rows. ■

The power of tables

Use tables instead of tabs or columns to control the flow of text. Create lists or design elaborate fill-in forms. Tables are one of the most versatile and powerful tools Word has to offer.

Formatting tables

Adjust the width of individual cells and columns. Add borders and shading to your table's cells, and format the cell contents to bring a creative touch to your documents.

Calculate and sort

Use your table as a database, and sort the table's contents. Perform calculations to sum a column of numbers or average a series of cells. Any simple spreadsheet function can be applied to table cells to increase the power and function of tables in your documents.

Why Use Tables?

Just about any document can be enhanced with a table. The ability to place text in columns and rows enables you to control the flow of text, eliminating your need to use other more cumbersome tools, such as tabs and columns. There are many uses for tables in just about any document. The following list contains just a few of them:

- Fax Cover sheets
- Memos
- Résumés
- Multi-column lists
- Parallel Paragraphs
- Newsletters
- Calendars

Many of the items in this list require you to fill in information, such as names and phone numbers on a fax cover sheet or in an address database. Creating a table to store and display the data makes inserting and viewing the date much easier. If the table is the only content of a document, the document can be saved and used as the data source for a mail merge. (For additional information on form letters, see Chapter 14, "Creating Form Letters.")

Figure 10.1 shows a name and address list stored in a Word table.

FIG. 10.1
Use a table to enter and store data.

Each column heading is the equivalent of a database field

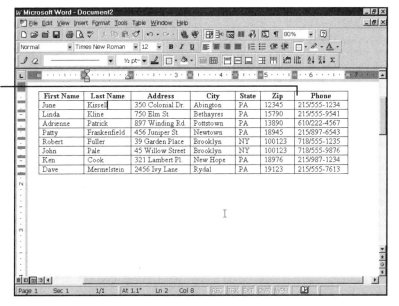

First Name	Last Name	Address	City	State	Zip	Phone
June	Kissel	350 Colonial Dr.	Abington	PA	12345	215/555-1234
Linda	Kline	750 Elm St.	Bethayres	PA	15790	215/555-9541
Adrienne	Patrick	897 Winding Rd.	Pottstown	PA	13890	610/222-4567
Patty	Frankenfield	456 Juniper St.	Newtown	PA	18945	215/897-6543
Robert	Fuller	39 Garden Place	Brooklyn	NY	100123	718/555-1235
John	Pale	45 Willow Street	Brooklyn	NY	100123	718/555-9876
Ken	Cook	321 Lambert Pl.	New Hope	PA	18976	215/987-1234
Dave	Mermelstein	2456 Ivy Lane	Rydal	PA	19123	215/555-7613

T I P Each column heading is the equivalent of a database field.

Tables also work well as Templates. Create the skeletal table, and save it as a template to be filled in later when the template is used to create a document.

Figure 10.2 shows a fax cover sheet template that uses a table to show the user where to enter their information. (For more information on saving a document as a template, see Chapter 2, "Creating Documents.")

FIG. 10.2

Tables can be used to create forms, such as fax cover sheets.

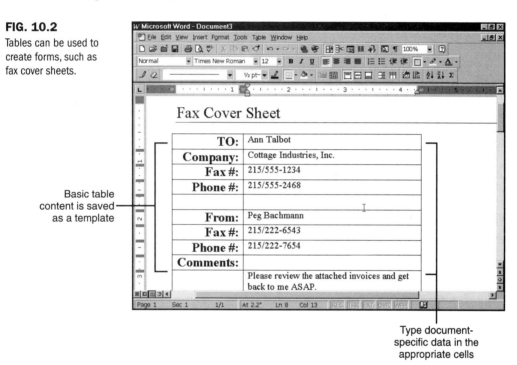

Basic table content is saved as a template

Type document-specific data in the appropriate cells

Part
II

Ch
10

Any document that requires consistent placement of text—reports or résumés, for example—will benefit from the use of a table. You will find Tables useful when you need to pair terms or items and a descriptive paragraph.

Figure 10.3 shows a résumé created with a table.

FIG. 10.3
Design your résumé
layout with a table

Pair a term and
descriptive paragraph

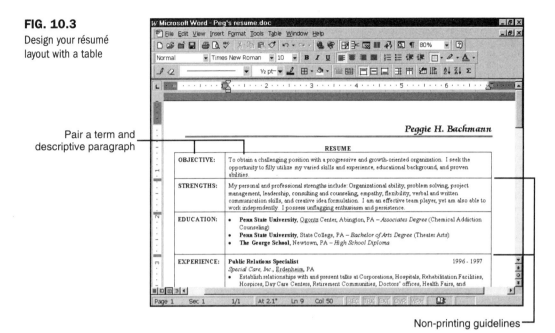

Non-printing guidelines

Planning Your Tables

Word gives you two methods of creating tables. You can Draw a table from the Table menu or Tables and Borders toolbar. You can Insert a table by clicking the Insert Table button on the standard toolbar. Either method requires some forethought:

- *How many columns will you need?* Each column will represent a "field" in your database, or category of information you'll be entering in each row. While you can add columns after you've created your table (and even after you've entered your table's contents), you're better off if you've designed your table's columns ahead of time.

- *How many rows will you need?* Knowing this ahead of time isn't as important as forecasting your number of columns. It's easy to add rows (press Tab at the end of the last row, and a new row is added). When estimating the number of rows you'll need, remember to add one for your column headings (the top rows).

Drawing a Table

When you choose Table, Draw Table or click the Draw Table button on the Tables and Borders toolbar, your mouse turns to a pencil. To draw the table, perform the following steps:

1. Drag your mouse to draw a box the size of your entire table.

2. Click at the top or bottom of the box, and draw vertical lines to separate your columns.

3. Click the left or right sides of the box to draw your rows.

T I P Drawing a table allows you to completely customize the look of your table—the width of each column and the height of each row can be set up individually.

Inserting a Table

Inserting a table (as opposed to drawing it) creates a more uniform table, as you don't have to manually draw the columns and rows. To Insert a table, follow these steps:

1. Place your cursor in the document where you want to insert your table.

 2. Click the Insert Table button on the Standard toolbar. A grid drops down from the toolbar button.

3. Drag your mouse through the grid to set your table's dimensions:

   • Drag across the top of the grid to choose the number of columns in your table

   • Drag vertically to choose the number of rows.

4. Watch the dimension display (*n × n Table)* to make sure you have the number of rows and columns you need.

5. Click and release the mouse. A table appears in your document.

 T I P You can also insert a table by choosing Insert, Table. Enter the dimensions of your table (number of rows and columns) and click OK to close the dialog box and insert your table.

CAUTION

When you create your table, make sure there isn't anything selected in your document. If any text is selected, Word assumes you want to place it in an individual cell, and clicking the Insert Table button will place a single cell around your selected text.

Entering Table Content

After you create your table, you'll want to enter text or numbers into the cells. Each cell functions like a small document—you can type single words or whole paragraphs, and you have full formatting capabilities. Fonts, indents, and alignment can all be set for text or numbers in a cell. If you type paragraph text, the text will wrap against the right border of the cell, as though it were the cell's margin.

To move from cell to cell, press the Tab key. This will move you from left to right. When you reach the last cell in a row, press Tab to go to the first cell in the next row. To move backward through the cells, press Shift+Tab.

T I P Since the Tab key is used to move from cell to cell in a table, you can't use it to indent text or create multi-column lists within a cell. To tab text within a table cell, press Ctrl+Tab.

You can also use your keyboard's arrow keys to move from cell to cell, but only if the cells are empty. If there is text in the cells, the arrow keys will move within the text before going on to the next cell.

Formatting Tables

Regardless of how you created your table, you'll want to format the table's size, shape, and content. To display a toolbar containing tools for customizing your table, choose View, Toolbars from the menu. Select the Tables and Borders toolbar. Table 10.1 shows each of the Table tools and explains their function:

 N O T E You can open the Tables and Borders toolbar by choosing the Tables and Borders button on the Standard toolbar. ▦

Table 10.1 Tables and Borders Toolbar Button

Icon	Option	Description
✎	Draw Table	Use this tool as an alternative to choosing Table, Draw Table from the menu. After activating this tool, your mouse pointer turns to a pencil. You can also add rows and columns to an existing table with this tool.
✐	Eraser	This tool allows you to remove columns and rows by clicking on the lines in your table. Any content in the cells you erase will be merged with the surrounding cells.
▭	Line Style	Choose from a variety of line widths and styles, such as thick, thin, dotted, dashed, and wavy.
½ pt	Line Weight	Select the point-size of your line. The default line thickness is 1/2 point.
✑	Border Color	Select this button to display an array of colors for your table's borders. The border color will apply only to the cells you have selected.
⊞	Borders	This button changes to display the last border you added, such as top, bottom, left, right, inside, and full outside borders.
⬦	Shading Color	Click this button to display your shading color choices. The shading will apply to whichever cells are selected.

Icon	Option	Description
	Merge Cells	Select two or more cells and merge them into one cell.
	Split Cells	Select an individual cell, and split it into two or more cells. A dialog box appears, allowing you to specify the number of columns and rows into which your cell will split.
	Align Top	This button applies to the cell's contents.
	Center Vertically	Your cell's contents will be vertically centered in the cell.
	Align Bottom	Click this button to place your cell's contents at the bottom of the cell.
	Distribute Rows Evenly	If you've drawn your table, click this button to give your rows a uniform height. You can select a specific range of rows, or the entire table before clicking the button.
	Distribute Columns Evenly	If you've adjusted your column widths or drew your table's columns in varied widths, you can select two or more of your columns and change them to a uniform width.
	Table AutoFormat	Click this button to open a dialog box containing pre-set table shading and border designs.
	Change Text Direction	If you want to turn your table text so that it prints vertically, click this button. This is a useful tool when your column heading is wide, but the column's contents will be single digits or characters.
	Sort Ascending	Use this tool to sort your table text alphabetically, A to Z. If your table contains numbers, you can sort them from smallest to largest.
	Sort Descending	This tool will sort your table text from Z to A. Numeric table contents will be sorted from largest to smallest.
	AutoSum	If you want to sum (add up) a column or row of numbers, click this button.

Part
II

Ch
10

Changing Column Width

You can change column width in any of the following ways:

- With no part of the table selected, point to the column border on the right side of the column you want to change. Your mouse pointer will turn into a two-headed arrow, as shown in Figure 10.4. Click and drag the border to the right to widen the column, to the left to narrow it.

- Drag the column markers on the ruler to the right to widen a column, to the left to make it narrower. Figure 10.4 shows a table's column markers.

 TIP   As you drag the borders or column markers, a vertical dashed line appears, showing you where your column border will fall when you release the mouse.

FIG. 10.4
Adjust column width by dragging the table's column borders or the column markers on the ruler.

Column marker

Column border

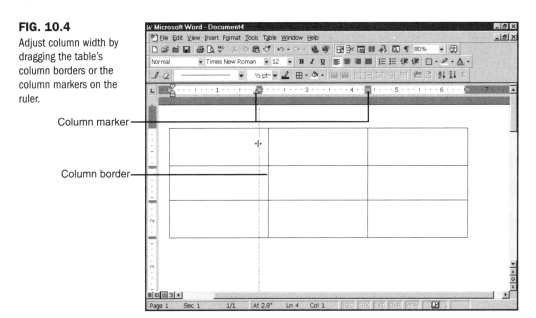

- Select the column you wish to change and select Table, Cell Height and Width from the menu. Click the Column tab, and enter the width of the cell, in inches.

Figure 10.5 shows the Cell Height and Width dialog box.

FIG. 10.5
Column width can
be set to a specific
measurement in the
Cell Height and Width
dialog box.

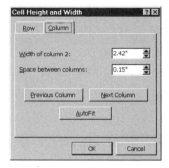

N O T E   You can also adjust the width of individual cells by selecting them and then dragging
their right borders—to the right to widen the cell, or to the left to narrow it.

Changing Row Height

You can adjust the height of a table row by using the following methods:

■ Point to the row border (the top border of any unselected cell) and when your mouse
pointer turns to a two-headed arrow, drag up to increase row height, or drag down to
decrease row height.

■ Drag the row markers on the vertical ruler. Drag up to make the row taller, drag down to
make it vertically shorter.

■ Select the row and choose T̲able, Cell Height and W̲idth. Click the R̲ow tab, and enter
the height of the selected row. Choose OK to accept the change and close the dialog box.

N O T E   You can choose from three row height settings in the Cell Height and Width dialog box—
Auto, At Least, and Exactly. To enter a specific height, choose At Least or Exactly. Choosing
Auto will tell Word that the row's height should be dictated by the cell's content, and you won't be able
to enter your own setting.

Figure 10.6 shows the R̲ow tab in the Cell Height and Width dialog box.

FIG. 10.6
Adjust the height of
your selected rows.

N O T E To center your table on the page, select the entire table (Table, Select Table) and click the Center button in the Cell Height and Width dialog box (Row tab). ▨

Inserting Columns

To add a column, perform the following steps:

1. Select the column to the right of where you want to insert your new column.

2. Choose Table, Insert Column. A new column is inserted to the left of your selected column.

 T I P To insert more than one column with one command, select the number of existing columns that you want to add. Choose Table, Insert Columns and the number of columns you selected will be inserted to the left of the selected columns.

 You can also insert a new column by drawing a new vertical line in your table with the Draw Table tool found on the Tables and Borders toolbar.

Inserting Rows

Adding a new row at the end of your table is simple—merely place your cursor in the last cell in the table and press the Tab key. A new row appears at the end of your table.

To add a row within your table, perform the following steps:

1. Select the row below where you want to insert your new row.

2. Choose Table, Insert Rows from the menu. A new row appears in your table, above the selected row.

 T I P To insert more than one row, select the number of rows you want to add, and choose Table, Insert Rows from the menu. The number of rows you selected will be added to your table.

N O T E The Table menu is context sensitive. If you have a column or columns selected, the Insert option is "Insert Columns." If you have a row or rows selected, the command changes to "Insert Rows." If any of the Table menu commands are dimmed, it means that you have something outside your table—usually the line above or below it—selected. ▨

Merging and Splitting Cells

Adding rows and columns to your table will change its overall dimensions. Splitting and merging cells will change the dimensions of an individual cell or group of cells within your table. Figure 10.7 shows a set of "before and after" tables—the "after" table's top row has been merged into one long row, to contain the table's title.

FIG. 10.7

A Before and After view of a table with its top row merged to create a title cell.

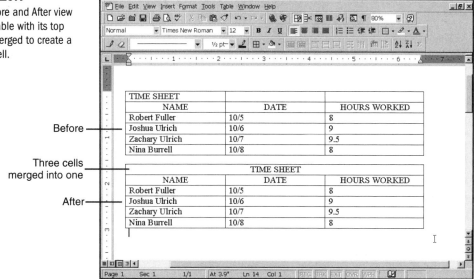

Before

Three cells merged into one

After

To split a cell, select the cell and click the Split Cells button. In the resulting dialog box, enter the number of columns and rows you want to split the cell into.

Figure 10.8 shows the Split Cells dialog box.

FIG. 10.8

Split your cell into two or more columns and rows.

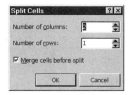

Part
II

Ch
10

To merge a series of contiguous cells, select them and click the Merge Cells button on the toolbar. The cells are automatically merged into one large cell.

 T I P You can also Split and Merge cells with the Table menu's Split Cells and Merge Cells commands.

Applying Borders and Shading to Tables

You can use borders and shading to draw your reader's eye to a particular cell, column, or row. Adding borders and shading also gives your table a polished, more graphical look.

To apply borders and shading, select the cell, column, or row you want to enhance, and use the Border placement, Line Style, Weight, Color, and Shading Color tools. (Refer to Table 10.1, earlier in this chapter, for more tool information.)

Figure 10.9 shows a table with shaded and bordered cells.

FIG. 10.9
Add borders and shading to cells, columns, and rows in your table.

Shading draws attention to specific cells

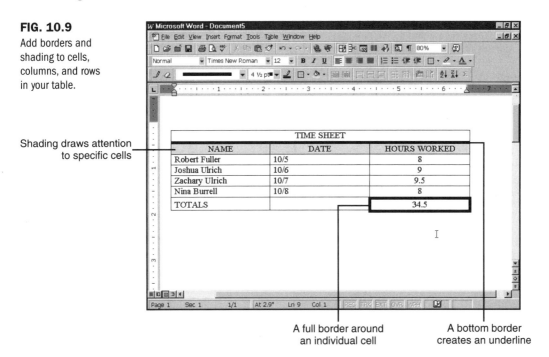

A full border around an individual cell

A bottom border creates an underline

Using Table AutoFormat

 Table AutoFormat saves you time in shading and applying borders to individual cells by applying pre-set table formats to your selected columns, rows, or your entire table. The AutoFormats also adjust your column widths to meet the needs of the content of your table. You can pick and choose which formats to apply. To access Table AutoFormat, select your table (or a portion of it) and choose T̲able, Table AutoF̲ormat or click the Table AutoFormat button.

Figure 10.10 shows the AutoFormat dialog box and a sample AutoFormat.

FIG. 10.10
Save time formatting
your table by using
Table AutoFormat.

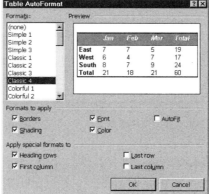

Part II
Ch 10

CAUTION
If you've already taken the time to set your columns to desired widths, be sure to turn off the AutoF̲it option in the Table AutoFormat dialog box.

Performing Table Calculations

If your table contains numeric data, you may wish to total it, average it, or perform some other calculation with the numbers. Word's Table tools allow you to apply any basic mathematical function to your table. To calculate cells in a table, perform the following steps:

1. Place your cursor in the cell that should contain the result of the calculation.

2. Choose T̲able, F̲ormula from the menu. The Formula dialog box opens, allowing you to choose the F̲ormula, N̲umber Format, and Paste Fu̲nction for the selected cell (see Figure 10.11).

FIG. 10.11

Enter a formula, function, and number format for your calculation.

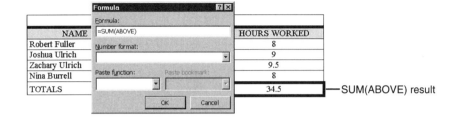

————SUM(ABOVE) result

3. The default formula is SUM(ABOVE), meaning to sum the numbers above the cell. You can change the formula as follows:

   - Change the Formula to SUM(LEFT) to sum a row.
   - SUM(A1,C1) where A1 and C1 are examples of cell addresses within the table, will add up random cell contents.
   - Choose a different function by clicking the Paste Function drop-down list. Choose from standard functions such as Average, Count, and Max(maximum). The function you choose from the list is inserted into the Formula box, and you can then add the (ABOVE), (LEFT), or specific cell addresses (in parentheses) to complete the formula.

4. If you want the calculation result to appear as currency, a percentage, or with a certain number of decimal places, click the Number Format drop-down box, and select a format from the list.

5. Choose OK to save your formula and format, and close the dialog box.

 The calculation results will change automatically if you change the content of any of the cells that were part of the formula. Place your cursor in the cell that contains your formula, and press F9 to update your calculation results after making any changes to the contributing cells.

Sorting Table Data

Word's tables can be used for entering and storing data, such as names and addresses, inventory lists, and scheduled events. When you create a table that will be used as a database, you must think of your table's columns as fields and your rows as records. To sort your records, you can use Word's Table, Sort command.

Figure 10.12 shows a video database, sorted by Movie Title.

FIG. 10.12

Use a table to enter, store, and sort a series of records.

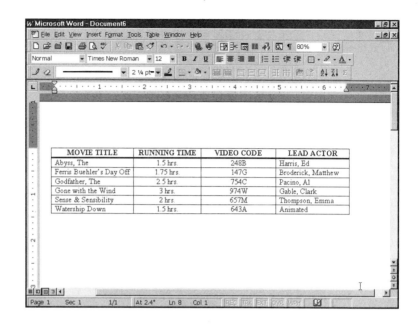

MOVIE TITLE	RUNNING TIME	VIDEO CODE	LEAD ACTOR
Abyss, The	1.5 hrs.	248B	Harris, Ed
Ferris Buehler's Day Off	1.75 hrs.	147G	Broderick, Matthew
Godfather, The	2.5 hrs.	754C	Pacino, Al
Gone with the Wind	3 hrs.	974W	Gable, Clark
Sense & Sensibility	2 hrs.	657M	Thompson, Emma
Watership Down	1.5 hrs.	643A	Animated

To sort your table's records, perform the following steps:

1. After entering your data, place your cursor in any one of the table's cells. Do not select any text or cells within the table.

2. Choose Table, Sort from the menu. The Sort dialog box opens (see Figure 10.13).

FIG. 10.13

Sort your records using as many as three separate fields.

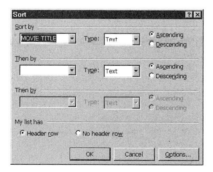

3. Click the Sort By drop-down box to select a field name (column heading) by which your records should be sorted.

4. Choose Ascending or Descending order for your sort, and click OK.

You can sort your data using as many as three of your fields. To do a multi-level sort, you should work from the largest number of qualifying records to the smallest. For example, in the table shown in Figure 10.14, an employee list can be sorted by Department, then by Salary, and then by Last Name.

FIG. 10.14

When sorting on more than one field, choose the fields in order from largest number of qualifying records to smallest.

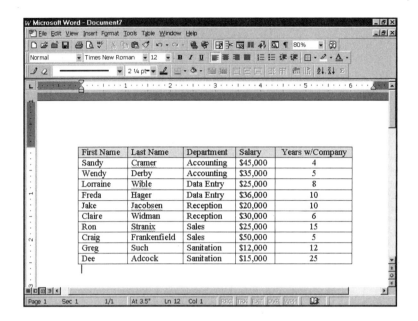

First Name	Last Name	Department	Salary	Years w/Company
Sandy	Cramer	Accounting	$45,000	4
Wendy	Derby	Accounting	$35,000	5
Lorraine	Wible	Data Entry	$25,000	8
Freda	Hager	Data Entry	$36,000	10
Jake	Jacobsen	Reception	$20,000	10
Claire	Widman	Reception	$30,000	6
Ron	Stranix	Sales	$25,000	15
Craig	Frankenfield	Sales	$50,000	5
Greg	Such	Sanitation	$12,000	12
Dee	Adcock	Sanitation	$15,000	25

Working with Columns

Word 97 gives you tools for converting and formatting text in columns, and a wizard to guide you through the process of creating a newsletter. Whether you apply columns to existing text or type your text into preset columns, you can create a polished, professional-looking document containing paragraph text, headlines, and graphics. ◾

Newspaper columns

Convert your text into two, three, or more columns. Apply column formats to existing text or set up your blank document so that the text you type automatically flows into columns.

Column wizardry

Use Word's Newsletter Wizard to create a newsletter for your company, family, or other organization. Graphics and sample instructional text are inserted to show you where and how to place your articles and related pictures.

Creating Columns

Columns are most often used in newsletters, although you may use them in any type of document. You can convert existing paragraph text to columns or set your columns before you start typing. To apply columns to existing text or at the beginning of a blank document, perform the following steps:

1. Choose View, Page Layout from the menu. Page Layout view is the only view that allows you to work with columns in WYSIWYG (What You See Is What You Get) mode.

 TIP If you view your columns in Normal view, you will see one long column down the left side of the page. This view isn't conducive to typing text into columns or formatting existing columns, because you can't see your results on-screen.

2. Select the text to be converted to columns, or place your cursor at the beginning of your blank document.

3. Choose Format, Columns from the menu. The Columns dialog box opens (see Figure 11.1).

FIG. 11.1

Format the width, spacing, and number of columns for your entire document or selected text.

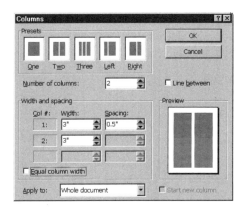

From within the Columns dialog box, you can set the following options for your columns:

- *Presets.* Choose from five pre-designed columns styles: One, Two, Three, Left, and Right. As you click each of the buttons, the Preview section shows you the effect your selection will have on your text.

- *Number of Columns.* Enter a number from one to ___.

- *Width* and *Spacing.* Depending on the number of columns in your chosen Preset or your Number of Columns entries, you can specify which column to edit, enter the width of each column, and set the amount of space between them.

- *Equal Column Width.* Click this check box if you want your columns to all be the same width. The space between your columns will also be uniform.

- *Line Between*. Click this check box to insert a vertical line between your columns.

 TIP If your document has three or more columns, or if your columns are close together, choosing to add the Line Between will make it easier to read your column text.

- *Apply To*. Choose Whole Document or This Point Forward. If you have existing text selected, Selected Text is the default option.

4. Set your Columns options, and click OK. The settings you selected will take effect on your existing text. If you are applying them to a blank document, the text you type will appear in columns formatted according to your settings.

 To set columns from the toolbar, click the Columns button, and drag through the number of columns you need. You can do this after selecting existing text that you want to convert to columns, or at the top of a blank document to format the document before any text is typed.

CAUTION

While Word 97's Columns feature allows you to place your text in as many as 12 columns, if you have more than three columns on letter-size paper (in Portrait orientation), your columns will be too thin, and the text will be too hard to read and follow from one column to the next.

Part
II

Ch
11

Formatting Columns

If your text is already in columns, you can change any of the Columns dialog box options by selecting the text and choosing Format, Columns from the menu. Enter any changes to the number, width, or spacing of your columns, or add a vertical line between columns. Your settings will apply only to the selected text in your document. Click OK to apply the changes and close the dialog box.

 To simply change the number of columns, select the text and use the Columns button on the toolbar. With either approach, your selected columns are changed to meet your new settings.

N O T E When you format your text as columns, a section break is inserted into your document at the beginning and end of the column text. For more information about section breaks, see Chapter 9, "Page Formatting," and Chapter 13, "Working with Long Documents."

You can have several different column settings for separate sections of text in one document. Selecting the existing section of text before applying columns, or placing your cursor at the point in your document where the new column settings should apply is the key to effective use of columns. Figure 11.2 shows a document with text in two columns and three columns.

 TIP Text in three or more columns will look smoother if you use Full justification, eliminating the ragged right edge.

FIG. 11.2
Use different column settings throughout your document.

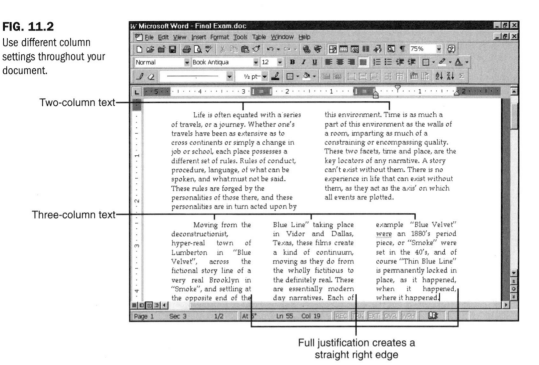

Two-column text —

Three-column text —

Full justification creates a straight right edge

Using the Newsletter Wizard

You can create a quick and easy newsletter by using Word's Newsletter Wizard. Using this wizard creates a formatted document with sample text, graphics, and headlines that you can replace with your own. To use the Newsletter Wizard, perform the following steps:

1. Choose File, New from the menu. The New dialog box opens (see Figure 11.3).

FIG. 11.3
Double-click the Newsletter Wizard icon in the Publications tab to create newsletters with Word.

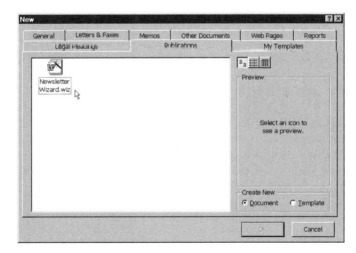

2. Click the Publications tab and double-click the Newsletter Wizard icon.

3. The first Newsletter Wizard dialog box opens showing a list of the steps that the wizard will take (see Figure 11.4). Click Next to proceed.

FIG. 11.4

The Newsletter Wizard opens with the Start screen.

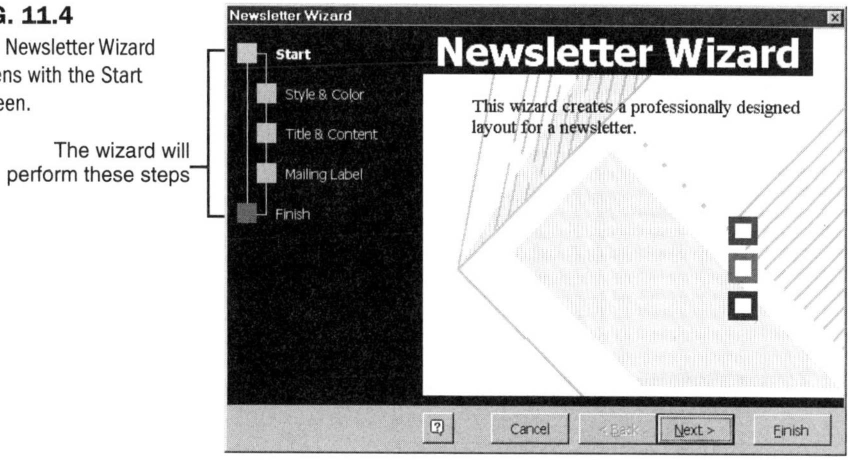

The wizard will perform these steps

NOTE You can also click the Newsletter Wizard icon once to select it, and click the OK button to start the wizard.

4. As the Newsletter Wizard begins, each dialog box asks you questions to which you respond by entering text, choosing options, and so on. To progress through the dialog boxes, click the Next button.

Figures 11.5 through 11.8 show the Wizard dialog boxes for a Professional-style newsletter. Following the Start screen (refer to Figure 11.4), the dialog boxes appear as follows:

- *Style & Color.* Choose a style for your newsletter (see Figure 11.5). Your options are Professional, Contemporary, or Elegant. You can also choose to print your newsletter in Black and White or Color.

- *Title & Content.* Enter a Title (main headline) for your newsletter (see Figure 11.6). Click the option buttons for Date and Volume and Issue number to have these items added to your title.

FIG. 11.5
Choose the style and color for your newsletter from this dialog box.

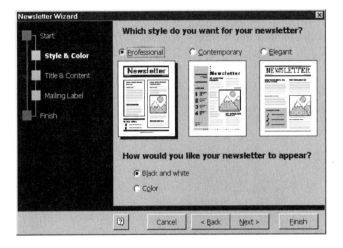

FIG. 11.6
Use this dialog box to type the name of your newsletter, as well as add any additional content.

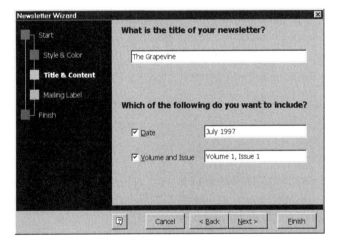

- ■ *Mailing Label.* Click the Yes option to leave room for a mailing label on the back cover (see Figure 11.7).
- ■ *Finish.* Click Finish to compose your newsletter based on your responses to the questions in the previous dialog boxes (see Figure 11.8).

 Click the Back button to go to a previous dialog box if you want to review or change your entries or responses to the wizard's questions.

FIG. 11.7
The Newsletter Wizard asks whether or not to leave room for a mailing label on your newsletter.

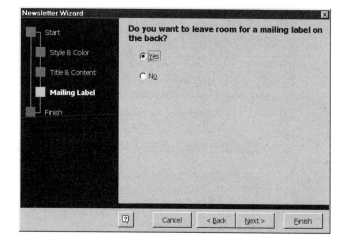

FIG. 11.8
After answering the wizard's questions, click the Finish button to create your newsletter.

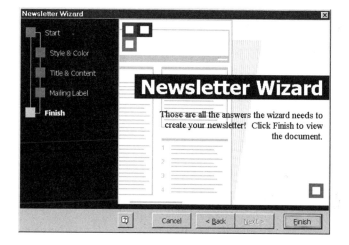

Click Finish in the last dialog box, and Word creates your newsletter. A five-page document is created, filled with instructions for inserting your own text, graphics, and article headlines (see Figure 11.9).

 When you use a wizard, there's no need to format your text, because the fonts are already selected for you. For more information on text formatting, see Chapter 6, "Enhancing Text with Character Formatting."

For more information on inserting and formatting graphics, see Chapter 12, "Using Graphics to Enhance Word Documents."

FIG. 11.9

The Newsletter Wizard creates a five-page newsletter, filled with instructions and sample graphics.

Replace this text with your own text

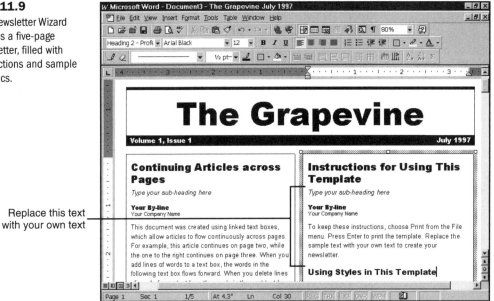

N O T E The Newsletter Wizard uses text boxes to house much of the text in the newsletter. Text boxes are drawn objects that contain text. They can be dragged to any position on your document. Text boxes can be linked so that text flows from one to another, allowing you, for example, to start an article on page one, and continue it on page four. In the newsletter that the wizard creates, the text boxes are drawn to fit within the columns on each page. For more information on using Text Boxes, see Chapter 12, "Using Graphics to Enhance Word Documents."

Using Graphics to Enhance Word Documents

A picture's worth a thousand words

Use pictures to convey an idea or a feeling in your documents. Use clip art from Word's set of installed graphics to enhance your memos, brochures, and newsletters.

Text as graphics

Add drop caps and pull quotes to your documents to add interest and draw the reader's attention to particular text.

Symbols and special characters

Fonts such as Animals, Typographical Symbols, and Wingdings enable you to use symbols in your documents and format them as you would text.

The ability to include photographs, drawings, maps, and other types of graphic images in a document can make the difference between a simple informative document and a great publication. Word 97 has enhanced its drawing and picture-formatting tools to give you more creative power and greater control over your graphic images. ■

Working with Pictures

Documents such as brochures, newsletters, and marketing flyers use pictures to communicate ideas and feelings. Adding a graphic to any document adds an extra dimension, and gives the document a polished, creative look.

You can add photographs, clip art images, or drawings to your documents by choosing Insert, Picture from the menu. Word also has a Drawing toolbar that gives you tools for drawing simple lines and shapes.

 Clip art are graphic files previously drawn either by hand or by using computer illustration software.

While the use of graphics in a brochure or newsletter is common, some other documents that can benefit from the addition of a picture or drawing include:

- *Memos.* In a memo about the company picnic, for example, add a graphic of food or people playing sports.
- *Reports.* Place an upward-pointing arrow behind your text as a graphic *watermark* to reinforce the concept that sales are on the rise.

 A *watermark*, in computer graphics lingo, is a graphic image that is placed behind the text layer on a document. The image is normally filled with a light-colored shade of gray or a muted color so as not to interfere with the legibility of the text.

- *Announcements.* Choose an appropriate picture to add interest to company bulletins. Incorporating an eye-catching graphic will entice people to read your document as they pass the bulletin board.

Some graphics are used to draw attention, others to impart information. Adding a chart or graph based on numeric data can express a complex range of financial information in a simple, quickly understood image. To learn more about adding a chart or graph to your documents, see Chapter 19, "Working with Other Office 97 Applications."

Schematic drawings, maps, and flow charts are other examples of graphics that can be added to a document to instruct or assist the reader in understanding the accompanying text.

Figure 12.1 shows a Memo with graphics inserted.

Understanding Graphic File Formats

A file's *format* determines its content, file size, and in some cases, appearance on-screen. You may find that saving a file in a particular format improves its appearance. Some formats can also result in a smaller file size, making it easier to transport the file on disk and faster to transmit via e-mail. A file's format is indicated by the file extension. Word supports the formats listed in Table 12.1.

FIG. 12.1

Something as simple as a telephone graphic can enhance your document and instruct the reader.

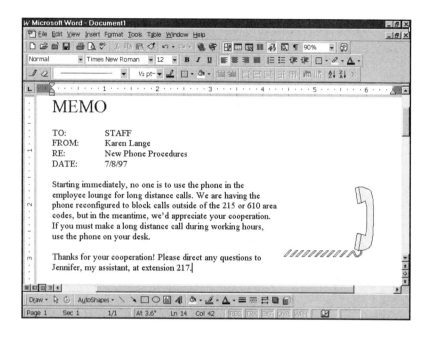

Table 12.1 Graphic File Formats Supported by Word 97

Format	Description
JPG or JPEG	Joint Photographic Experts group. JPEG (pronounced "Jay-Peg") is a popular format for scanned photographs. The image quality is usually very high and is an often-used image format amongst Web page designers.
WMF	Windows Metafile. Most Microsoft applications come with a group of WMF-format clip art images. Microsoft developed the file format for their own licensed graphic images.
BMP	Bit Mapped. Bitmap images are made up of many small square dots, or pixels. The images can have a ragged edge, especially on curved lines. If you enlarge a BMP graphic, the jagged effect is increased.
EPS	Encapsulated PostScript. This file format requires that you have a PostScript printer. EPS file images have smooth edges, and a clear background, making it easy to use EPS files where graphics will be layered.
TIF or TIFF	Tagged Image File Format. A very popular graphic file format that is great for large images.

Part

II

Ch

12

continues

Table 12.1 Continued

Format	Description
GIF	CompuServe Graphics Interchange Format. Originally designed by CompuServe to enable their members to transfer pictures within the online service and across the Internet. The PNG (Portable Network Graphics) format was designed to do the same job, without dealing with CompuServe's licensing issues (they own the GIF format). GIFs also are very popular with Web page designers.
DXF	AutoCAD version 2.0 generates this format.
PCX	Windows 95 Paint and PC Paintbrush create PCX files.

Unless your document will be printed by a commercial printing company or will be exported to another software product for final composition, you may not be concerned with the actual format of your files. If you're having a photograph or hand-drawn image scanned for use in your Word documents, refer to the preceding list or check the list of File Types in the Insert Picture dialog box to choose the format in which you'll save your scanned image. To access this list, choose Insert, Picture from the menu, and choose From File from the submenu. In the Insert Picture dialog box, click the Files of Type drop-down list.

Figure 12.2 shows the Insert Picture dialog box with the Files of Type list displayed.

FIG. 12.2
View the file formats supported by your installed version of Word in the Insert Picture dialog box.

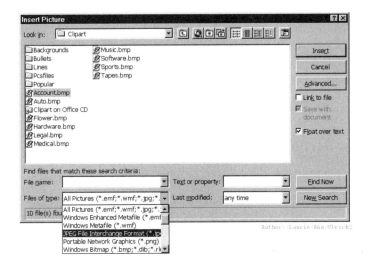

Inserting a Picture

To insert a picture into your document, perform the following steps:

1. Position your cursor at the location where you want to place the image. You will be able to move the image later.

2. Choose Insert, Picture from the menu. The submenu contains the following choices:

   - *Clip Art.* Choose this submenu option if you want to add one of Word's installed clip art images. The Microsoft Clip Art Gallery opens (see Figure 12.3).

FIG. 12.3
Choose from Word's installed clip art in the Microsoft Clip Art Gallery.

Clip art categories —
A selected clip art image —

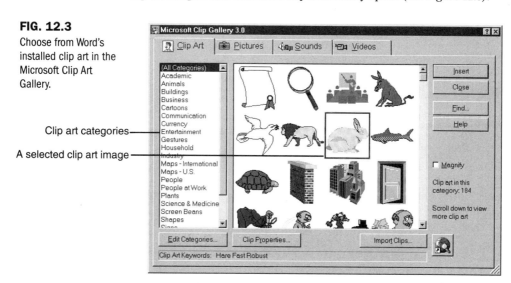

   - *From File.* If you have a scanned photo or some other graphic file on a disk, your local hard drive, or a network drive, select this option. The Insert Picture dialog box will open and you can select the file of your choice.

   - *AutoShapes.* Choose this option to open a toolbox of geometric shapes, such as stars, arrows, and flowchart shapes.

   - *WordArt.* This applet runs within Word and other Microsoft applications, and enables you to create banners, signs, and change the shape, size, and fill of text. (See "Using WordArt to Create Headlines and Graphic Text," later in this chapter.)

> **TIP** An *applet* is a program that runs within a larger application. The item produced by the applet becomes an embedded object within the application file.

   - *From Scanner.* This option opens Microsoft's Photo Editor program. If you have a scanner attached to your computer, you can use the program to scan and save graphic files, and by opening the program from the Insert, Picture submenu, insert the newly-scanned image directly into your open document.

Part
II

Ch
12

- *Chart.* Choose this option to open Microsoft Chart, another applet that provides a simple spreadsheet and a toolbar of charting tools for creating graphs from numeric data.

3. Whichever Picture option you choose, the graphic image will be placed in your document at the cursor. The image will now be an object in your document that can be moved or resized.

N O T E   To edit the object, double-click it to reopen the program that created it (or that Windows 95 associates with that file format) and use that program's tools to manipulate the content of the image. These tools will open within Word, either joining or replacing your Word toolbars and menus.

Moving and Resizing Graphics

Once you add a graphic image to your document, you may want to change its size or location. To move your graphic, simply point your mouse to any part of the graphic itself. The mouse pointer will turn to a four-headed arrow. As soon as the four-headed arrow appears, drag the graphic to your desired location (see Figure 12.4).

FIG. 12.4

Move a graphic by dragging it with your mouse.

Your mouse pointer becomes a four-headed arrow

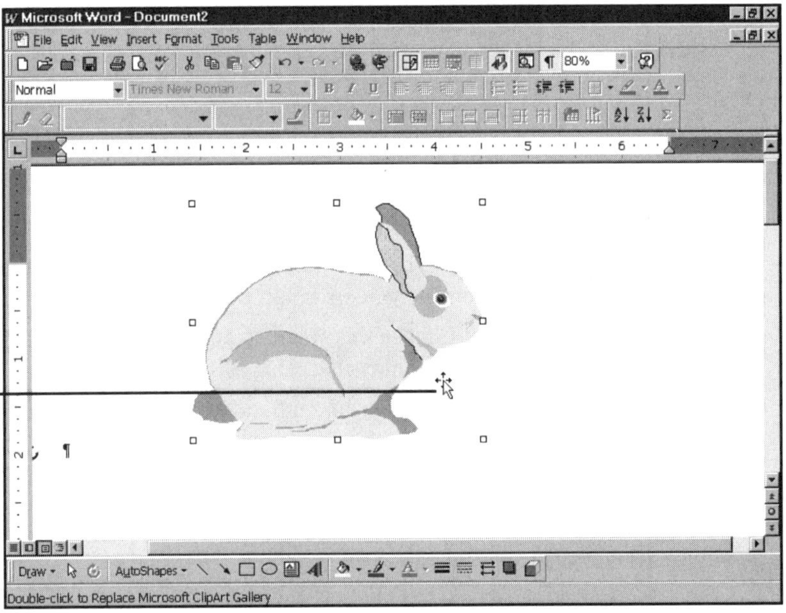

T I P   In previous versions of Word, a graphic had to be placed in a frame before it could be moved. Framing a graphic is no longer necessary in Word 97—graphics can be moved freely immediately upon insertion into your document.

To resize a graphic, point to the handles that surround your selected graphic. If the handles aren't showing, click the graphic once. Your mouse pointer will turn into a two-headed arrow (see Figure 12.5).

FIG. 12.5
Drag a graphic's handles to resize it.

Dragging from a corner handle maintains aspect ratio

Point to a handle and your mouse becomes a two-headed arrow

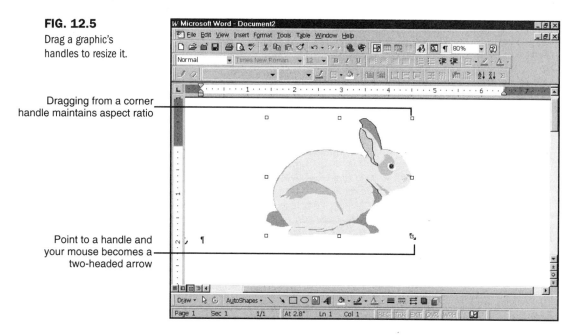

Understanding the following basic rules will make it easier to resize any graphic object in your document:

- To make the object larger, drag the handles outward.
- To make the graphic smaller, drag inward, toward the graphic's center.
- To keep the graphic's aspect ratio, drag from a corner handle.

N O T E *Aspect ratio* is the graphic's current horizontal and vertical proportions. If you drag the side handles on your graphic, the image will become wider or narrower. Dragging from a corner handle keeps the object in its current proportions, regardless of how small or large you make it.

Formatting Graphics

The color, size, location, and content of the graphic can be adjusted from the Format Picture dialog box (see Figure 12.6). This six-tabbed dialog box is accessed by choosing Format, Picture from the menu. Your graphic must be selected in order for this menu option to be available.

Part
II

Ch
12

FIG. 12.6

Select the Size tab in the Format Picture dialog box to format such aspects as your graphic's size, rotation, and scale.

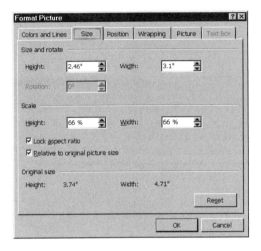

The Format Picture dialog box tabs and their options are as follows:

- *Colors and Lines.* Choose this tab to adjust the fill color of your object, the color, weight (in points), and style of the graphic's outline. Check the Semi-transparent box to give your graphic a "see-through" fill color.

- *Size.* This tab offers options for entering a specific height and width (in inches) for your graphic, and rotating your graphic on its center axis. To lock the object's aspect ratio and to keep it's proportions the same as the original picture size, place an X in the appropriate check boxes.

- *Position.* Choose the Horizontal and Vertical position for your graphic. You can specify the distance that the graphic will be placed relative to your document's margins, columns, or paragraphs.

- *Wrapping.* See the next section in this chapter, "Using Text and Graphics Together" for more information on text wrap.

- *Picture.* This tab offers you the ability to Crop (cut away) the top, bottom, left, and right sides of your image, and to control the Color, Brightness, and Contrast of your image.

N O T E By default, the Float Over Text check box is selected, indicating that the feature is on. This is what gives you the ability to move the object freely by dragging it with your mouse. If you turn this option off, your object will be locked into its current position, and will move with the text. ▪

 If you've cropped your graphic and want to retrieve some or all of the cropped areas, merely reduce the crop measurements in the Picture tab. Cropping a graphic in your document doesn't actually remove any of the graphic's content, it just reduces the displayed area of the graphic.

Using Text and Graphics Together

If your graphics are used in a newsletter or among text paragraphs in any document, the relationship between the text and the graphic is important. By default, text is set to break around your inserted graphic, so that if placed in the middle of a paragraph, the text will appear above and below the graphic. If you adjust the graphic's wrapping, you can make the text flow around it on all sides, or run behind the text. To adjust your picture's wrap settings, perform the following steps:

1. Select the graphic by clicking it once. The graphic's handles will appear.

2. Choose Format, Picture from the menu. The Format Picture dialog box opens.

3. Click the Wrapping tab (see Figure 12.7). The dialog box contains three sections:

FIG. 12.7

Choose the relationship your graphic will have with surrounding text by setting your Wrapping options.

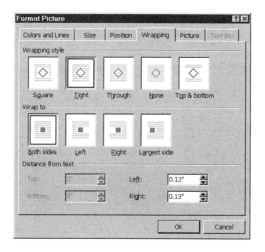

- *Wrapping Style.* Choose the way your text and graphic will work together. Each wrap style is represented by a picture button, which shows how text will wrap around your selected graphic.

- *Wrap To.* Choose Both Sides, Left, Right, or Largest Side. If your wrap style is None or Top & Bottom, these options will be dimmed.

- *Distance from Text.* Set the amount of space you want to appear between the text and the graphic's edges. The Left and Right distances are set to .13", and the Top and Bottom distances are set to 0" by default.

TIP If your graphic is very detailed or very small, you may want to increase the Distance from Text settings on all four sides so that the text doesn't visually overwhelm the graphic.

4. Set your wrap options, and click OK to save your settings and close the dialog box.

Part
II

Ch
12

Creating a Drop Cap

A *drop cap* is the first letter in a paragraph, enlarged and dropped down along side the first two or three lines of the paragraph (see sample in Figure 12.8). Drop caps are most often used in newsletters.

FIG. 12.8

A drop cap draws attention to a particular paragraph, and adds graphic interest to your document.

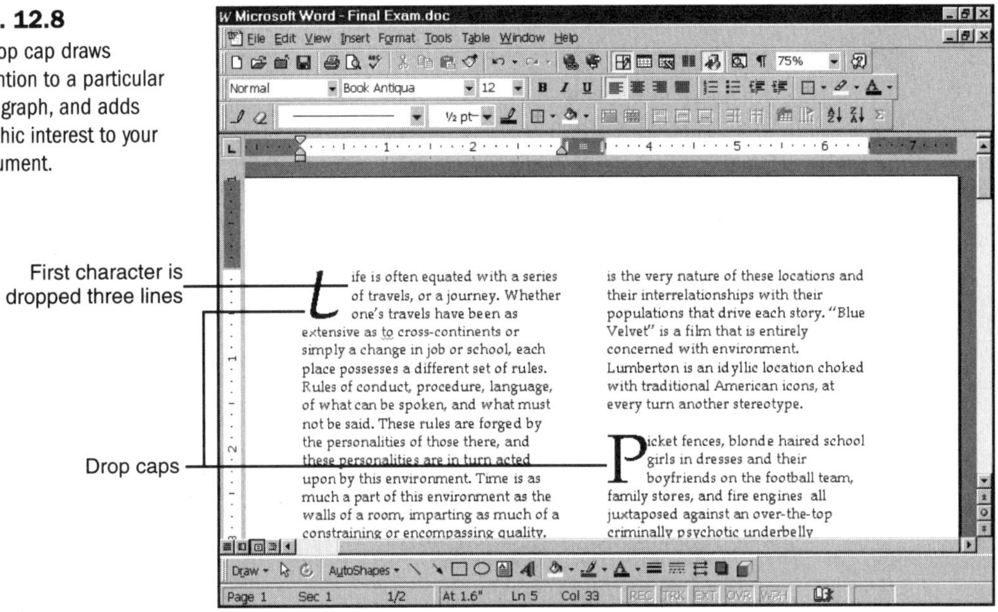

First character is dropped three lines

Drop caps

To create a drop cap in your document, perform the following steps:

1. Place your cursor to the left of the first character in the desired paragraph.

2. Choose Format, Drop Cap from the menu. The Drop Cap dialog box opens (see Figure 12.9).

FIG. 12.9

Choose your options from the Drop Cap dialog box.

3. Choose the Position of your drop cap—None, Dropped, or In Margin. You can specify the Font of the character that will be dropped, enter a number of Lines to Drop, and set the Distance from Text (which is the space between the dropped character and the paragraph text).

4. Click OK to save your settings and close the dialog box.

If you want to change some aspect of your drop cap after you've created it, click the dropped letter. A border appears around the character. Choose Format, Drop Cap from the menu, and make your changes. Click OK to apply your new settings and close the dialog box.

To remove a drop cap, place your cursor to the left of the dropped letter, and choose Format, Drop Cap. Choose the None option and click OK. Your dropped letter returns to the style of the rest of the paragraph.

Working with Text Boxes

 Another method of using text as a graphic is to insert a text box into your document by clicking the Text Box button on the Drawing toolbar. This creates a floating paragraph that can be moved and resized just like a picture, yet can be formatted just as you would format any other text. Some popular uses for text boxes are as follows:

■ *Pull Quotes.* In a newsletter or magazine article, sections of the article's body text are repeated in a text box and placed, like a graphic, within the article's columns. The paragraph text flows around the box, as though it were a graphic. The text within the box is normally a different or a larger font than the paragraph text (see Figure 12.10).

FIG. 12.10
Pull Quotes draw a reader's attention to important points covered in the surrounding text.

Text box has a light gray fill and a thin black border

Text wrap is set to Square

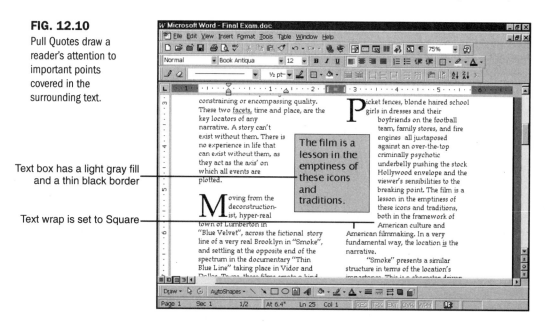

■ *Extra instructions.* Text boxes can be placed in the margins surrounding your paragraph text in any type of document. These boxes can contain supplementary instructions, tips, or explanations of terms within the paragraph text.

To create a text box, perform the following steps:

1. Display Word's Drawing toolbar by choosing View, Toolbars from the menu. Select Drawing from the list of toolbars.

2. Place your cursor within your existing paragraph text.

3. Click the Text Box tool on the Drawing toolbar. Your mouse pointer turns into a crosshair.

4. Click and drag the crosshair to draw a box. You will want to make it large enough to accommodate your intended text contents, but it can be enlarged or reduced in size later as needed.

5. As soon as you finish drawing the box (by releasing your mouse), a cursor appears in the box. You can begin typing the text contents for your text box.

Your text box contents can be typed, selected, and formatted as you would any other text. When you finish entering your text, click anywhere outside of the box to deactivate it. You can now move it (click and drag it) to any location in your document, and adjust its text wrap features as though it were a picture.

To format the text box itself, select the box with a single click of your mouse, and choose Format, Text Box from the menu. The Format Text Box dialog box opens, displaying six tabs, five of which apply to the selected text box (see Figure 12.11).

FIG. 12.11

Five of the Format Text Box dialog box tabs apply to text boxes.

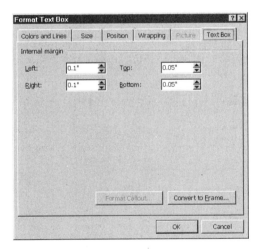

The Format Text Box dialog box options are as follows:

- *Colors and Lines.* This tab allows you to change the Fill Color and Line Style, Weight and Color for your text box.
- *Size.* Adjust the Height, Width, and Scale of your text box from this tab.
- *Position.* Choose the Horizontal and Vertical position for your text box. You can specify the distance that the text box will be placed relative to your document's margins, columns, or paragraphs.
- *Wrapping.* By default, text boxes lie on top of your text layer, potentially obscuring your paragraph text. The most appropriate choices for a text box are Square or Top & Bottom.
- *Text Box.* Set the Internal Margins for your text box contents. The default settings for the Left and Right margins are .1", and the Top, and Bottom are .5".

After adjusting the formatting of your selected text box, click OK to save your settings and close the dialog box.

Using WordArt to Create Headlines and Graphic Text

WordArt is an applet that runs within Word and other Microsoft products. WordArt is used to create fancy text effects by allowing you to apply interesting fills and shapes to your text. The WordArt tool is on the Drawing toolbar. (See the next section in this chapter, "The Drawing Toolbar," for more information.)

You can also open the WordArt applet by choosing Insert, Picture from the menu. Choose WordArt from the submenu. When you activate WordArt, an array of pre-designed text effects is displayed (see Figure 12.12). There are various fills and text shapes from which to choose.

FIG. 12.12

Choose an effect for your text from the WordArt Gallery.

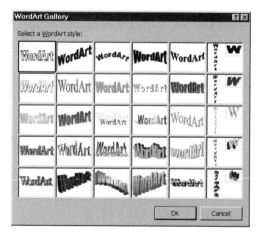

Part
II

Ch
12

To create a headline or banner with WordArt, perform the following steps:

1. In an open document, type the word or words that you wish to turn into WordArt. Highlight the text.

2. Choose Insert, Picture from the menu. In the resulting submenu, choose WordArt. A large graphic array, called the WordArt Gallery, opens.

3. Click the box displaying your desired WordArt effect, and click OK.

4. The WordArt applet opens, displaying the Edit WordArt dialog box (see Figure 12.13). You can change your font, font size, and make your text bold or italic.

FIG. 12.13

Format your WordArt text from the Edit WordArt dialog box.

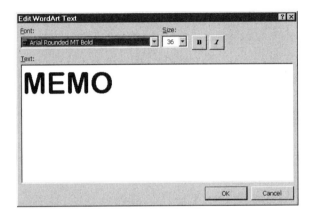

5. Click OK to accept any changes and close the dialog box.

Your text now appears as a graphic, in the WordArt style you chose, and the object has handles. There is also a floating toolbar on-screen, displaying tools for enhancing your WordArt effects. Figure 12.14 shows a selected WordArt text object with the WordArt toolbar.

The tools you can use with WordArt are defined in Table 12.2.

FIG. 12.14
The WordArt toolbar offers features for changing and enhancing your WordArt object.

WordArt object —
WordArt toolbar —

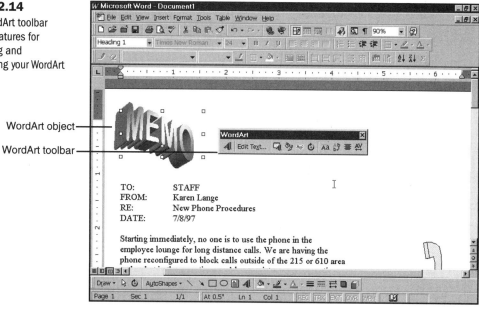

Table 12.2   WordArt Tools

Icon	Option	Description
	Insert WordArt	Opens the WordArt Gallery, enabling you to create another WordArt object in addition to the selected object.
Edit Te_x_t...	Edit Text	Reopens the Edit WordArt dialog box. You can add, delete, or change the WordArt text for your selected WordArt object.
	WordArt Gallery	Opens the WordArt Gallery, allowing you to change the effect applied to your selected WordArt object.
	Format WordArt	Opens the Format WordArt dialog box. Is the same six-tab dialog box used to format pictures and text boxes. Choose from the Colors and Lines, Size, Position, and Wrapping tabs to format your WordArt object.
Abc	WordArt Shape	Applies a variety of shapes to your WordArt text. Choose from Arches, waves, boxes, and other shapes. Your text will be reshaped to fit inside the shape you choose.

Part
II

Ch
12

continues

Table 12.2   Continued

Icon	Option	Description
	Free Rotate	Spins your object on its center axis. When you click this tool, your selected object's handles turn to small green circles. Your mouse will turn to a four-headed arrow. Click and drag any one of the handles in a circular direction, releasing the mouse when the desired rotation is achieved.
	WordArt Same Letter Heights	Makes your lower- and upper-case characters the same height in your WordArt object. This button functions as a toggle, allowing you to switch between same and different letter heights.
	WordArt Vertical Text	Turns your text so that it reads vertically. This button is also a toggle, allowing you to switch between vertical and horizontal text placement.
	WordArt Alignment	Offers alignment options for your text that apply only to WordArt objects, within the WordArt object shape.
	WordArt Character Spacing	Spreads out or tightens the tracking of your text.

Any changes you make using the WordArt tools are immediately reflected in your selected WordArt object. To close the toolbar, click away from your WordArt object. The object's handles disappear.

N O T E   You can move and resize your WordArt object like any other graphic object in your document. See "Formatting Graphics" earlier in this chapter for more information. ▧

The Drawing Toolbar

In addition to the Text Box and WordArt tools on the drawing toolbar, there are other tools for drawing squares, circles, lines, and a variety of pre-designed geometric shapes. Tools for changing the color, style, and placement of these objects are also available. You don't have to be an artist to use these tools, although good hand-eye coordination helps. To display the Drawing toolbar, choose View, Toolbars from the menu. Select Drawing from the list of available toolbars (see Table 12.3).

Table 12.3   The Drawing Toolbar

Icon	Option	Description
Draw ▾	Draw	Opens a pop-up menu containing options for Grouping and Ungrouping drawn objects, changing the order of layered objects, snapping your drawn items to an invisible grid, moving and aligning objects, rotating and flipping, reshaping (Edit Points), and changing AutoShapes. Toolbar icons in previous versions of Word represented most of these items but have been added to this menu to save on-screen space.
⌖	Select Objects	Use this tool to click and select one or more drawn objects. To select more than one, press and hold the Shift key as you "collect" objects for your selection.
↻	Free Rotate	Allows you to spin a drawn object on its center axis. When you click this tool, the handles of your selected drawn object turn to small green circles. Position your mouse over the circles (it turns to a four-headed arrow), and drag in a circular motion to rotate the object.
AutoShapes ▾	AutoShapes	Rather than trying to draw stars, arrows, and other geometric shapes, choose them from the pop-up menu that opens when you click this button. Each item in the menu opens an array of shapes. Click the shape you want and then drag your mouse (which turns to a crosshair) to draw the shape.
╲	Line	Draws a straight line at any angle. If you press and hold the Shift key as you draw the line, you will find it easier to constrain the line to any 45° angle. Press and hold the Ctrl key to draw the line from the center out.
↘	Arrow	Works just like the Line tool, except an arrowhead appears at the end of the line you draw.
▭	Rectangle	Draws boxes. To draw a perfect square, press and hold the Shift key as you draw the box. Be sure to release the mouse before releasing the Shift key. To draw a box from the center out, press and hold the Ctrl key as you draw the box. You can hold both the Shift and Ctrl keys to create a square, drawn from the center out.
⬭	Oval	Creates ovals and circles. To draw a perfect circle, press and hold the Shift key while drawing. Be sure to release the mouse before you release the Shift key. To draw an oval from the center out, press and hold the Ctrl key while drawing. You can hold both the Shift and Ctrl keys to create a perfect circle, drawn from the center out.

Part

II

Ch

12

continues

Table 12.3   Continued

Icon	Option	Description
	Text Box	See the previous section, "Using Text Boxes" for more information on the use of this tool.
	WordArt	Opens the WordArt applet, which enables you to create graphical text objects for signs, banners, and headlines. See the previous section, "Using WordArt to Create Headlines and Graphic Text" for more information on this tool.
	Fill Color	Actually two tools. The button with the bucket on it is used to quickly change the selected object to the displayed color. The drop triangle next to the bucket allows you to select the color that will be displayed on the bucket tool.
	Line Color	Like the Fill tool, it is really two buttons. Click the drop-down list to choose a color, or use the paintbrush button to change the selected line to the displayed color. This tool is also used to change the outline color of a filled object.
	Font Color	Changes the color of your selected text. Can be used for paragraph text or text box contents.
	Line Style	After you draw a line or arrow, use this tool to choose a style for the line. Choose thick, thin, double, or triple lines from the pop-up list.
	Dash Style	Turns a selected line into a dashed line. After list of dash styles pops up. Click the style you prefer, and it will apply to the selected line.
	Arrow Style	If you've drawn an arrow line, choose this tool to apply different arrowheads to your line.
	Shadow	Places a drop shadow behind your selected drawn object.
	3-D	Gives your drawn object a three-dimensional. An array of 3-D perspectives pops-up after selecting object and clicking this button.

Objects you draw using the Word Drawing toolbar can be moved in any direction and resized just like a picture. To delete a drawn object, select it by clicking it with your mouse, and press the Delete key.

Inserting Symbols and Special Characters

Another way to enhance your document is to insert a symbol. The Wingdings and Dingbats fonts contain many symbols such as smiley faces, stars, geometric shapes, astrological symbols, and so forth. The Symbol font contains symbols for degree marks, copyright symbols, and typographical characters. Depending on what fonts you have installed on your computer, you may also have groups of symbols such as animals and plants. To insert a symbol into your document, perform the following steps:

1. In your open document, place your cursor where you want the symbol to be inserted.

2. Choose Insert, Symbol from the menu. The Symbol dialog box opens (see Figure 12.15).

FIG. 12.15

Insert a symbol or special character into your document using the Symbol dialog box.

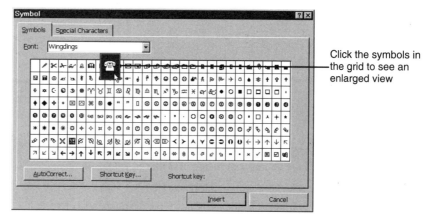

Click the symbols in the grid to see an enlarged view

3. The Symbol dialog box has two tabs—Symbols and Special Characters. Make sure the Symbols tab is in front by clicking the tab.

4. Click the Font drop-down list to see a list of available fonts. Click the font you wish to display in the grid. All the characters for the font you select display in the large grid.

 T I P The display of each character is very small, so to see an enlarged view of a particular symbol, click the mouse and hold the mouse button down (refer to Figure 12.15).

5. After you select the symbol you want to insert, click the symbol in the grid. Click the Insert button.

6. Inserting a symbol doesn't close the dialog box. To close the dialog box, choose Close.

N O T E While the Symbol dialog box is open, you can insert a single symbol more than once by pressing the Insert button repeatedly. You can insert several different symbols by clicking each new symbol (from any font you choose) and clicking the Insert button for each one. ■

Part
II

Ch
12

Special Characters can be inserted by choosing Insert, Symbol from the menu, and clicking the Special Characters tab (see Figure 12.16). Special Characters are typographical symbols such as em and en dashes. Select them from the list of characters, and click the Insert button. To close the dialog box, click Close.

FIG. 12.16

Special Characters such as an Em Dash (–) or an Ellipsis (...) can be added from the Special Characters tab.

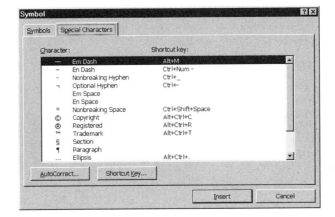

After you inserted a symbol or special character, you can increase its size by selecting it and choosing a larger font size. You can also apply any other Font formats, such as Bold or Shadow. You can change the color of the symbol as you would any text.

To delete a symbol or special character, use the Backspace or Delete keys (depending on your cursor position), or select it with your mouse and click the Delete key.

If a particular symbol or special character is one that you'll be using often, you may want to assign a keyboard shortcut to that character. To apply a shortcut key to your symbol, perform the following steps:

1. Open the Symbols dialog box by choosing Insert, Symbol from the menu. You don't need to insert a symbol or special character at the time that you assign the shortcut keys.

2. Click the Symbols or Special Characters tab.

3. Select your symbol or special character, and click the Shortcut button.

4. The Customize Keyboard dialog box opens (see Figure 12.17). Notice that your cursor is blinking in the Press New Shortcut Key box. Press the keyboard shortcut that you want to apply, such as Alt S to insert a Smiley Face.

When assigning a keyboard shortcut, choose an alpha key that will help you remember the symbol associated with it, such as Alt+D for a degree symbol, or Alt+M for an em dash.

FIG. 12.17

Assign a keyboard shortcut to any symbol or special character that you will use often.

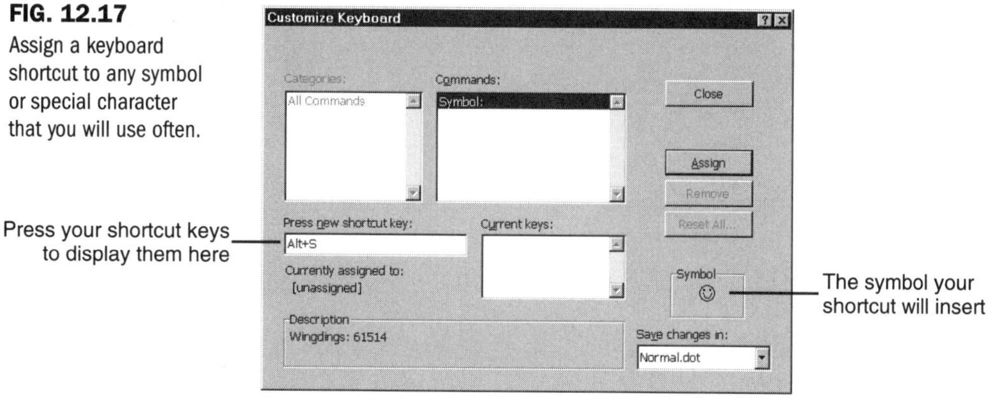

Press your shortcut keys to display them here

The symbol your shortcut will insert

5. The dialog box will inform you if you selected a keyboard shortcut that is already assigned to another function, and tell you what function it is. If it's already assigned, try another one, until you find one that is available.

6. Click the Assign button, and then choose Close. In the Symbols dialog box, click Close to save your changes and close the dialog box.

T I P If the Alt+key combination that you want to assign is already in use, try adding the Shift key to your shortcut.

After creating your shortcut, you can insert the associated symbol or special character at any time by placing your cursor where you want to insert it, and pressing the assigned key combination.

Part
II

Ch
12

Special Documents

CHAPTER 13

Working with Long Documents

A document need not be 100 pages long to require special treatment and formatting. Any document exceeding a single page can have page numbers, headers and footers, and even a section break added to it. The longer your document is, however, the more you'll need to assist your reader in navigating the document's pages, and to control the flow of text. ■

Page numbers

Decide when, where, and how to number the pages of any document. Customize your page numbers to assist your readers in navigating your document easily and logically.

Sections and chapters

Keep track of the physical and conceptual breaks in your long document by creating chapters and inserting section breaks.

Headers and footers

Placing your document title, chapter numbers, or author information at the top or bottom of each page helps your readers keep track of where they are in a long document. Add horizontal lines below the header and above the footer to separate the header and footer text from the rest of the page.

Indexes and tables

Just like this roadmap tells you what to expect in this chapter, a table of contents tells your reader what your document covers, and on which pages to find specific content. For really long documents, you'll want to add an Index and turn your document into a real reference.

Inserting Page Numbers

It's a good idea to number your pages in any document that exceeds one page. In most business letters, for instance, if your letter is two or more pages long, the pages, beginning with page two, are numbered to help the reader keep the pages in order.

The longer your document is, the more important page numbering becomes. Word gives you the ability to format and customize the page numbers in your document to accommodate your printing and binding considerations. It also enables you to set up separate numbering styles for different parts (or sections) of your document.

 T I P If you're applying different page numbers to different sections of your document, click the Show/Hide tool, so that you can see your section breaks.

 To apply page numbers to your open document, perform the following steps:

1. Place your cursor in the section of the document that you want to number. If your document has no separate sections, place your cursor on page one. (For more information on document sections, see the "Creating Section Breaks" section later in this chapter.)

 T I P You can quickly see which section you're in by checking the status line at the bottom of your Word screen.

2. Choose Insert, Page Numbers from the menu. The Page Numbers dialog box opens (see Figure 13.1).

FIG. 13.1
Use the Page Numbers dialog box to insert page numbers for your whole document or a just a section of it.

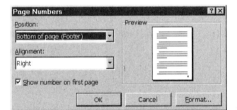

3. The Page Numbers dialog box contains the following options:
   - *Position*. Choose Bottom of Page (Footer) or Top of Page (Header). Page numbers are placed in the Header and Footer areas of your document, not on the text layer.

   For more information on how you can add other text to the header and footer areas of your document, see "Working with Headers and Footers," later in this chapter.
   - *Alignment*. Choose from Left, Center, Right, Inside, or Outside. Your choice will depend on your printing and binding intentions. If you're not sure how your document will be printed—double-sided, single-sided, or bound—choose Center alignment.

- *Show Number on First Page*. This is on by default, but should be turned off for letters and most other business documents.

4. To insert your page numbers according to your position and alignment settings, click OK.

N O T E   After inserting your page numbers, you can see them by switching to Page Layout view, or by choosing File, Print Preview. Page numbers are inserted as a field, meaning that the number displayed and printed will change as you add or delete pages from your document.

Formatting Page Numbers

If your document has separate sections, or if your page numbers require further formatting, you will want to customize the way Word applies your page numbers. To view your page numbering format options, perform the following steps:

1. If your page numbers have already been inserted or if you're inserting them for the first time, choose Insert, Page Numbers from the menu.

2. Set your Position and Alignment options if necessary, and click Format. The Page Number Format dialog box opens (see Figure 13.2).

FIG. 13.2
Use the Page Number Format dialog box to format your page numbers to meet the needs of your long document.

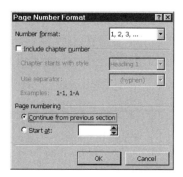

3. Your formatting options are as follows:

- *Number Format*. Choose from Arabic numbers, Roman numerals, and letters of the alphabet.

- *Include Chapter Number*. If your document is broken down into chapters, click this check box. You can then choose the numbering format for your chapters.

For more information on using chapters in your long document, see "Working with Chapters," later in this chapter.

- *Page Numbering*. You can choose Continue from Previous Section (so that the numbers flow over your sections uninterrupted) or Start At and enter a starting page number for your whole document or active section.

T I P   If your first page is a cover page (for a report or manual) and you want the second page to appear as page one, set your Start <u>A</u>t number to zero.

4. After setting your format options, click OK. You will return to the Page Numbers dialog box. Click OK to close it and put your formats into effect.

At some point in the future, you may want to remove numbers you added. As the Header/ Footer layer will be activated during this process, you may want to refer to "Working with Headers and Footers," found later in this chapter.

To remove page numbers from your document, follow these steps:

1. Double-click any page number in your document or within the section of your document for which you wish to remove the page numbering.

2. Your document will switch to the Header/Footer layer, and the Header and Footer floating toolbar will appear on-screen. Click the page number field once. A border will also appear around the page number (see Figure 13.3).

3. Click the number's border again—handles (small black boxes) appear on the sides and corners of the border.

FIG. 13.3

To remove page numbers, double-click the number and delete it from the Header/ Footer layer.

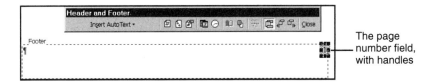

The page number field, with handles

4. Press the Delete key.

5. Click the <u>C</u>lose button on the Header and Footer floating toolbar.

To change or reformat your existing page numbers in your whole document, or to change or reformat a specific section of your document, follow these steps:

1. Place your cursor in the section in which you want to change the existing page number settings.

2. Choose <u>I</u>nsert, Page N<u>u</u>mber from the menu.

3. Make any changes to <u>P</u>osition and <u>A</u>lignment, or click the <u>F</u>ormat button to make changes to the numbering style, as necessary. If you make formatting changes, you must click OK in the Page Number Format dialog box to return to the main Page Numbers dialog box.

4. Click OK in the Page Numbers dialog box. This will close the dialog box and insert your new page numbers.

5. If you chose a new <u>P</u>osition or <u>A</u>lignment, you will now have a second set of page numbers on your document, requiring you to delete the old page numbers from your document's Header/Footer layer.

N O T E You can change the format of existing page numbers without adding a new set of numbers as long as you don't change the position or alignment settings. Word sees any change to these options as a new page number insertion, resulting in two sets of page numbers. ▪

Creating Section Breaks

Long documents often consist of several sections. These sections can be conceptual, where only the text content of the document is changed, while other sections require a physical break in the document. Physical section breaks are normally inserted so that page numbers, margins, and page orientation can be changed to meet the functional needs of the document.

To insert a section break, perform the following steps:

1. Place your cursor in your document at the point where you wish to insert the section break.

2. Choose Insert, Break from the menu. The Break dialog box opens (see Figure 13.4).

FIG. 13.4
Use the Break dialog box to insert and format your document's section breaks.

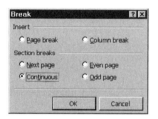

3. Your Section Breaks options are as follows:

   - *Next Page.* The break will begin at the top of the next page in your document. If no next page exists, one will be added automatically.

   - *Continuous.* The section break will be inserted at your current cursor location, and no physical break will be inserted into your document.

   - *Even Page.* If your document will be printed on both sides, bound, or both, you may want to have separate settings for page numbers and margins for your odd and even pages. Even pages normally have their page numbers on the left and a wider right margin. To create an even page section break (breaking at the end of every even page), click this button.

   - *Odd Page.* To insert your odd page section breaks, click this button. Your odd pages will normally be numbered on the right side, and the left margin will be wider.

N O T E Inserting section breaks for odd and even pages will neither automatically insert page numbers on the left (for odd pages) or the right (for even pages), nor will it adjust the margins. The section breaks are inserted to assist you in creating separate settings for odd and even pages: They make it possible for you to have separate rules for each section in your document. ▪

Part
III

Ch
13

4. After selecting your Section Breaks option, click OK to insert the break and close the dialog box.

Your section breaks contain the formatting for that section. If, for example, your section break was inserted to place a physical break between your Table of Contents and your first page of paragraph text, that section break will contain the formats for the page numbering and margins for that section. To re-use those section formats for your Index or an Appendix later in the document, you can copy the section break and paste it where you need it.

To copy and paste any section break in your document, follow these steps:

1. Click the Show/Hide button on the standard toolbar to make your section breaks visible.

2. Select the section break you want to copy (see Figure 13.5). You can click and drag through it with your mouse, or click once in the left margin. Make sure no other text or blank lines are selected.

FIG. 13.5

Select a section break to copy and paste it to another place in your document.

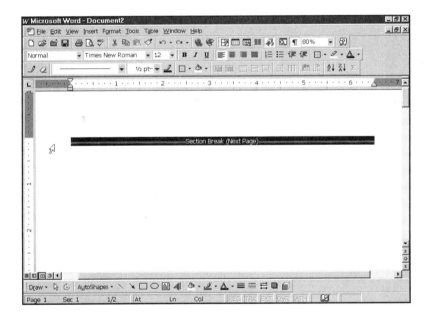

3. Choose Edit, Copy from the menu, or press Ctrl+C.

4. Place your cursor in your document at the point where you wish to paste the copied section break.

5. Choose Edit, Paste from the menu, or press Ctrl+V. The section break is inserted, and the formats are applied to the pages following it.

To remove a section break, turn on your Show/Hide feature so that you can see the breaks. Place your cursor on the line with the section break, and press Delete.

CAUTION

Deleting section breaks should be done with care and forethought. Remember that if your section breaks were inserted to allow you to use different page numbering styles, margins, or page orientation, removing the section break will also remove those features.

Working with Headers and Footers

Headers and Footers are areas at the top and bottom of a document's pages that contain text such as page numbers, chapter titles, or copyright information; and graphics, such as your company logo or a piece of clip art. If your document is one large section, the headers and footers will remain constant throughout it. If your document is broken into several sections, each section can have its own header and footer. In many cases, the need for separate headers and footers throughout a document is the motivation for inserting section breaks in the first place.

NOTE You don't have to have different headers and footers throughout your multi-section document. By default, header and footer content remains constant throughout your document. You must choose to create unique headers and footers for any separate sections within your document.

To create a header or footer in your document or a particular section of it, follow these steps:

1. Place your cursor at the top of your document (if the headers and footers will apply throughout your single-section document) or within the section for which you want to create the header or footer.

2. Choose View, Header and Footer from the menu. Two things happen to your document—a floating Header and Footer toolbar appears, and your document switches to the Header/Footer layer. Your text layer will appear dimmed (see Figure 13.6).

3. The Header and Footer areas appear with a dashed border. Word goes to the Header box first. You can begin typing your header text, or switch to the Footer box to insert text there. Before proceeding, however, you should become familiar with the Header and Footer toolbar. See Table 13.1 for more information on the Header and Footer toolbar.

Part
III

Ch
13

Table 13.1   The Header and Footer Toolbar

Icon	Option	Description
Insert AutoText ▾	Insert AutoText	If you use the same Header and Footer text often, you may choose to create an AutoText entry for it. For more information on creating an AutoText entry, see Chapter 2, "Creating Documents."

continues

Table 13.1 Continued

Icon	Option	Description
	Insert Page Number	An alternative to Insert, Page Numbers from the menu, this option also allows you to type **Page** or **Pg** before inserting the number. The Page Number is inserted as a field, meaning that the page numbers will change as pages are added to your document.
	Insert Number of Pages	If you want your Header or Footer to say, for example, "Page 5 of 10," click this button after the word "of." Like Page Numbers, this number is inserted as a field, so as your total number of pages changes, this number will also change.
	Format Page Number	This button opens the Page Number Format dialog box. See "Formatting Page Numbers" earlier in this chapter for more information.
	Insert Date	Click this button to insert a date field. If you open the document on a later date, the date in your header or footer will change to that date.
	Insert Time	To insert a time field, click this button. The time will update each time the document is opened.
	Page Setup	Clicking this button will open the Page Setup dialog box. This link to that dialog box exists to enable you to adjust the Header and Footer settings in the Margins tab.
	Show/Hide Document Text	If you find that the dimmed text-layer text is distracting during the header and footer creation process, turn off the display for that layer. You can turn it back on by clicking the button again.
	Same as Previous	This button allows you to break or maintain the default link between one section and the section before it. If you have created a header and footer for your previous section, you must break this link (by clicking this button) if you want a different header and footer for your active section. If you make the change to the active header and footer before breaking the link, you will change the header and footer in the previous section.

Icon	Option	Description
🔲	Switch Between Header and Footer	To go from the Header box to the Footer box (and back again as necessary), click this button.
🔲	Show Previous	Click this button to see the previous section's header or footer.
🔲	Show Next	To see the header or footer in the following section, click this button.
Close	Close Header and Footer	After entering and formatting your header and footer content, click this button to close the toolbar.

4. After typing your header or footer content and inserting any date, time, or page number fields, click the Close button to close the Header and Footer toolbar and return to your text layer.

FIG. 13.6

The text layer appears dimmed when the Header/Footer layer is active in your document.

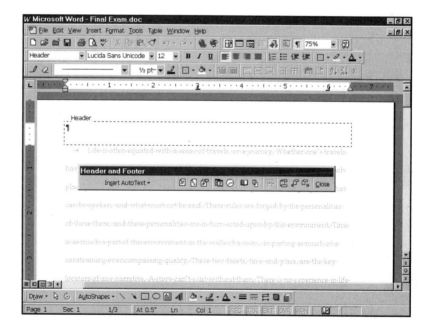

Your Header and Footer content can be formatted just like any text. You can change the fonts, size, or alignment of the text, and although default tabs are set for your Header and Footer boxes (a centered tab at 3" and a right-aligned tab at 6"), you can set your own tabs as needed. Figure 13.7 shows a document's Footer.

Part
III

Ch
13

FIG. 13.7

Format your Header and Footer content as you would any text.

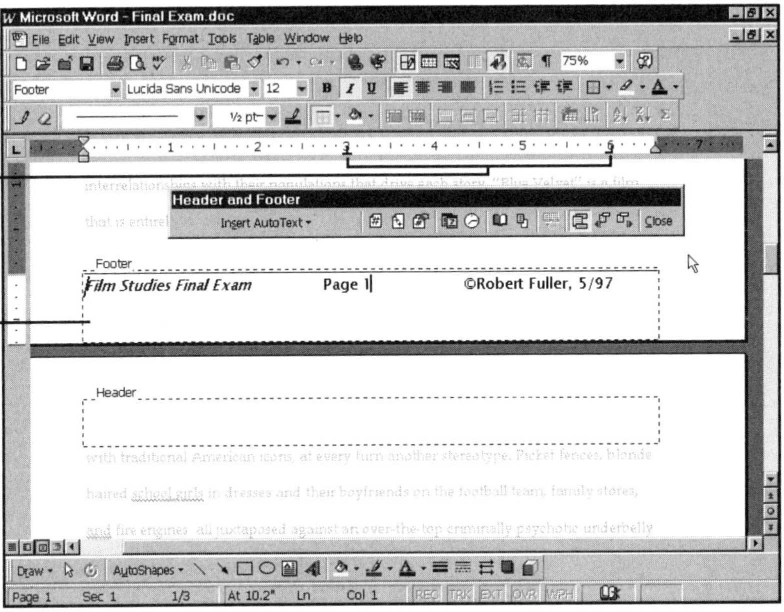

Default Footer tabs

Formatted Footer text

Film Studies Final Exam   Page 1   ©Robert Fuller, 5/97

To visually separate your header or footer content from the rest of the page, add a horizontal border. You'll want to place a bottom border on your header, and a top border on your footer. To place a border on your header or footer, follow these steps:

1. With your Header or Footer layer active, select the entire content of your Header or Footer box.

2. Click the drop-down list on your Word's Border tool (found on Formatting toolbar). Select the top border for your Footer, or the Bottom border for your Header (see Figure 13.8).

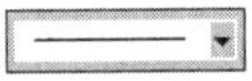

3. To format the line, click the Line Style and Line Weight buttons on the Tables and Borders toolbar.

TIP To turn on your Tables and Borders toolbar, choose <u>V</u>iew, <u>T</u>oolbars from the menu, and select the toolbar from the submenu.

For more information on applying and formatting text borders, see Chapter 7, "Paragraph Formatting."

FIG. 13.8
Choose a bottom border for your Header and a top border for your Footer.

Tables and Borders toolbar is displayed

Header border

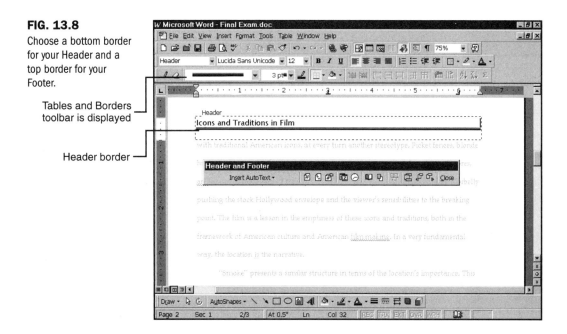

Generating a Table of Contents

The Table of Contents contains a page-order list of topics covered by your document. Word constructs a table of contents by tracking your use of Heading styles throughout your text. By default, the use of Heading 1, 2, and 3 for your subject heading text will enable Word to automatically create a table of contents. You can determine the level of detail included in the table of contents, as well as its overall appearance. To create a table of contents for your document, perform the following steps:

1. Place your cursor in your document at the point where you want the Table of Contents to start.

N O T E   If your document contains page numbers or other headers and footers, you may want to place the Table of Contents in a separate section within the document. This will enable you to choose different page numbers (normally a Table of Contents is numbered with lowercase Roman numerals) and to eliminate or change the header and footer content. For more information about inserting section breaks, see "Creating Section Breaks" earlier in this chapter. ■

2. Choose Insert, Index and Tables from the menu. The Index and Tables dialog box opens. Click the Table of Contents tab (see Figure 13.9).

Part
III

Ch
13

FIG. 13.9

Set up your Table of Contents by choosing a format for the table's text.

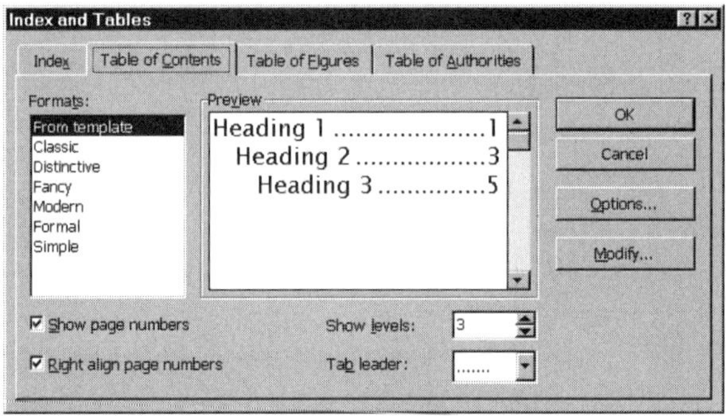

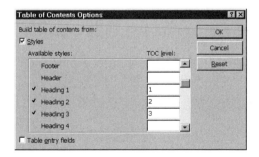

The Table of Contents tab contains the following options:

- *Formats*. Choose from a list of styles such as Classic, Fancy, Modern, and Simple. You can see how the formats will look in the Preview area within the dialog box.

- *Show Page Numbers*. This option is on by default.

- *Right Align Page Numbers*. This option is also on by default for most of the formats.

- *Show Levels*. By default, Word looks for Heading 1, 2, and 3 styles in your document, and places the text formatted in those styles in your Table of Contents. To increase or decrease the heading levels, click the up or down arrows or type the desired level in the box.

- *Tab Leader*. The page numbers in your Table of Contents are entered with a right-aligned, dot leader tab. The leader is a character leading up to the tabbed text. The character is a dot (.) by default. To change it to another character (an underscore or dash, for example), type the new character in the box.

3. To change the styles that Word will look for to establish Table of Contents entries, click the Options button. The Table of Contents Options dialog box appears (see Figure 13.10). You can choose different Styles from the list supported by your current document's template.

4. To enter your own Table of Contents field entries, thus telling Word to ignore Styles in building the Table of Contents, click the Table Entry Fields check box. Click OK to save your settings and return to the Index and Tables dialog box.

FIG. 13.10

Click the Options button to choose other styles to build your Table of Contents, or choose to create your own Table of Contents field entries.

5. To change the fonts, indents, and tabs for your Table of Contents entries, click the Modify button. The Style dialog box appears (see Figure 13.11). After making your changes, click Modify to return to the Index and Tables dialog box.

FIG. 13.11

Modify the appearance of your Table of Contents, by formatting the text, indents, and tabs for each level.

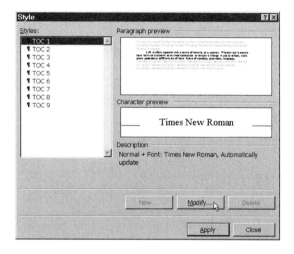

6. After creating your Table of Contents settings, click OK. The dialog box closes, and Word will create and display your Table of Contents in your document.

Figure 13.12 shows a completed Table of Contents.

FIG. 13.12

After you select various options and styles, Word displays the complete Table of Contents.

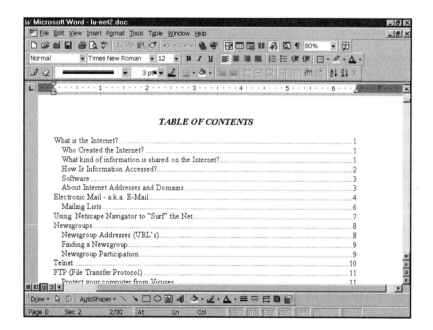

Part
III

Ch
13

If you want to create your own Table of Contents field entries (rather than have your use of Heading styles create the Table of Contents), follow these steps prior to opening the Index and Tables dialog box:

1. Place your cursor in your document where you want to insert the Table of Contents field.

2. Choose Insert, Field from the menu. The Field dialog box opens.

3. On the left side of the box, choose Index and Tables from the list of Categories; click TC from the list of Field Names on the right.

4. In the Field Codes box, place your cursor after the TC that appears in the box. Press the spacebar once. Then type the field entry (the text that you want to appear in the Table of Contents), in quotation marks.

5. Follow the closing set of quotation marks with a backward slash (\), followed by the number **1**.

   Type another single space, and type a number representing the level of that particular entry as it should appear in the Table of Contents. You can enter any number between 1 and 9.

   Figure 13.13 shows a Table of Contents field entry in the Field dialog box.

FIG. 13.13

Be sure to type the field code carefully when creating your own Table of Contents field entry.

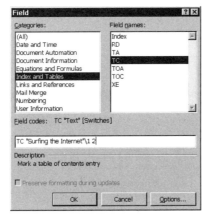

6. Click OK to close the Field dialog box.

Repeat the preceding steps for each Table of Contents entry throughout your document.

Figure 13.14 shows a Table of Contents field entry as it appears in a document.

To update an existing Table of Contents (whether it is built through your use of styles or by Table of Contents field entries), place your cursor anywhere in the Table of Contents and press the F9 key.

To delete a Table of Contents, highlight the entire table and press Delete.

FIG. 13.14

Insert Table of Contents field entries throughout your document to build a customized Table of Contents.

Table of Contents field

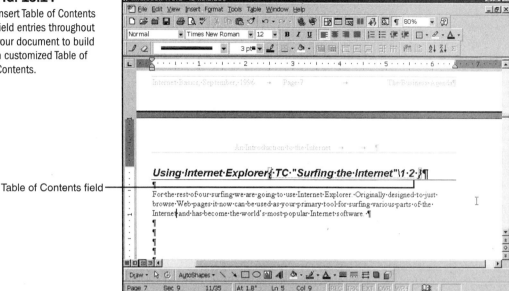

Creating an Index

You can turn your long document into a useful reference by adding an index at the end of the document. An index is an alphabetical list of the topics covered in your document, accompanied by the page number on which the topic can be found.

Unlike a Table of Contents, which normally lists major topics that appear in your document's headings, an index can be very detailed, listing a topic or name that appears only once, even as a parenthetical reference. This detail is possible because you, as the document's author or editor, can choose which items from your document are represented by a listing in the index.

There are two ways to create an index in your document:

- Mark the text throughout your document that you wish to include in the index and then let Word compile and insert the index at the end of your document.

- Create a concordance table to keep track of words or phrases for Word to find in your document when the index is created, along with a list of the entries Word should place in the index for each word or phrase found.

To create an index by marking your own text, perform the following steps:

1. Select the text (a word or short phrase) that you want to include in your index.

2. Choose Insert, Index and Tables from the menu. Click the Index tab (see Figure 13.15).

Part
III

Ch
13

FIG. 13.15
Use the Index and Tables dialog box to add an index to your document.

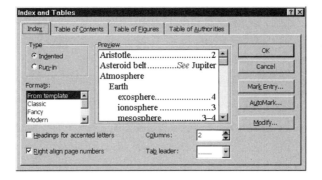

3. Click the Mark Entry button. The Mark Index Entry dialog box opens (see Figure 13.16), displaying the following options:

FIG. 13.16
Create your own index entries by marking text within your document

- *Main Entry.* This is the text you selected in your document. You can leave this text as is, or type the exact entry as you want it to appear in the index.

- *Subentry.* If your Main Entry has related items that you want to have listed under the main entry, enter this text in the Subentry box. To enter more than one Subentry, separate each one with a colon.

- *Options.* You can choose one of the following: Cross-reference, Current Page, and Page Range. To create a range, type the page range (such as **13–18**) in the box, or click the drop-down list to select an existing bookmark.

N O T E A bookmark is a marked location in your document. To create a bookmark, select a word, paragraph, page, or range of pages, and choose Insert, Bookmark from the menu. Give the bookmark a name, and click Add. The dialog box closes, and the bookmark is available (by name) for your use in creating Index entries.

- *Page Number Format.* Choose Bold or Italic, or both.

4. You can leave the Mark Index Entry dialog box open as you move through your document, marking entries. Click outside of the dialog box to reactivate the document, and then click back in the dialog box to mark your next entry.

T I P As you select text for new index entries, your last entry will remain in the Main Entry box until you type the new entry or click your mouse once in the Main Entry box to insert your latest highlighted index entry.

5. When you complete your entries or wish to close the dialog box, click Cancel.

To create an index by using a concordance table, open your main document (the document to be indexed) and then perform the following steps:

1. Click the New button to create a new, blank document. In the new document, create a two-column table.

N O T E For more information on creating tables, see Chapter 10, "Using Tables."

2. In the left column of your table, enter the text you want Word to look for in the document you want to index. Press the Tab key to move to the second column, and enter the index entry as you want it to appear in the document's index.

T I P When building your concordance file, be sure to use all forms of the word you want Word to search for. Enter each form of the word in a cell in the first column, paired with the index entry in the opposing cell in the second column.

3. If you need subentries to appear under your main entries, type them, separated by colons in the second column.

   Figure 13.17 shows a concordance table for a Word document.

4. Enter each entry in a row in the table. The table can span several pages of the document, if necessary.

   When you've finished creating your entries, save the concordance file document.

T I P To speed up your indexing process, leave the concordance file document open when you go back to your main document.

5. To use your concordance file in your main document, switch back to or open your main document, and choose Insert, Index and Tables from the menu.

6. Click the AutoMark button. The Open Index AutoMark File dialog box opens.

7. Enter the file name for your concordance file document or select it from the displayed files.

   Click Open to open the concordance file document. Even if the concordance file document is already open, this step is required so that Word knows which document to use for the concordance file information.

Part

III

Ch

13

FIG. 13.17

Create a two-column concordance table as the basis of your document's index.

Words to search for

Forms of the word

Subentries separated by a colon

Index entries

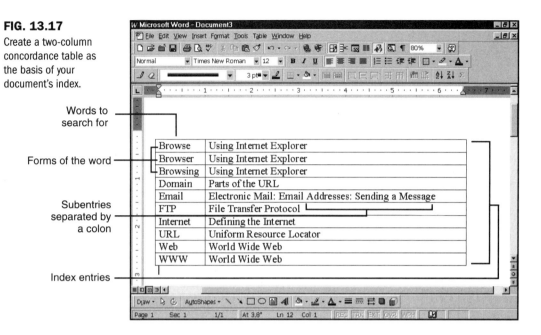

8. A prompt will appear, indicating the number of index entries found by Word as it compares your concordance table's first column entries to your document's text. Click OK to close the prompt box and return to your document.

Whether you've built your index entries by manually marking them in your document text or by creating a concordance file, you can create and insert the index by following these steps:

1. Place your cursor where you want the index to begin.

2. Choose Insert, Index and Tables from the menu.

3. Click the Index tab.

4. Choose from the list of Formats, such as Fancy, Modern, Classic, or Simple.

5. Check the Headings for Accented Letters or Right Align Page Numbers check boxes, and set your number of Columns and Tab Leader characters, as needed. These changes will alter whichever format you've chosen, as it applies to this specific index.

6. Click OK. The dialog box closes, and the index is automatically created (see Figure 13.18).

You can add to your index entries by updating your concordance file or marking new entries in your document. To update your existing index with these new entries, perform the following steps:

1. After updating and re-saving your concordance file document or marking new entries within your document, select the entire index.

2. Press F9. This will update the index to include your new entries.

FIG. 13.18
This figure shows a completed index.

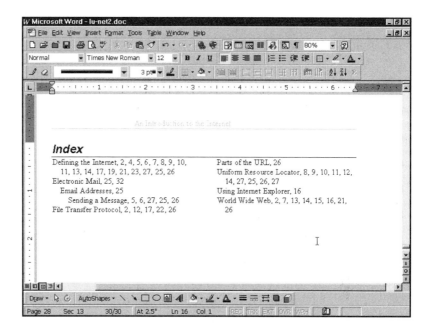

NOTE If you want to lock your index, thus preventing any other user from changing it, place your cursor anywhere within the index itself and press Ctrl+F11. The index cannot be updated. To unlock it, press Ctrl+Shift+F11. ■

You can delete your entire index by selecting it and pressing Delete.

Working with Chapters

If your long document will cover several topics, you may wish to break these topics down into chapters. This can be a purely cosmetic process, in which you simply type a chapter title at the top of the page where a new topic starts. If, however, you want each of your chapters to be a distinct part of your document, you can use your Heading 1 style to format the chapter titles. By doing so, you will be able to use the chapter numbers in your page numbers and Table of Contents. (For more information on applying Styles to your text, see Chapter 6, "Enhancing Text with Character Formatting.")

By using the Heading 1 style in your document, you give Word a format to track. If you decide to use your chapter numbers in your page numbers for example, the only way to tell Word where each chapter starts is to use the Heading 1 style for the chapter title.

You aren't restricted to using the Heading 1 style for chapter titles, although that is the default. If you want to use another heading style for your chapter titles, follow these steps.

1. Choose Insert, Page Numbers from the menu. In the Page Numbers dialog box, click the Format button. The Page Number Format dialog box appears (see Figure 13.19).

Part
III

Ch
13

2. Click the Include Chapter Number check box. This turns on the features below it in the dialog box.

3. In the Chapter Starts with Style drop-down list, choose the heading style you want to use for your chapter titles.

FIG. 13.19

Choose an alternate style for your chapter titles from the Page Number Format dialog box.

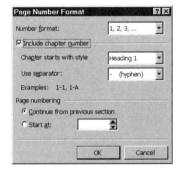

4. Click OK.

As you type your chapter titles, be sure to use the selected heading style for the title text. If your titles are already typed, be sure to go back and format all of them in this style.

 You can also insert a section break at the beginning of each chapter if your formatting needs for each chapter require different headers and footers. (For more information on inserting section breaks and using headers and footers, see "Working with Section Breaks" and "Working with Headers and Footers," earlier in this chapter.)

CHAPTER 14

Creating Form Letters

Form letters enable you to send a seemingly personal letter to many people with one simple procedure. You can create the basic letter and insert fields to mark the places where recipient-specific data such as names and addresses will be inserted. If you already have a database of customers or other contacts, you can use that data to personalize your mailing. Word 97 gives you the tools to build the letter, create the database, and insert the database fields into the letter. Form letters can be updated and used repeatedly, saving you a great deal of time and effort. ▪

Writing form letters

You receive them almost daily—letters that appear to be written to you personally, but they're not. You can create your own form letters to communicate with your current and potential customers.

Using data

Create a database of names and addresses, or use an existing data source that may contain much more information. Link the data to your form letter by inserting data fields into the form letter.

Selecting and merging records

Deciding who gets the mailing, and in what order the merged form letters print is an important step. Sort your records by ZIP Code for a mass mailing, or filter them to send letters to a select few names from your database.

Creating a Form Letter

Form letters are popular marketing tools because they take a standard sales or informational letter and create the illusion of a personal mailing. The process of creating this personalized form letter is called a *mail merge* because a letter is merged with a database to create the personal inserts ("Dear Bob" instead of "Dear Customer").

The form letter contains the recipient's address, which also comes from the database. If the letter is placed in a window envelope, the task of addressing the letter for mailing is resolved. A mail merge can also be used to create envelopes and labels for mailing form letters or other documents or products.

Word's Mail Merge process consists of three main steps:

1. *Create the form letter and its generic content.* This step has two parts—typing the generic content and inserting the database fields. The latter part of the process is normally performed after a database has been selected or created, so that the proper database field names can be inserted.

2. *Create or select a database.* If you already have a database containing your target recipients' names and addresses, you can use that. If you don't have a database, you can create one.

3. *Merge the database with the form letter.* The merging process also has two parts. Before actually merging the letter and the database, you can choose the order that all records (letters) will print, or you can specify which records will be included in the merge.

 TIP After you designate the document that will contain your form letter, the remaining buttons in sections 2 (Data Source) and 3 (Merge the Data with the Document) become available.

To begin the mail merge process by creating a form letter, perform the following steps:

1. Open a new, blank document.

2. Choose Tools, Mail Merge from the menu.

3. The Mail Merge Helper dialog box opens, showing the three steps in the mail merge process: creating your document, choosing or creating a data source, and merging your data with the document (see Figure 14.1).

   Click the Create button in the Main Document section of the dialog box; choose Form Letters from the drop-down list.

4. A prompt appears asking you to indicate where you want to create the document—either by using the Active Window or by creating a New Main Document. Because you have already opened a blank document, choose Active Window.

5. Click the Get Data button in the Data Source section of the Mail Merge Helper dialog box. A drop-down list appears, from which you can choose to create a database, open an existing data source, or use the address book.

6. Choose Create Data Source.

FIG. 14.1

The Mail Merge Helper shows the three-step checklist used in setting up a mail merge.

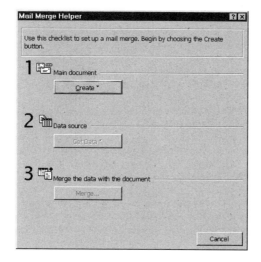

N O T E   If you already have a database that you want to use for your mail merge, choose Open Data Source from the Get Data drop list. The Open dialog box will appear, and you can select the database file of your choice. Word supports many database file formats, or you can use a data table created in Word or WordPerfect. You can also use files created in software products such as Excel and Access as your data source, or use your Address Book data in Exchange or Outlook. As soon as you open the database, Word links it to your main document, and you can proceed with the mail merge process as described in this chapter.

Your open blank document will now be linked to the database you create and save. The next section of this chapter will show you how to create the database, enter your records, and save the database.

Creating a Database

To continue the mail merge process and build your database, follow these steps:

1. After choosing Create Data Source in the Mail Merge Helper, Word displays the Create Data Source dialog box (see Figure 14.2).

   The Create Data Source dialog box contains the following tools for building your database:

   - *Field Name*. Enter a name for any field you wish to create for your database records.
   - *Field Names in Header Row*. Word provides a comprehensive list of fields for your database. You can add your own (using the Field Name box and Add Field Names button) or delete field names by clicking the Remove Field Name button.
   - *Move*. You can change the order of the field names in your database by selecting the field to be moved, and clicking the up and down arrows as necessary.

Part
III

Ch
14

FIG. 14.2

Begin to create your database by choosing the field names for your data.

2. Add, Remove, and Move (re-order) your database fields as necessary, using the tools in the Create Data Source dialog box. Then click OK.

3. The Save As dialog box opens. Enter a name and choose a drive and folder for your database and click Save.

4. Now that your database fields are saved, Word informs you that your database is empty. You can edit the database (enter your records) or return to your main document. Choose Edit Data Source.

5. A data entry window opens, containing a list of the fields you created. Figure 14.3 shows the data entry window and all of its tools.

FIG. 14.3

Enter your database records using the Data Form dialog box.

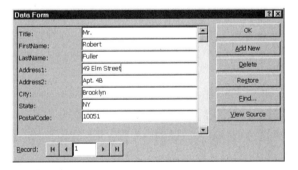

6. Enter your records. You don't need to enter them in any particular order, as the computer will alphabetize them for you should you need to later. As you enter each field's data, press the Tab or Enter key to move to the next field. At the end of each record, press Enter or click Add New to begin the next record.

7. After you finish entering records, click OK.

It's a good idea to save your database as soon as you finish entering records. If you have a lot of records to enter, save early in the process and continue to save periodically as you enter the data.

To save your database, perform these steps:

1. Choose File, Open from the menu.

2. Open the Word document that contains your data (you named it earlier in the mail merge process). The database document is actually a Word table, and you'll see your field names at the top of each column, and the data records you've entered in each row (see Figure 14.4).

FIG. 14.4
Your database is stored in a Word table.

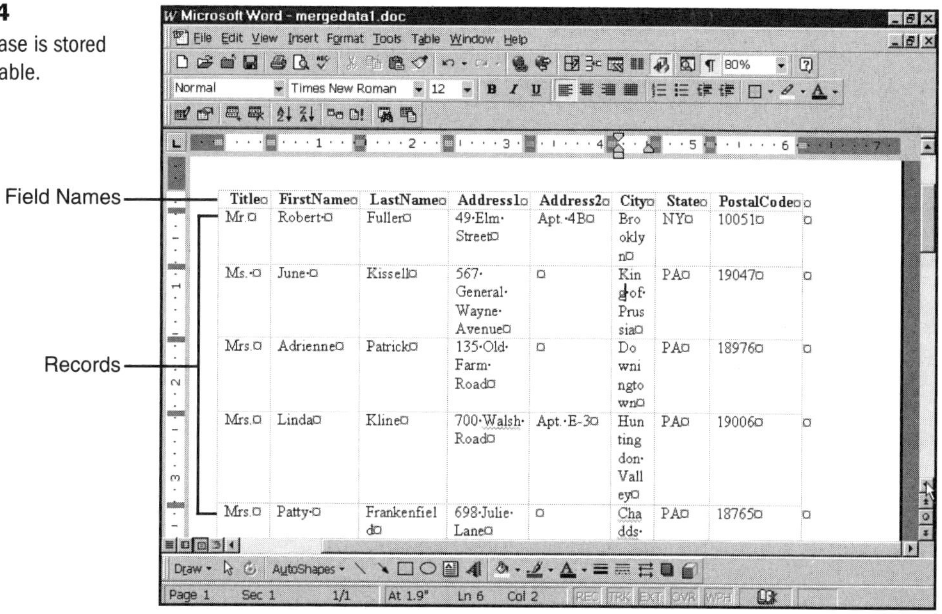

To continue the mail merge process using the database you've just created and saved, move ahead in this chapter to section entitled "Inserting Data Fields in Your Form Letter."

3. Choose File, Save from the menu, or press Ctrl+S. You can also click the Save button on the toolbar.

4. You can leave the database file open as you continue the mail merge process. If you are not going to continue the process at this time, close the file by choosing File, Close from the menu.

Inserting Data Fields in Your Form Letter

Once you have created or selected a database for your mail merge, you need to build your document and insert the fields that will plug in the data. In the steps that follow, it is assumed that your blank main document is open, the Mail Merge toolbar is displayed, and your database file has been selected (or created) and saved.

Part

III

Ch

14

To build your form letter and insert your database fields, follow these steps:

1. Begin typing your form letter by entering the date.

 TIP If you want your letter's date to update to your computer's system date each time you use the letter, insert the date as a field by choosing Insert, Date and Time from the menu. Choose the date format you need, and click the Update Automatically check box at the bottom of the dialog box. Click OK to insert the date field.

NOTE To reset your computer's system date and time, choose Settings, Control Panel from the Start menu. Double-click the Date/Time icon in the Control Panel window, and set your computer's date and time in the resulting dialog box. Click OK to put your changes into effect.

2. After typing the date, press Enter twice to place two blank lines between the data and your recipient's address (standard business letter format).

3. Next, you'll want to insert the recipient's name and address. Click the Insert Merge Field button on the Mail Merge toolbar. A list of your fields descends (see Figure 14.5).

FIG. 14.5

Choose your field name from the Insert Merge Field list.

4. Select the appropriate fields for your recipient's name and address—if you are using Title, insert that first. Then type a space.

5. Click the Insert Merge Field button again, and choose FirstName (or the appropriate field name). Type a space.

Continue to add fields, (LastName, Address1, Address2, City, State, and PostalCode as appropriate) each time clicking the Insert Merge Field button and selecting the next field to be inserted into your letter. Be sure to type spaces between fields, and to press Enter to move to the next line of the address.

 TIP Don't forget to type a comma after the City field.

6. After entering your name and address fields, type the salutation and then begin typing the body of your letter.

 TIP A salutation normally begins with "Dear" and is followed by your insertion of the FirstName or other appropriate field names, such as Title and LastName.

N O T E   You'll notice that each of the fields that you've inserted is preceded by two less-than signs (<<), and followed by two greater-than signs (>>). These symbols indicate to Word that the text between the symbols is a database field. You cannot create the data field inserts by typing these symbols and your field names in manually—you must use the Insert Merge Field button and select the field names from the list. ■

Insert Merge Field ▾

7. If there are any database fields required in the body of your letter (references to the recipient's city, for example), click the Insert Merge Field button when you reach that point in the letter. Press a space after the field, and continue typing your generic content.

Figure 14.6 shows a completed form letter with fields inserted and generic text.

FIG. 14.6

Data fields create your address, salutation, and other data inserts throughout your letter.

Database fields create the address and salutation

Data field inserted in the body of the form letter

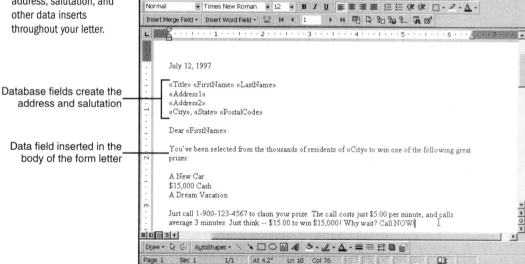

 When you finish typing your letter and inserting your fields, click the Mail Merge Helper button on the Mail Merge toolbar. You can now proceed with your mail merge, by merging records with your letter.

It's a good idea to save your form letter prior to merging it with your data—you may want to use it again with this or another similar database. To save your form letter, follow these steps:

1. Choose File, Save from the menu, or press Ctrl+S.

2. Choose a location (folder and drive) for your form letter, and give it a relevant name.

Part

III

Ch

14

T I P When you choose a name for the form letter, it's a good idea to use the words "form letter" in the name (**Sales Form Letter** or **Spring Promotion Form Letter**, for example). This will make the file easier to find in the future.

3. Click the Save button.

Editing Your Database

If you wish to add, delete, or change records in your existing database, you can do so from within the Mail Merge Helper or by editing the database table directly. Editing the table directly is often easier, if your database table was created with Word or a word processor with which you are familiar. To edit your database, perform the following steps:

1. If the database is not already open, open it by choosing File, Open from the menu. Select your file by name and click the Open button, or double-click the file name.

2. In the open file, view the table. Your field names are across the top row of the table, and your database records are in the subsequent table rows.

3. Scroll up and down in your table using your scrollbars or the up and down arrows on your keyboard to locate the records you wish to edit.

4. You can edit your Word database table as follows:

    *   To remove a record, click the left margin next to the row you want to delete. The entire row becomes highlighted. Choose Table, Delete Rows from the menu.

    *   To add a record, move to the last record in the database, and click in the last cell in that record's row. Press the Tab key, and a blank row appears. Enter the record's data in each cell.

    *   To edit a record, click in the cell that you want to change. Select the text to type a replacement, or click within the text and edit it with the Backspace or Delete keys.

5. Save your database as soon as you finish editing. Choose File, Save from the menu or press Ctrl+S.

If you wish to edit your database from within the Mail Merge Helper, perform the following steps:

1. Open your main document or switch to that document from the Window menu's list of open documents. The Mail Merge toolbar should appear on-screen with that document.

 2. Click the Mail Merge Helper button on the Mail Merge toolbar.

3. Click the Edit button in the Data Source section of the Mail Merge Helper dialog box.

4. Choose your database from the list. The database will open in the Mail Merge data entry window.

5. To move from record to record, use the left- and right-pointing triangle buttons in the lower left corner of the dialog box (see Figure 14.7).

FIG. 14.7

Use your record navigation buttons to move through your database and edit your records.

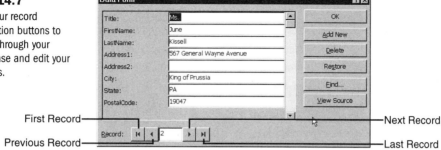

First Record —
Previous Record —
Next Record
Last Record

You have three options for revising records:

- To edit fields within your records, click in the cell and add or delete text as necessary.

- To remove an entire record, display the record and click the Delete button.

- To add a record, click the Add New button and enter the record content.

6. When you finish editing your database, click OK. The data entry window closes, and you are returned to your form letter document.

After editing your database through the Mail Merge Helper, you should save it. If the database is a Word table document, open the file and save it as described earlier in this chapter. See the end of the section entitled "Creating a Database" for details.

If your database is of some other format, such as a DBF file or a table document created in another word processor, follow that program's instructions for opening and saving the database file.

Merging Your Form Letter with the Data

Combining (merging) your letter and your database is the final step in the mail merge process. To merge them, the letter must be open and displayed on-screen. If you have performed all previous phases of the mail merge process in one session, the Mail Merge toolbar will be on-screen with your letter. If for any reason the Mail Merge toolbar is *not* displayed, you can select it by choosing View, Toolbars from the menu and selecting the Mail Merge from the submenu.

To merge your letter and database, perform the following steps:

1. With your form letter open and on-screen, click the Mail Merge Helper button on the Mail Merge toolbar.

Part

III

Ch

14

2. Click the Merge button in the third section of the dialog box. The Merge dialog box opens (see Figure 14.8), offering the following choices for customizing your mail merge:

FIG. 14.8

Choose the destination for your merged letter and the range of records to print.

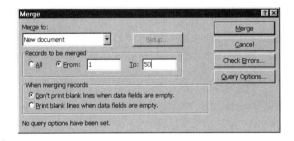

- *Merge To.* Choose to print your merged documents to a New Document (the default), the Printer, Electronic Mail, or Electronic Fax.

- *Records to Be Merged.* If you know the record numbers of your data records, you can choose which ones to print. The default is All, but you can choose a range of records by entering a starting (From) number and an ending (To) number.

- *When Merging Records.* Your two options in this section refer to blank data fields within your database. If, for example, you have both Address1 and Address2 fields in your database, you may have records that don't use both. You can choose Don't Print Blank Records when Data Fields Are Empty, which will pull the City, State, and ZIP (or Postal) Code line up to fill in the line where Address2 is not used. You can also choose Print Blank Lines when Data Fields Are Empty, which will potentially create blank spaces in your letter. This second option is most often used for checking the completeness of your database—printing a list of records to see if anyone's ZIP Code is missing, for example.

3. After making your selections in the Merge dialog box, click the Merge button. If you chose New Document as your output destination, Word will create a document with as many pages as you have merged records (in addition to the number of pages in your form letter). This document can then be sent to your printer or modem for e-mail or faxing.

CAUTION

In case you have any problems with your data or the setup of your letter, it's a good idea to output to a new document rather than directly to the printer. You can print the new document after you've checked it for errors, and you've avoided wasting expensive letterhead paper or other costly marketing materials.

N O T E The Check for Errors feature will look for problems with your mail merge such as blank fields and duplicate data. You can choose to have the errors reported in a new document or to have Word pause and inform you of the errors in a series of on-screen prompts during the merge. Click the Check for Errors button in the Merge dialog box to initiate this feature. ▪

Sorting Records

If you want to merge all of your records with your database but you want to control the order in which they print out, you need to Sort your data. You can Sort any field in your database, or a combination of fields. If, for example, you have customers in several states, you can sort by State, and then by Postal Code within each state. If you don't sort your data before merging, the records will print out in the order they were entered when you built the database.

To sort your database, perform the following steps:

 1. With your form letter open and on-screen, click the Mail Merge Helper button on the toolbar.

2. In the third section of the dialog box, click the Query Options button. The Query Options dialog box opens (see Figure 14.9).

FIG. 14.9
Sort your database records by up to three fields.

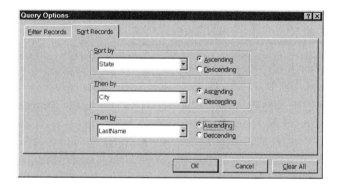

 You can also click the Merge button and then click the Query Options button in the Merge dialog box.

3. Click the Sort Records tab.

4. Click the Sort By drop-down list to review the fields in your database; click the field by which you want to sort your records.

5. Choose Ascending (A to Z) or Descending (Z to A).

 If the field on which you're sorting contains numerical data, Ascending will put your records in smallest to largest order, and Descending will sort them in order from largest to smallest.

6. If you want to sort by more than one field, click the first Then By drop-down list, and select your second field, and choose Ascending or Descending.

   Enter a third sort field if necessary, and then click the OK button.

7. Back in the Mail Merge Helper dialog box, click the Merge records, and proceed as described in the previous section, "Merging Your Form Letter with the Data."

Part
III

Ch
14

T I P Click Clear All in the Query Options dialog box to remove your current Sort Records settings.

Filtering Records

If you don't want to merge all of your database records with your form letter, filter them. Filtering is just like querying, which is another database term you may have heard. When you filter or query your database for a mail merge, you are presenting the database with a list of criteria, and only the records meeting that criteria will be merged with the form letter. For example, if you only want to send your letter to your customers in New Jersey, filter the State field for "NJ". Any records containing any other letters in the State field will not be merged with your form letter.

You can filter your database on more than one field. For example, you can filter the Title field for Mrs. or Ms. (so your mailing only goes to your female customers), and then on the State field for people living in Montana (MN). You can also filter and then sort your records, so that the records meeting your filter criteria are printed in an order you specify.

To filter your database, follow these steps:

1. With your form letter open and on-screen, click the Mail Merge Helper button on the Mail Merge toolbar.

2. Click the Query Options button in the third section of the Mail Merge Helper dialog box.

3. In the Query Options dialog box, click the Filter Records tab (see Figure 14.10).

FIG. 14.10

Filter your records so that only the records you need are merged with your form letter.

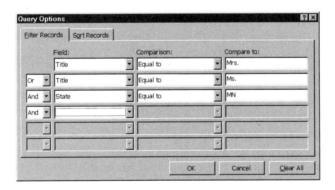

4. Click the drop-down list and choose from the list of fields in your database.

5. Moving to the right, click the Comparison drop-down list and choose the most appropriate operator—Equal To, Greater Than, Less Than, and so forth.

6. Enter the Compare To value in the box. If, for example, you're filtering for customers living in the State of New Jersey, type **NJ** in the Compare To box.

7. If you want to filter on more than one field, select the relationship between your first and second filtered field by choosing And or Or in the box between filter rows.

8. Select your Field Name and Comparison options, and enter your Compare To data. You can filter on up to six fields.

9. After setting up your filters, click OK. You are returned to the Mail Merge Helper.

 TIP To remove your Sort or Filter settings, click Query Options in the Mail Merge Helper dialog box, and click the Clear All button in the Sort and/or Filter tabs.

If you want to Sort your filtered records, click the Query Options button again in the Mail Merge Helper dialog box, and enter your sort as described in the previous section, "Sorting Records."

To perform a merge based on your filter or sort, click the Merge button in the Mail Merge Helper dialog box, and proceed as described in the previous section, "Merging Your Form Letter with the Data." ●

CHAPTER 15

Addressing Envelopes and Labels

After you've taken the time to create a professional-looking document, why send it in a handwritten or typed envelope? Create a single envelope or label for an individual letter, or use the Address Book to generate envelopes or labels for a mass mailing. Word 97 makes it simple to format the content and appearance of your mailing. ■

Envelopes and labels

Word will automatically use the address in your letter to generate a single envelope or label. Before printing the envelope or label, you can choose the type of envelope or label you'll be using, and format the text in your address. You can also print an entire sheet of the same label to accommodate repeated mailings to the same address, or print many envelopes and labels for your mass mailing.

The Address Book

Accessible from any Microsoft Office product, the Address Book contains names and addresses that you enter and store for use in generating single envelopes, labels, or creating a mass mailing. The Address Book can also serve as your electronic contact database.

Printing an Individual Envelope or Label

You can turn the recipient address that you type at the top of your letter into an envelope's mailing address or an address label with just a few clicks of your mouse. You can enter your own return address or omit the return address to make use of pre-printed stationery.

To generate a single envelope for a letter you've typed, perform the following steps:

1. With your letter open, choose Tools, Envelopes and Labels from the menu.

2. The Envelopes and Labels dialog box opens, with the Envelopes tab in front (see Figure 15.1). The dialog box offers the following options for creating an envelope:

FIG. 15.1

Word will pick up the recipient address from your letter and insert it into the Delivery address box to assist you in creating your envelope.

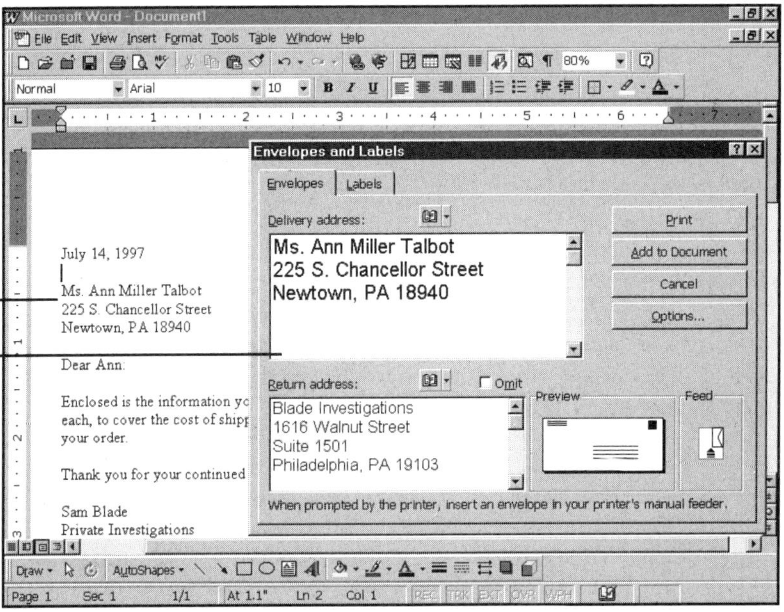

Recipient address in the document

The address is automatically inserted in the Envelopes and Labels dialog box

- *Delivery Address.* Word uses the address it finds in your letter. If your document has no address in it, you can type your own in the Delivery Address box. You can also add extra text, such as **Personal** or **Dated Material**, to assist the mailroom at your recipient's company.

- *Address Book.* An Address Book button accompanies both the Delivery and Return address boxes. This button opens the Microsoft Address Book, from which you can select an address you have stored there. All Microsoft products can use the Address book. For more information, see the "Working with the Address Book" section later in this chapter.

- *Return Address.* This box is empty by default, because many people use pre-printed stationery. If you are using a blank envelope, type your return address in this box. If you type a return address into the box, Word will ask you if you want to make the address your default return address. If you answer Yes, that return address will appear in the box each time you use the Envelope feature. You can tell Word not to print the default return address at any time by clicking the Omit check box.

3. Click the Options button to set your Envelope and Printing Options (see Figure 15.2).

FIG. 15.2

Choose your envelope size, set the font for your addresses, and add a bar code to speed the processing of your mail.

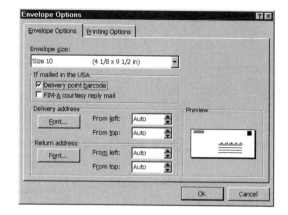

4. Click the Envelope Options tab to adjust the following settings:

- *Envelope Size.* The default is a Size 10, standard business envelope.
- *Delivery and Return Address Fonts.* Set the font for your delivery and return addresses. The Font buttons for both the delivery and return addresses will open the standard Font dialog box. For more information on setting fonts for your text, see Chapter 6, "Enhancing Text with Character Formatting."
- *Delivery Point Barcode.* Word will create and add a bar code based on the numeric content of your street address and zip code.
- *From Left/From Top.* Position your return and delivery address by setting their distance from the edge of the envelope. The default Auto setting can be increased or decreased by your entering a measurement into the From Left and From Top boxes.

N O T E You can also insert a FIM-A courtesy reply code on your envelope. To add it to your envelope, click the FIM-A Courtesy Reply Mail check box in the Envelope Options dialog box. This code tells the U.S. Postal Service sorting machines which is the front side of your envelope. Theoretically, this can speed your mail through USPS processing.

5. Click the Printing Options tab to choose the direction your envelope will feed into your printer (see Figure 15.3). When in doubt as to which feed option to use, go with the default setting because it is based on the information in your printer driver file. If you want to change the setting, consult your printer's manual if you're not sure which one to use.

FIG. 15.3

Choose a direction for your envelope to feed into your printer

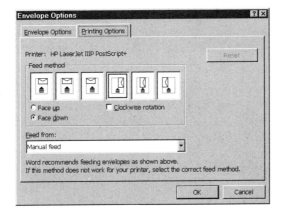

6. Click OK in the Options dialog box to return to the Envelopes and Labels dialog box.

7. Click P̲rint to generate the envelope according to your settings and close the dialog box.

N O T E You can make the envelope part of your document so that you can print both the document and the envelope in one print job. To do so, click the A̲dd to Document button. The envelope is added as "page" one, and will therefore print first. For more information on setting up your printer for working with envelopes, see Chapter 5, "Printing Documents."

To print an address label, perform these steps:

1. With your letter open, choose T̲ools, E̲nvelopes and Labels from the menu.

2. The Envelopes and Labels dialog box opens. Click the L̲abels tab (see Figure 15.4). This tab offers the following options:

FIG. 15.4

View the address inserted from your letter and edit as necessary. Choose a single label or a full sheet of the same label.

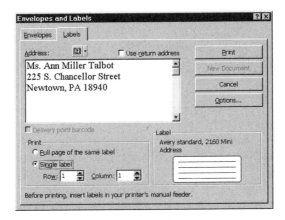

Part

III

Ch

15

- *Address*. This address is normally inserted by Word based on the recipient address in the open document. If you don't have a letter to go with this label, or if you want to edit or add to the address, type your text in this box. If you want to make the label serve as your Return Address label, click the Use <u>R</u>eturn Address check box. If a default return address has been set previously, that address will appear in the box.

- *Delivery Point Barcode*. Click this check box to have Word generate a barcode based on your address.

- *Print*. Choose to print a <u>F</u>ull Page of the Same Label or to print a Si<u>n</u>gle Label. If printing a single label, enter the coordinates of the next available label on the sheet in the Ro<u>w</u> and <u>C</u>olumn boxes.

3. Click the <u>O</u>ptions button. This opens the Label Options dialog box (see Figure 15.5), in which you can adjust the following settings:

FIG. 15.5

The Label Options dialog box contains printer and label information, as well as labeling specifications and product numbers.

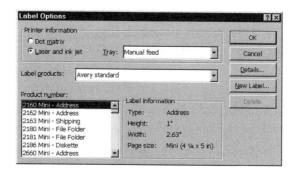

- Choose the Printer type (Dot <u>M</u>atrix or <u>L</u>aser and Ink Jet). If you choose <u>L</u>aser and Ink Jet, you can change the intended <u>T</u>ray from which your printer will draw the sheet of blank labels.

- Select the Avery product number for the label you'll be using. The dimensions are stored in the Word program, so that the proper height and width will be set based on the product number you choose. If you don't use Avery labels, click the Avery Standard drop-down list and choose Avery A4 and A5, or MACO labels. The Other option offers a list of many different label vendors.

N O T E If your label isn't available from any vendor's product list and you can't find one that's a reasonable match, you can create your own label configuration by clicking the <u>N</u>ew Label button in the Envelopes and Labels dialog box. This opens a new dialog box in which you can enter custom height and width settings for your special label. ▣

4. Click OK in the Label Options dialog box to return to the <u>L</u>abels tab in the Envelopes and Labels dialog box.

5. Click <u>P</u>rint to generate your label or sheet of labels, and close the dialog box.

Working with the Address Book

 If you use a contact database product such as Microsoft's Outlook or Schedule+, you have access to the Address Book in any Microsoft product. In Word, the Address Book can be your data source for a mass mailing, or it can provide a single address for an envelope or label. The goal of this section is to acquaint you with the uses of the Address Book in generating Word documents.

The Address Book exists in two possible forms:

- *Outlook.* Microsoft Outlook is a personal information tool that allows you to keep track of your contacts, appointments, files, and send e-mail.

- *Schedule+ Contacts.* If you're using Schedule+ to keep track of your calendar, you can use it to maintain a list of your contacts as well. You also can store names, addresses, phone numbers, birthdays, and spouse names for each of your contacts.

If you performed a typical installation of Office 97, Outlook is on your system; although you may not have it set up. By installing Windows 95, you install Exchange, which includes Microsoft Schedule+. Schedule+ and Outlook do many of the same things—keep track of your appointments and activities, and maintain a list of contacts.

Whether you're using Outlook or Schedule+ as your Address Book, they are accessed in the same way when you want to extract many addresses for use in a mass mailing or a single address for an individual envelope or label.

To use the Address Book as your data source for a mass mailing, perform the following steps:

1. Choose Tools, Mail Merge from the menu. This opens the Mail Merge Helper dialog box (see Figure 15.6).

FIG. 15.6

When performing a Mail Merge, you can use your Address Book as the source of your data.

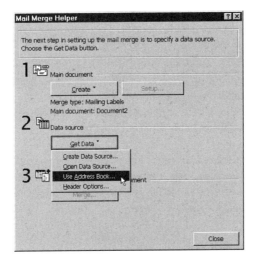

2. Click Create and choose the document type that you will be creating—a form letter, envelope, or label.

3. Choose to use the Active Document (the document you had open when you accessed the Tools menu) or a New Active Document.

4. Click the Get Data button in the Mail Merge Helper dialog box.

5. Choose Use Address Book from the drop-down list. A dialog box opens, asking you to choose which Address Book you'll use (see Figure 15.7).

FIG. 15.7

Select your Address Book from this dialog box.

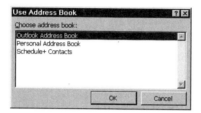

6. Select the Address Book of your choice, and click OK. This links the contacts stored in the Address Book with your document, and the fields in your Address Book will be the fields you insert in your letter, envelope, or label.

Continue the Mail Merge process as described in Chapter 14, "Creating Form Letters."

 To use the Address Book for a single envelope or label, choose Tools, Envelopes and Labels from the menu. In both the Envelopes and Labels tabs in the resulting dialog box, you will see the Address Book icon.

Figure 15.8 shows the Envelopes tab in the Envelopes and Labels dialog box.

FIG. 15.8

Use the Address Book as your source for an envelope's delivery and return address.

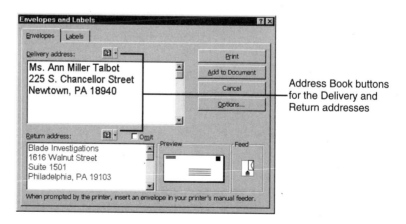

Address Book buttons for the Delivery and Return addresses

You can use the Address Book to find your Delivery or Return address for envelopes, or for the single address on your label. When you click the Address Book icon in either tab, you will see the Use Address Book dialog box, as shown in Figure 15.6.

N O T E If your installation of Office 97 (for Outlook users) or Exchange (for Schedule + users) was set up for more than one user, you may also have to supply a Profile Name upon clicking the Address Book button. The profile name is probably your user name, and this tells Word to open your Address Book, rather than that of another user. ▪

To change, add, or delete contacts in your Address Book, you can access the programs directly (by starting Outlook or Schedule+ from the Programs menu) or through Word's Mail Merge feature.

To edit your Address Book from within Word, follow these steps:

1. Open a blank document.
2. Choose Tools, Mail Merge from the menu. The Mail Merge Helper dialog box opens.
3. Click the Create button, and choose a document type from the list.
4. Click the Active Document button when prompted.
5. Back in the Mail Merge Helper dialog box, click the Get Data button.
6. From the drop-down list, choose Use Address Book. A dialog box will open (refer to Figure 15.6), from which you will choose your Address Book (Outlook, Schedule+, or Personal Address Book). Make your selection and click OK.
7. Word has now linked your Address Book to this particular mail merge. Click the Edit button in the Data Source section of the Mail Merge Helper dialog box.

   The Data Form dialog box opens (see Figure 15.9), displaying a data entry form. You can scroll through your existing records, using the record navigation tools in the lower left corner of the dialog box.

FIG. 15.9

Edit your database records in the Data Form dialog box.

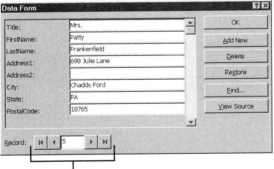

Record navigation buttons

8. Edit your records as necessary:
   - To change the content of a record, go to that record and click the field or fields that need to be changed. Edit the content as you would any document text.

- If you need to add records to your list of contacts, click Add New and enter the data for each field.

- You can delete records by going to the record to be removed and clicking the Delete button.

9. When your edits are complete, click OK. This closes the Data Form dialog box and returns you to the Mail Merge Helper.

   If you were using this technique for database editing only, click Cancel in the Mail Merge Helper and Close your blank document by choosing File, Close from the menu.

If you wish to actually complete a mail merge with your open document, follow the mail merge instructions in Chapter 14, "Creating a Form Letter."

 Unlike a Word table, your Outlook or Schedule+ databases do not need to be saved in a separate function. It is wise, however, to frequently backup your schedule and contact database to a disk or tape.

CHAPTER 16

Using Master Documents to Combine Word Files

Word 97's Master Documents feature enables you to take two or more existing documents and combine them into one large document. ■

Combining documents

Make one long document by combining several other documents into a master document. Using master documents to combine your Word files saves disk space and gives you a powerful set of tools to control the large documents you create.

Manage subdocuments

Using Master Documents makes it simple for you to reorganize your files and the order they'll appear in the Master.

Add page numbers to the master document

Your master document can be numbered as one long, continuous document, or its individual sections can be numbered independently. You can also format separate headers and footers for each section of your master document.

Creating a Master Document

A master document combines two or more other Word files, called *subdocuments,* into an outline. Rather than repeating the content (and file size) of the subdocuments, the master document maintains a framework for the subdocuments. You can rearrange the order of the subdocuments, or add and delete subdocuments as you develop your master. To the reader, the printed master document is just one long file. To you, the author or editor, the document is a skeleton—it provides the backbone on which all of the appending documents are supported.

You can create a master document before the subdocuments exist, using the master document as a sort of planning device that also works to combine them after they're written. You can also use a master document to combine existing files.

When you begin the process of creating a master document, it's a good idea to know which documents you'll be adding as subdocuments. You can always add and delete files as the process continues, but having a plan before you start will make the process much simpler for you. To create the master document, follow these steps:

1. Open a new, blank document.
2. Choose <u>V</u>iew, <u>M</u>aster Document from the menu. The Outlining and Master Document toolbars appear on-screen (see Figure 16.1).

FIG. 16.1

Choosing Master Document view adds the Master Document and Outlining toolbars to your Word screen.

The Outlining toolbar   The Master Documents toolbar

Tables 16.1 and 16.2 describe each tool and its function.

Table 16.1   The Outline Toolbar

Icon	Option	Description
←	Promote	If you think of each part of your outline as an item with a rank, you will understand Promote and Demote. Each item in an outline is either a Heading (its rank determined by the Heading style number) or its Body Text. Use Promote and Demote to raise or lower the rank of a selected item in your outline.
→	Demote	Click this button to make a heading into a subtopic by demoting the selected text to the next lowest heading style.

Icon	Option	Description
	Demote To Body Text	Body Text is the lowest ranked item in a document.
	Move Up	Use this tool to move the selected heading up in the chronological order of your heading topics. This tool does not change an item's rank, merely its order in the document.
	Move Down	This tool will move the selected heading down in the order of topics. The item will retain its rank.
	Expand	When used with the Collapse tool, this controls the amount of detail (lower-ranked headings) you see below any of your headings. Expanding the item will display the lower-ranked headings.
	Collapse	Click this tool to hide the lower-ranked headings that follow the selected heading.
	Display Heading	There are seven heading styles (numbered 1 through 7). Click the number corresponding to the level of detail you wish to see. If, for example, you're using Headings 1 through 5 in your outline, click the 5 button to see them all.
	Display All	Click this button to reveal all of your headings and body text.
	Show First Line Only	You can switch between showing all your body text or only the first line of each segment of body text by clicking this button.
	Show Formatting	Some users find it visually confusing to see your headings and body text in the actual fonts and sizes that they appear in the Page Layout or Normal view of the document. To toggle between seeing and not seeing the fonts and sizes, click this button. When you're looking at your text without formatting, the text all appears in your default font, with no additional formatting displayed.
	Master Document View	Click this button to switch between viewing your document in Outline or Master Document view. If you're in Master Document view, you'll see the Master Document toolbar buttons.

Table 16.2 The Master Document Toolbar

Icon	Option	Description
	Collapse Subdocuments	If you want to only see the heading levels in your documents, click this button.
	Create Subdocuments	If you're creating your subdocuments from the Master document (as opposed to combining existing documents), this button will take the selected headings and create a new document from them. You can then type the body text to support the topics in your headings.
	Remove Subdocument	After you've created a new subdocument or inserted an existing subdocument, you can use this button to delete it from the Master document.
	Insert Subdocument	Use this button to add an existing file to your Master documents. An Insert Subdocument dialog box opens, looking and working like a standard Open dialog box. Select your file and click Open.
	Merge Subdocument	This button combines two or more of your subdocuments into one.
	Split Subdocument	Use this button to break off a selected section of a subdocument into a separate subdocument.
	Lock Document	This button toggles between locking and unlocking the selected subdocument. Locking a subdocument prevents it from being split or removed.

 3. Click the Insert Subdocument button. From the Insert Subdocument dialog box (a typical Open dialog box), select the file you wish to add to the master document.

4. Click Open to insert the document. You are returned to your Master document, and the content of the inserted document appears on-screen (see Figure 16.2).

N O T E   As you insert a subdocument, a section break is inserted. Each subdocument will have its own section break following it. This will allow you to control the page numbers and headers/footers for each subdocument as it appears in the larger master document.

 5. To add other documents, move your cursor to the first blank line after the subdocument (and its accompanying section break) you've just inserted. Click the Insert Subdocument button again. Follow the preceding steps 3 and 4 for each subdocument you wish to insert.

FIG. 16.2

This figure illustrates adding your existing files to your master document.

Heading text

Body text

Section breaks between each subdocument

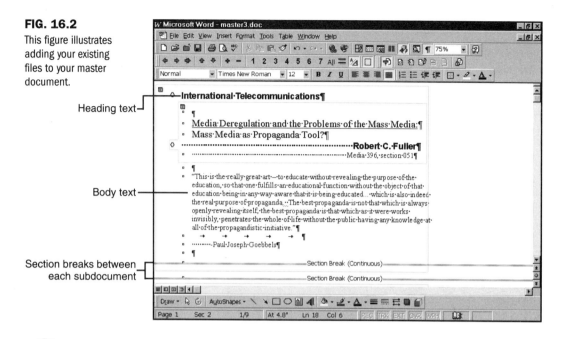

Part

III

Ch

16

T I P While you are in a Collapsed view of the subdocuments, you cannot insert new subdocuments.

---

6. After you add all of your subdocuments, you can collapse them. Each one will appear in a box, represented by a path statement (the drive letter, folder names, and file name). The path text will appear in color (see Figure 16.3).

7. As soon as you choose to collapse your subdocuments, you will be prompted to Save your Master document. Click OK. A standard Save As dialog box opens, allowing you to name your master document.

N O T E If you point your mouse at one of the subdocument paths, you'll see your mouse pointer turn to a pointing hand. Word treats any document path as a hypertext link. Click the mouse (while pointing to the link) and you will automatically open the subdocument as a separate open document. You can then edit and save the document or merely view it. After closing the document, you are returned to your master document, and file path and name have changed colors, showing you've followed that link.

For more information on hypertext links and Word's treatment of links to files and Web pages, see Chapter 18, "Using Hyperlinks in Word Documents." ■

After saving your master document, you can add or remove subdocuments, reorder the subdocuments that have already been added, or print the master document. Procedures for editing, printing, and sharing your master documents appear in this chapter's following sections.

FIG. 16.3

Collapse the view of
your master and see
the path to each
subdocument.

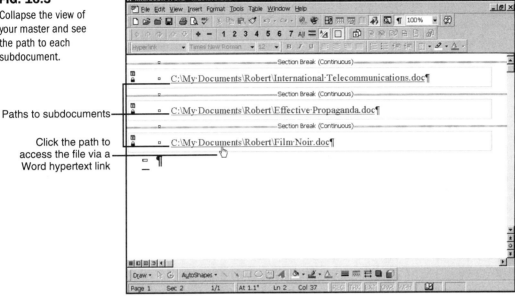

Paths to subdocuments

Click the path to
access the file via a
Word hypertext link

 N O T E   If you need to create a subdocument from within your master document, type the heading
text for the topics to be covered in the subdocument, and use the outline tools to promote
and demote the headings as necessary. Select the headings, and click the Create Subdocument
button. Your headings will become the text content of a separate document, which you can then build
by adding body text to support your topic headings. ■

Rearranging Subdocuments

Subdocuments can be rearranged within your master document. Doing so will change the
order in which their content will appear in the printed version of the master document.

To change the order of subdocuments in your master document, follow these steps:

1. Click the Collapse Subdocuments button on the Master Documents toolbar.

2. In the box for the subdocument you want to move, click and hold your mouse on the
   document icon in the upper left corner (see Figure 16.4). Your mouse pointer will turn to
   a four-headed arrow, and the entire text content of the box will become selected.

3. Drag your mouse up to move your subdocument ahead in the order of files. Drag it down
   to move it to a later position in the master document.

FIG. 16.4
Collapse your
subdocuments and
then drag them up or
down to rearrange
them.

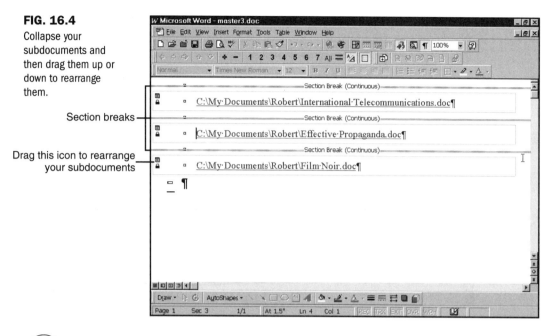

Section breaks ——

Drag this icon to rearrange
your subdocuments ——

Part

III

Ch

16

TIP Watch your section breaks! As you insert each subdocument, a section break is added to follow it. When moving a subdocument, be sure to place the subdocument you're moving above the section breaks (when moving a subdocument up) or below it (when moving a subdocument down) before releasing the mouse. This will maintain the separate sections for each subdocument.

4. Save your master document to keep your latest changes by choosing File, Save from the menu or pressing Ctrl+S.

Splitting and Merging Subdocuments

After you add a subdocument to your master document, you may decide that it contains more than you need, or that parts of it should really be separate subdocuments unto themselves. Separating them (*splitting* them) then enables you to move the new distinct subdocuments around, rearranging them with your other subdocuments.

To split one subdocument into two or more subdocuments, perform the following steps:

1. With your master document open, switch to Master Document view by choosing View, Master Document from the menu.

2. Display the full content of your subdocuments by clicking the Expand Subdocuments button on the Master Documents toolbar.

3. If you're working with existing documents, you may need to add a heading at the point where you want to split the subdocument. To add the heading, position your cursor at the intended split, and press Enter. Type your heading text, and then select it with your mouse. Choose the Heading 1 style from the Style drop-down list on the Formatting menu.

 TIP If your text already contains text that could serve as a heading, select it with your mouse and apply the Heading 1 style to it.

4. With your heading text selected, click the Split Subdocuments button on the Master Documents toolbar.

5. Save the master document.

If you find that you have two or more subdocuments that are related in topic (and therefore should appear in the printed master as one section), you may want to merge them into one subdocument.

Merging related subdocuments into one larger subdocument can be a useful step in that it will simplify the structure of your master document, making the application of page numbers and headers and footers easier.

To merge two or more separate subdocuments, follow these steps:

1. In your open master document, switch to Master Document view. If your subdocuments are collapsed, click the Expand Subdocuments button.

 TIP You must be in expanded view to merge your subdocuments.

2. Make certain that the subdocuments that you intend to merge are contiguous. Rearrange them if necessary.

3. Select all of the subdocuments that you want to merge.

N O T E   To select two or more subdocuments without dragging your mouse, click the document icon in the first of your subdocuments to be merged. Press and hold the Shift key as you scroll down to see the top of the next subdocument. With the Shift key still depressed, click the second subdocument icon. Continue gathering subdocuments in this way until all of the subdocuments you want to merge are highlighted. Release the Shift key after you've selected all of your subdocuments. ▥

4. Click the Merge Subdocument button. The selected subdocuments are now one subdocument.

 N O T E   After merging your subdocuments, click the Collapse Subdocuments button. You'll see that the path and file name for the first of your merged subdocuments now represents the entire merged group. ▥

CAUTION

When you merge or split subdocuments, you are affecting the original files as well. If you must keep an original file intact, save a separate copy (by choosing File, Save As from the menu and giving the file a new name) before performing the split or merge function.

Removing a Subdocument

After you insert or create subdocuments in your master document, you may decide that one or more of them are no longer needed. You can remove them quickly by performing the following steps:

1. In your open master document, switch to Master Document view.

 2. If your subdocuments are expanded, click the Collapse Subdocuments button.

TIP Collapsed view creates a simplified view of your master document, and can therefore simplify the selection and deletion process.

3. Click the document icon for the subdocument you wish to remove.

4. Press the Delete key.

 NOTE You can remove subdocuments in expanded view. Select the subdocument to be deleted, and then click the Remove Subdocuments button.

Sharing a Master Document

A master document can include subdocuments created by other authors. As discussed in Chapter 3, "Editing Documents," Word retains information about each document's author. This feature can be implemented when sharing a master document or when a team of authors is editing and compiling a master document.

When a group of people are working with your master document's subdocuments, you can lock the master document, enabling the team members to edit only the subdocuments of which they were the original author. You can also unlock subdocuments to allow a non-author to edit someone else's document.

To lock a master document, perform these steps:

1. With your master document open, switch to Master Document view.

 2. If your subdocuments are collapsed, click the Expand Subdocuments button.

 3. To lock the entire master document, click anywhere in the master document, and click the Lock Document button.

When you lock a master document, the words "Read Only" appear in the master document title bar.

4. To lock an individual subdocument, select the subdocument, and click the Lock Document button.

 When you lock a subdocument, a padlock icon appears in the upper left corner of the subdocument boxes.

Figure 16.5 shows a locked subdocument.

FIG. 16.5

Locked subdocuments can only be edited by their original author.

Padlock icon ——

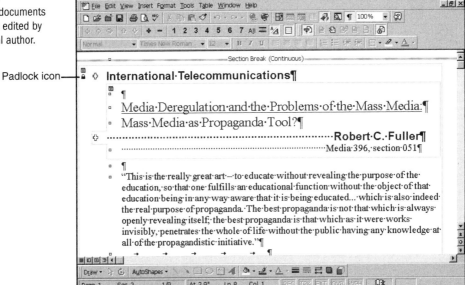

 When you lock the entire master document, all of the subdocuments are automatically locked.

To unlock a master document or one of its subdocuments, follow these steps:

- To unlock a master document, place your cursor anywhere in the expanded view of the locked master document. Click the Lock Document button.

- To unlock an individual subdocument, select the locked subdocument (click the document icon for that subdocument) and click the Lock Document icon.

If you, as the author of the master document, want to have complete control over the locking, unlocking, and editing of the master document, you can apply a password to the document. See Chapter 4, "Managing Word Files," for more information.

Inserting Master Document Page Numbers

To quickly apply continuous page numbers throughout your master document, follow these steps:

N O T E If your subdocuments were numbered before they were inserted into your master document, those page numbers will be retained in the master document. To reformat the page numbers, see Chapter 13, "Working with Long Documents," for more information on removing and reformatting page numbers. ■

Part

III

Ch

16

1. Open your master document and switch to Normal View by choosing <u>V</u>iew, <u>N</u>ormal from the menu.
2. Choose <u>E</u>dit, Select <u>A</u>ll or press Ctrl+A.
3. Choose <u>I</u>nsert, Page Nu<u>m</u>bers from the menu.
4. Choose the <u>P</u>osition and <u>A</u>lignment for your page numbers.
5. If you want to use your subdocument headings to create chapter numbers, click the <u>F</u>ormat button. You can choose which heading style will trigger the numbering of your chapters, and choose the style of your page and chapter numbers.

T I P If you want your page numbers to start with 1 for each new chapter (subdocument), you'll have to reset your starting page number for each subdocument. See Chapter 13, "Working with Long Documents," for more information on formatting your page and chapter numbers.

6. Click OK to return to the Page Numbers dialog box.
7. Click OK again to insert your page numbers and close the dialog box.

Applying Headers and Footers in a Master Document

When you print your master document, you want the reader to see it as one large document, unaware of the structure behind it. For this reason, Word applies your headers and footers to the entire document, flowing between sections, as it does in any other long document. You can, however, make each subdocument into a separate chapter, and you can have different headers and footers throughout the master document's sections.

For more information on Headers and Footers, see Chapter 13, "Working with Long Documents." But for purposes of this discussion, follow these steps to apply Headers and Footers to your master document:

1. With your master document open and in Master Document view, make sure you are in expanded view.
2. Choose <u>V</u>iew, <u>H</u>eaders and Footers from the menu. The Headers and Footers toolbar appears on-screen (see Figure 16.6).

3. Type your header content (if any). Click the Switch Between Header and Footer button to switch to the footer, and type any content there.

Section number (for subdocument 1)

FIG. 16.6

Create your master document's headers and footers as you would in any document.

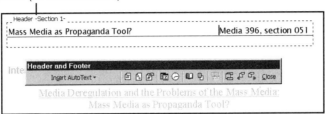

 4. If you want to insert page numbers, place your cursor where you want to insert the page numbers (left, right, or center), and insert any pre-number text ("Page" or "Pg."). You can place your page numbers in either the header or the footer. Click the Insert Page Number button on the Header and Footer toolbar.

 5. If desired, apply a horizontal border below your header and above your footer, by selecting the header or footer text and clicking the Borders button on the Formatting toolbar.

 6. Click the Close button when you finish entering and formatting your Header and Footer text.

To create separate headers and footers for each subdocument, perform the following steps:

1. In your open master document, make sure you're in expanded view.

2. Choose View, Headers and Footers from the menu.

  3. Using the Show Previous or Show Next button in the Header and Footer toolbar, move to the header or footer for the section you wish to edit.

 4. Click the Same as Previous button to turn off the default link between the previous section and the section you're in.

 5. Edit your header or footer as desired, and click the Close button. The active section's header or footer is now changed, leaving the remaining sections intact.

TIP If you have any difficulty with your master document's headers and footers, read Chapter 13, "Working with Long Documents," to fully understand the concept of sections and their impact on headers, footers, and page numbers.

Inserting Tables of Contents and Indexes into a Master Document

After you combine your documents, rearrange your subdocuments, and apply your page numbers, you'll want to add a Table of Contents to your master document. The longer your master document is, the more inclined you might be to add an index. These features will enable your document's readers to use it as a reference, as well as give it a professional, "published" appearance.

The process of inserting a Table of Contents or Index into a master document isn't very different from the process of adding one to any document. Please refer to Chapter 13, "Working with Long Documents," for complete coverage of this topic. Some considerations when adding a Table of Contents or Index to your master document:

- When you open your master document, click the Expand Subdocuments button if your subdocument text is currently collapsed.

- You must be in Normal or Page Layout view to add a Table of Contents or Index.

- If you add, delete, or rearrange your subdocuments later, you must update your Table of Contents and Index.

- If you will be applying separate chapter numbers to your subdocuments and formatting your page numbers according to chapter numbers, make sure these are set up before you generate the Table of Contents or Index.

Printing Master Documents

Printing a master document is simple, and doesn't vary from standard printing methods for a "regular" document. In fact, many people create a master document as a quick way of printing several separate files so that they can all be printed with one command. When printing your master document, keep these things in mind:

- If your subdocuments had page numbers before you combined them into a master document, those page numbers will be retained when the master document is printed.

- Make sure your subdocuments are expanded before you print the master document.

- Switch to Normal or Page Layout view before printing.

PART

IV

Word and The Web

CHAPTER 17

Creating Web Pages with Word

Word 97 gives you simple, yet powerful tools for creating and editing Web pages. You no longer need to know HTML (HyperText Markup Language) to design and create a great Web page for your personal use or for your company. ■

Word and the Web

Word's standard tools for formatting text, inserting graphics, and using color and lines can now help you design and edit a Web page. Find out about the additional formatting tools available for adding hypertext links, sound, and animation.

Intranet basics

Your company's private network can function like the global Internet on a smaller scale. Find out how Word can be a powerful tool for creating content and navigating your company's intranet.

Creating Web pages

What makes a good Web page? Discover important tips on designing and creating your Web pages and how to use Word to simplify the process.

Hypertext links

Create the internal connections that give your Web page depth. Your Web page can be a launching point to other Web sites and useful data, sound, or graphic files.

The World Wide Web

The World Wide Web is host to various businesses, interest groups and associations, families, and individuals. An effective Web page contains information to sell or enlighten, and graphics that grab the viewer's attention. The same Word 97 tools that enable you to create a dynamic newsletter, a professional-looking report, or other creative document can also design an exciting and effective Web page for the World Wide Web or your company's intranet. Word 97 enables you to save Word documents as HTML (HyperText Markup Language), the programming language used to build Web pages.

Your Word Web pages will, of course, contain text. It will also contain graphics, borders, backgrounds, and hypertext links to other Web sites. After you create your Web page, it appears online for you to preview. When your page is ready, it can be published on a Web server so that others can access it. Figure 17.1 shows the Macmillan Publishing Web page, containing informative text and eye-catching graphics that link to other Web pages.

FIG. 17.1

Macmillan Publishing's Web page contains graphics and text that inform you about their products and show you how to get to other Web pages for more information

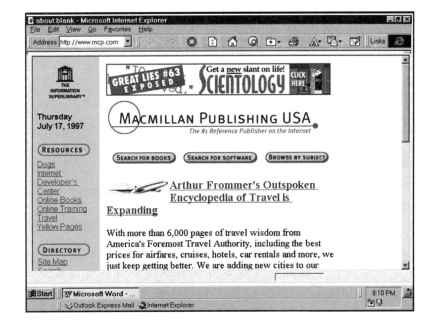

Browsing Web Pages

You can reach the World Wide Web and the Web pages on it by using an Internet *browser*, such as Microsoft Internet Explorer or Netscape Navigator. These are the two most popular browsers, but there are many others. The browser software's job is to give you a friendly interface—buttons and menus—to assist you in searching for information on the Internet and World Wide Web. Each Web site has an *URL (Uniform Resource Locator)*, or *Web address*. The Web address consists of some common elements. If you take the URL **http://www.microsoft.com**, you can break it down into the following parts:

- **HTTP://** is the first leg of any URL. The http stands for HyperText Transfer Protocol. It's the set of rules established for transmitting Internet information and files. The colon (:) and the slashes // are part of the operating system's lingo for separating one part of the URL from another.

- **WWW** tells the browser that the place you're going is on the World Wide Web.

- **MICROSOFT** is the name of the Web page. The name is determined by the Web page designer. For commercial Web pages, it is normally the company name.

- **COM** is the Web page file name extension. COM is for commercial organizations, ORG is for non-profit groups, EDU is for colleges and schools, GOV is for government, and NET is for Internet-related companies, such as an ISP (Internet Service Provider), a company who will rent you space on their Web server to store your Web site.

Web sites are also called *home pages*. The difference between a Web page and a home page is that the home page is the starting point from which you can go to *linked* Web pages. The person who designs the home page decides which other Web pages to link to, and provides the physical link for you to follow. These links are called *hypertext* links, created through a programming language called HTML (HyperText Markup Language), designed especially for the Internet and World Wide Web.

Figure 17.2 shows a home page with a hypertext link to another Web site.

Part
IV

Ch
17

FIG. 17.2

Your mouse pointer turns to a hand when you're pointing to a hypertext link. Click the link to go to the linked Web site.

Hypertext link —

Mouse Pointer —

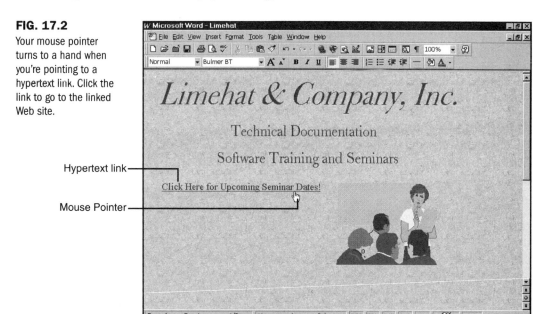

As you follow the hypertext links in a Web site, the URL grows. If you start at Microsoft's home page (**www.microsoft.com**) and follow the link to find technical support, the URL would appear as:

www.microsoft.com/support

Your browser will help you to move backward and forward through these links. It will even allow you to store the exact location of a particular link so that you can quickly return to it the next time you're browsing the Web.

Using Word to Create Your Web Pages?

With Word 97, you no longer need to know HTML to create a Web page. Word 97 enables you to create your own Web pages, including hypertext links to other Web pages, right within Word, through a very simple interface. You can use Online View to design the page, or let Word coach you through the whole process with its Web Page Wizard. You can create a document and then save it as HTML, converting your typing to HTML code.

Word also enables you to add hypertext links within your regular documents, so that you can link one file to another, or add a link to an actual Web site, right in your document. Whether you're using the Internet at home or the office, or you're working with your company's private intranet, you can use Word to jump onto the "information highway" faster and easier than ever before.

The Internet is a global network of computers, set up to share information. An *intranet* is a smaller, closed version of that global network. Your company may have an intranet that gives its employees access to departmental or divisional Web pages, each containing information (in the form of text and graphics) pertaining to that department or division of the company. Most intranets also have a connection to the global Internet, through a device called a *gateway*. The private aspects of a corporate intranet are protected from outside viewing or manipulation by *firewalls*.

Like the Internet, a corporate intranet is designed to share information: a calendar of events, vacation day applications, an employee phone list, details on a product your company manufactures or sells, and so on. Using the same software products, you browse an intranet as you would the Internet.

Word's Web page design tools can create a Web page for your company's intranet the same way you would create a World Wide Web page for the Internet.

When designing your Web page, be it for the World Wide Web or your company's intranet, you'll want to keep some basic things in mind:

■ *Clarity.* Don't let your message or specific information get lost in your layout. State the goal or reason for the Web page's existence right at the beginning. Let people know what they can find on your Web site, and show them how to find it. Limit your Word documents (that will later be Web pages) to approximately two screens of content.

■ *Simplicity.* While you may be tempted to use various fonts, graphics, sounds, and elaborate backgrounds, you want your Web page to be accessible to everyone: You don't want to exclude people with slow modems from viewing your Web page or getting information from it. Try to keep your graphics files under 30K each, so that they don't take too long to download.

■ *Accuracy.* Always run spell check on your Web page before "publishing" it or posting it on your Web server. Follow that with a thorough proofreading, to look for any other errors. Also, try looking at your Web page with more than one browser before publishing it on the Web. Make sure all your features, such as links, sounds, and animation, work properly.

Before you sit down to create your Web page, it's a good idea to have it planned out on paper. You should generally know what you want to say, what other documents or Web pages you want to link to, and where those links should appear on the home page. After that, you can begin the process of creating your page.

Word provides you with two ways of creating a Web page:

■ *Save your document as HTML.* Using the Blank Web Page template, type your text and insert your graphics as you would in any document, formatting your text, setting your alignment, indents, margins, and so forth. Insert your hypertext links. Then, save your document as HTML—Word will convert your text, graphics, and Web addresses to HTML code, and your document instantly becomes a Web page, ready for placing on your Web server.

■ *Use the Web Page Wizard.* This tool guides you through the process of building a Web page, and gives you pre-designed templates to assist you in your layout, fonts, and overall design. Using the Web Page Wizard will be covered later in this chapter.

Inserting Text, Graphics, and Sound

To create a Web page from a Word document, you must first create the document itself. A document on its way to becoming a Web page should include text, graphics, Web addresses (for hypertext links), and sound files, if desired. To begin creating a Web page, follow these initial steps:

1. Choose File, New from the menu. The New Document dialog box opens.
2. Click the Web Pages tab (see Figure 17.3).
3. Double-click the Blank Web Page icon. A blank, new document opens in Online Layout view.

Figure 17.2 shows a Web page in progress, in Online Layout View. You will notice the following changes in your Word screen's appearance:

■ Your toolbars change. Some of your Standard and Formatting tools disappear, and other buttons are added, to create a toolbar that contains the most useful Web page-creation tools.

■ Your ruler (if it was displayed previously) disappears.

FIG. 17.3
Select the Blank Web Page icon to build your Web page from scratch and save it as HTML.

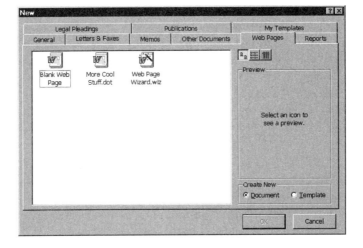

FIG. 17.4
Online Layout view offers tools for formatting your Web page and inserting graphic objects.

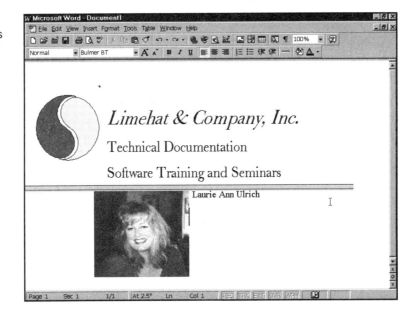

Table 17.1 defines the tools specifically applicable to Web page design in Online Layout view. The remaining tools (refer to Figure 17.2 for a view of the entire document window) are available in Page Layout and Normal View on your Standard and Formatting toolbars.

Table 17.1 Web Page Design Tools

Icon	Option	Description
	Insert Hypertext Link	Places a link in your Web page document. You can type the URL for the page you want

Icon	Option	Description
		to link to, or the path and file name if you're linking to a file.
	Web Toolbar	To open the basic Internet Explorer toolbar, click this button.
	Web Page Preview	Click this button to open Internet Explorer and display your Web page as it would appear to someone using a browser.
	Form Design Mode	This tool opens a floating toolbar of tools for creating check boxes, option buttons, drop lists, and so forth for adding user-interactive features to your Web page.
	Insert Picture	Click this button to add a graphic file such as a photograph, clip art, or drawing to your Web page.
	Insert Table	To create a series of columns and rows to hold your text and graphics, click this button and choose the dimensions of your table.
	Document Map	Click this button to open a vertical strip on the left side of your document. Any heading text you type (and format in Heading 1 through 6 style) appears in this strip, enabling you to quickly go to a particular section by clicking the heading text.
	Increase Font Size	Rather than forcing you to choose a particular point size for your text, you can click the Increase Font Size button to make text bigger. Each click of the button increases the font size by 6 points.
	Decrease Font Size	To make your text smaller, select it and click this button. Each click reduces the text's point size by 6 points.
	Horizontal Line	Add a graphic "rule" to your Web page by clicking this button. To format the line style and thickness, double-click the line after you've added it to your Web page. A formatting dialog box opens, with the Colors and Lines tab in front.

Part
IV
Ch
17

continues

Table 17.1 Continued

Icon	Option	Description
	Background Color	Click this button to choose from an array of colors to fill in the background of your Web page. You can also choose Fill in Effects, and work with various textures, patterns, and shaded fill styles.
	Font Color	Keeping your background color in mind, click this button to choose a color for your selected text.

You type your text using Heading styles 1 through 6 for your major headlines and important text. Format any body text (paragraphs) as you would in any Word document.

 N O T E Tables are an effective tool to use in your Web page for inserting text and graphics. For example, a two-column table can contain a graphic on the left and descriptive text or a related hypertext link on the right. Placing the text and graphics in a table helps you control their placement and visual relationships. For more information on using tables, see Chapter 10, "Using Tables."

 In addition to text, you may also want to insert graphic files to enhance your Web page. To do this, choose Insert, Picture from the menu, or click the Insert Picture icon on the toolbar.

N O T E Each time you insert an object into your Web page document, you'll be prompted to save your file. It's a good idea to save your work each time you add anything to it, just to save your having to repeat your efforts should a computer malfunction or power outage cause you to shut down unexpectedly.

 Add horizontal lines (known as "rules") to define sections of your page and underline important text blocks. Click the Horizontal Line tool on the Drawing toolbar and drag your mouse on the page to draw the line. (For more information about inserting, resizing, and moving graphics, see Chapter 12, "Using Graphics to Enhance Word Documents." The Drawing toolbar's features are also covered in Chapter 12.)

T I P While in Online Layout view, your Drawing toolbar will contain fewer drawing tools than Page Layout or Normal view.

 You select a background color or fill for your Web page by choosing Format, Background from the menu, or by clicking the Background Color button on the toolbar. Figure 17.5 shows the Background Color dialog box.

FIG. 17.5

Choose a background color for your Web page.

If you want a shaded or textured background, click Fill Effects in the Background Color dialog box. In the Fill Effects dialog box, you can choose from a series of tabs, each representing a different background effect (see Figure 17.6). Click OK to apply your effect and return to the Web page.

 TIP Keep your text colors in mind when you choose your Web page background. You want the page to be legible and "easy on the eyes" for your viewers.

FIG. 17.6

Apply a textured fill effect to your Web page background.

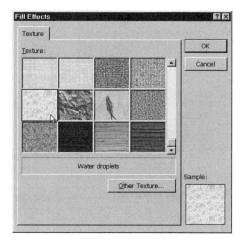

In addition to the visual effects covered in this section, Word offers a variety of features that you can insert to even further enhance your Web page. While in Online Layout view, click the Insert menu to see the list of potential items you can add to your Web page (see Figure 17.7).

FIG. 17.7

Add pictures, video clips, background sound, and more to your Web page.

If you are interested in embellishing your Web pages, see the following examples of Insert menu options:

■ *Video*. Choose Insert, Video to add animation or a small "movie" to your Web page. The Video Clip dialog box opens (see Figure 17.8), into which you can enter the name of the video file or browse to find it on your local or network drives. You can also set the video's playback options (when and how long it will play).

■ *Scrolling Text*. Choose Insert, Scrolling Text to create a moving strip of text in your Web page. You can choose the type of motion (scroll or slide), and set the colors, direction, speed, and duration of the display (see Figure 17.9).

FIG. 17.8

Use this dialog box to add a video to your Web page.

FIG. 17.9

Scrolling text will draw your viewer's attention to an important word or phrase

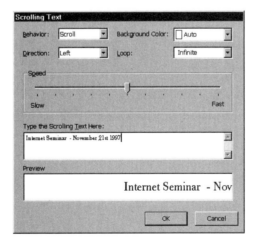

Saving a Word File as HTML

When you finish creating your Web page (or to end your current session with the Web page in progress), follow these steps to save the file as HTML, turning your document into a Web page:

1. Choose File, Save As from the menu. The Save As dialog box opens (see Figure 17.10).

2. In the Save As Type box, you'll see that the default file format is an HTML Document, not a Word document. Give your Web page a name (choose something descriptive and relatively short to keep the page's URL simple).

FIG. 17.10
Your document is automatically saved as HTML. Give it a name that will be easily typed and remembered as part of the site's URL.

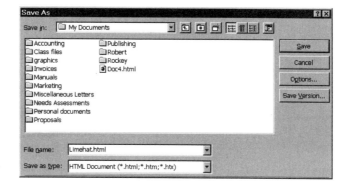

3. Click the Save button. Your document is now a Web page, ready for publishing on your Web server.

Creating Hypertext Links

To insert a hypertext link into your Web page, follow these steps:

1. Position your cursor where you want the link inserted.

2. Click the Insert Hyperlink button on the toolbar, or choose Insert, Hyperlink from the menu. The Insert Hyperlink dialog box opens (see Figure 17.11).

3. Choose to insert a link to a Web address (URL) or to a document on your local or network drives. You can also link to a Bookmark (named range of pages) in a document on your local or network drive.

4. If you don't know the exact path to the URL or file, click the Browse button to find it. If you are looking for a Web address (URL), click the Search the Web button in the Link to File dialog box. After accessing the site on the Web, note the URL and enter it in the Insert Hyperlink dialog box.

 TIP To avoid possible typing errors when entering the URL text, you can copy (Ctrl+C) the URL from the Browse address box and then paste (Ctrl+V) it into the document.

Figure 17.12 shows the Link to File dialog box.

FIG. 17.11

Add a hypertext link to a Web address or a document on your local or network drive.

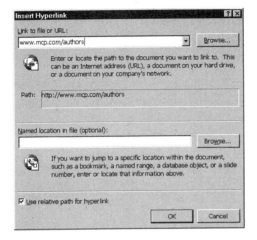

FIG. 17.12

Browse your local or network drives for the file to which your hypertext link will point.

Click the Search the Web icon to open Internet Explorer

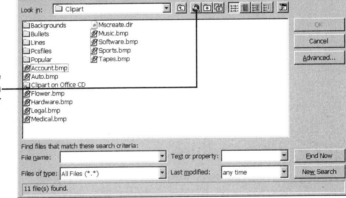

5. Click OK to insert the link and close the dialog box.

After you place a hyperlink in your Word document, you might want to change its appearance. A long path and file name can be unattractive, and it may not be very informative to the viewer. To reduce the hyperlink to a single word or short phrase, follow these steps:

1. Point to the hyperlink you want to edit and click your right mouse button.
2. Choose Hyperlink from the pop-up menu.
3. From the submenu, choose Select Hyperlink. The hyperlink becomes highlighted.
4. Type the word or short phrase that you want to appear as your hyperlink.
5. Click away from the selected hyperlink or press one of your arrow keys to deselect it. Your hyperlink is now represented by the text you typed.

Figure 17.13 shows a renamed Hyperlink.

FIG. 17.13
Select and rename your hyperlink to save space on-screen or to create a more attractive or informative link.

Renamed hyperlink

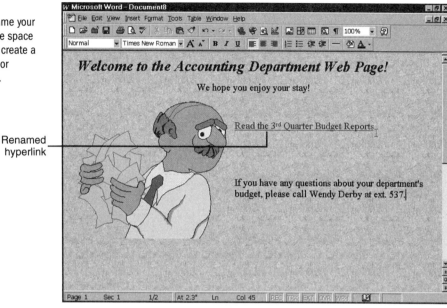

Part
IV

Ch
17

Using the Web Page Wizard

The Web Page Wizard is a user-friendly tool for users who are new to Web page design. You may also find this Wizard useful if you want to use Word's pre-designed layouts for Web pages.

To use Word's Web Page Wizard, follow these steps:

1. Choose File, New from the menu. The New Document dialog box opens (see Figure 17.14).

FIG. 17.14
Choose Web Page Wizard from the Web Pages tab to begin building your Web page.

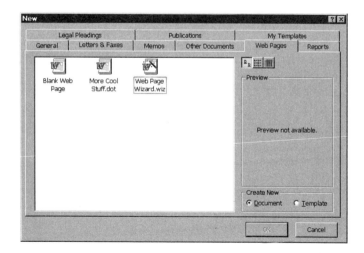

2. Click the Web Pages tab.

3. Double-click the Web Page Wizard icon.

4. Select a type of Web page from the first Web Page Wizard dialog box (see Figure 17.15); click <u>N</u>ext.

FIG. 17.15

Choose from various pre-designed layouts and forms for your Web page.

5. Choose a Web page Style, such as Contemporary, Festive, or Jazzy (see Figure 17.16); click <u>F</u>inish.

FIG. 17.16

The Web Page Wizard asks you to select a visual style for your Web page.

6. The Web Page Wizard creates your Web page for you. Your layout, backgrounds, and colors have been selected, and sample text shows you where to place your own content (see Figure 17.17).

7. Save your Web page by choosing <u>F</u>ile, Save <u>A</u>s from the menu. The Save As Type format defaults to HTML.

Give your Web page a short, easily typed and easily remembered name. The name you give it will be part of its URL.

FIG. 17.17
The Web Page Wizard creates a Web page for you based on your layout and style selections.

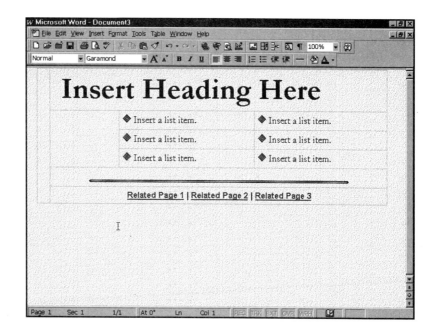

After the Web Page Wizard has completed creating a basic Web page for you, you can insert your own text, graphics, and hypertext links as desired. The Web page contains sample instructive text to help you. Remember to save frequently during your development process. ●

CHAPTER 18

Using Hyperlinks in Word Documents

Links are not limited to Web pages. You can insert hyperlinks in any Word document, providing fast access to other files from within a letter, report, or any other type of document. These links make it easy to view supporting information, graphics, video clips, and so forth while you (or another user) read your document on-screen. ■

Link Office 97 files to Word documents

Create a hyperlink in your Word document that takes you to an Excel spreadsheet, a PowerPoint presentation, an Access database, a Word document, or even files created with other applications.

Link programs to your document

Word documents contain hyperlinks to specific programs. Add a link that takes you to an accessory, such as the Calculator, or open an Office 97 application from within your document.

Rename and redirect your links

What if you want your link to say `Click Here!` instead of `c:\my documents\reports\budget.xls`? Rename the hyperlink to be more instructive or creative. After you create a link, the file or application that it points to may move or be renamed by another user. Update your hyperlink to reflect these changes.

Creating Links to Office 97 Application Files

In the previous chapter, you learned about adding hypertext links to a Web page, enabling the user to jump to a particular Web site or a file on your local or network drive. The same sort of link can be established in a Word document (called a hyperlink), adding the same depth and power to a report, reference guide, or memo. By linking a file to your document with a hyperlink, you make it simple for your document's user to access the file.

You can add a hyperlink in three ways:

■ *Insert the hyperlink.* Create a hyperlink from the menu or toolbar. This is the same method covered in Chapter 17, "Creating Web Pages with Word."

■ *Type the path and file name.* This requires Word's AutoFormat to convert the path to a link.

■ *Paste.* Use copy or cut and paste a section of another document, spreadsheet, or presentation (or any Windows-based application file) into your Word document as a hyperlink.

To insert a hyperlink into a Word document, follow these steps:

1. With your document open, position your cursor where you want to place the hyperlink.

2. Click the Insert Hyperlink button on the Standard toolbar. The Edit Hyperlink dialog box opens (see Figure 18.1).

> **T I P** You can also choose Insert, Hyperlink from the menu to insert a link into your Word document.

FIG. 18.1

Insert a hyperlink into your Word document. The link can be to a Web site or a document on your local or network drive.

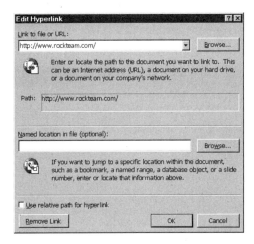

3. To insert a file, type the path and file name in the Link to File or URL box. If you don't know the exact path or file name, click the Browse button to search for it.

4. After entering the path and file name, click OK to insert the hyperlink and close the dialog box.

> **TIP** When you point to a hyperlink in your document, your mouse pointer turns to a hand. Click it once to access the linked file.

You can also add a hyperlink to your document by typing the path and file name anywhere in your text. By default, Word 97 sees any path (such as C:\my documents\reports\expenses.xls) as a hyperlink. As soon as you type the path and file name, the text will change color and become underlined. This default is a function of Word 97's AutoFormat feature. If your path and file name do not change color, the default has been changed. To reset it, follow these steps:

1. Choose Tools, AutoCorrect from the menu.
2. Click the AutoFormat As You Type tab.
3. Place a check in the Internet and Network Paths with Hyperlinks check box.
4. Click the AutoFormat tab.
5. Make sure the Internet and Network Paths with Hyperlinks item is checked in this tab as well.
6. Click OK to save your settings and close the dialog box.

The previous methods—Inserting and using AutoFormat to convert a typed path to a hyperlink—result in an entire file being linked to your document. However, if you want only a section of a document or a few columns from a spreadsheet to be linked to your Word document, you should paste the hyperlink instead. Follow these steps:

1. Open the Word document into which you want to paste the hyperlink.
2. Position your cursor where you want to place the link.
3. Open the application and specific file that contains the section you wish to paste into your Word document.
4. Select the section that you wish to paste as a hyperlink. Choose Edit, Copy from the menu or press Ctrl + C.
5. Using the Taskbar, switch back to your Word document. Ensuring your cursor is still located where you want to paste the hyperlink, choose Edit, Paste as Hyperlink from the menu.
6. Your pasted section appears in its entirety. To activate the hyperlink, point to the pasted item with your mouse, and click once. The source document (and application) opens.

Figure 18.2 shows a section of a spreadsheet, pasted as a hyperlink.

Part

IV

Ch

18

FIG. 18.2

Your hyperlinked section of a document or spreadsheet will appear in your Word document. Click it once to open the source file and application.

Spreadsheet section pasted as hyperlink

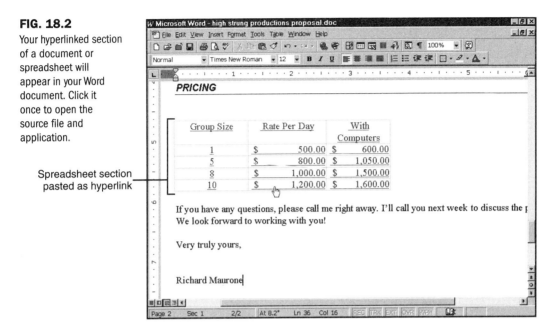

Starting a Program with a Hyperlink

A hyperlink can be added to your Word document to open an application rather than a specific file. You can, for example, add a Windows' Calculator program hyperlink to your Word document so that you or another user of the document can have instant access to an on-screen calculator while reviewing the document.

 T I P If you'll be sharing your Word document with other users, make sure your hyperlinked files are on a network drive that they can access. If your link points to your local drive or a drive that only you can access, the link will fail when your users attempt to access the linked program.

To add an application hyperlink to your Word document, follow these steps:

1. With your document open, place your cursor where you want to insert the hyperlink.
2. Click the Insert Hyperlink button on the Standard toolbar, or choose Insert, Hyperlink from the menu. The Insert Hyperlink dialog box opens (see Figure 18.3).
3. Type the exact path to your program's executable file (EXE extension). At the end of the path, type the executable file name. Program files may also have extensions such as COM and BAT.
4. If you don't know the exact path and file name, click the Browse button. The Link to File dialog box opens (see Figure 18.4).
5. Click the Files of Type drop-down list, and scroll up to choose All Files.

FIG. 18.3
Insert a hyperlink that will activate a program from within your Word document.

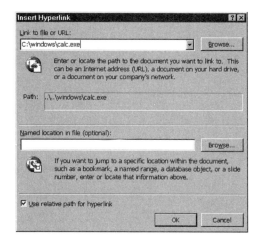

FIG. 18.4
When browsing to insert a hyperlink that points to a program file, choose All Files in the Files of Type box.

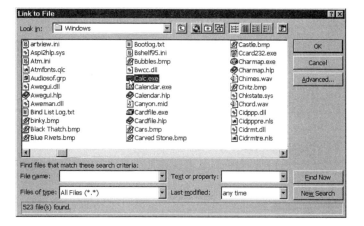

Part
IV

Ch
18

 By default, Word searches only for Office 97 application files when you insert a link. If you're attempting to insert a hyperlink to another type of application or a program, you must redirect it to look for either All Files or another specific file type.

6. Navigate to the folder that contains the program to which you want to link. When you've found it, click OK to return to the Insert Hyperlink dialog box.

7. Click OK to insert your hyperlink and close the dialog box.

 When creating a hyperlink to an intranet drive, make sure your users will have access to the same drives and files in the same locations as referenced in your link.

To use your program hyperlink, click the link once with your mouse. The application will open, on top of your Word document.

Figure 18.5 shows the hyperlink to the Windows Calculator program, and the open Calculator window.

FIG. 18.5

Click the program hyperlink to open the program on top of your Word document.

Hyperlink ——

Calculator program window ——

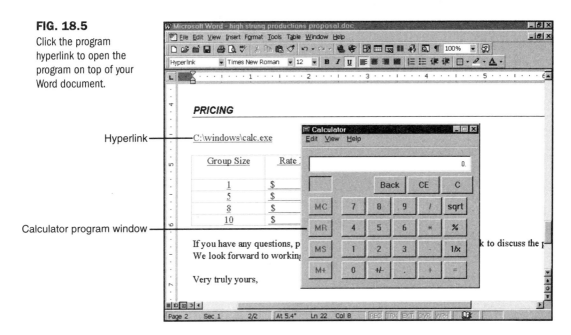

Editing Hyperlinks

When adding hyperlinks to your Word documents, it's a good idea to keep track of your linked files and programs periodically, making sure they're in the same place and have the same file names as when you established the link. If a file or program has moved or been renamed, you will need to edit the hyperlink so that any users of the document will be able to successfully use the link.

To edit your hyperlink, perform these steps:

1. Open the document that contains the hyperlink you wish to edit.

2. Point to the hyperlink you wish to edit, and click your right mouse button.

3. From the pop-up menu, choose Hyperlink, and then choose Edit Hyperlink from the submenu. The Edit Hyperlink dialog box opens.

 TIP The Edit Hyperlink dialog box looks and functions the same as the Insert Hyperlink dialog box discussed earlier in this chapter.

4. Type the correct path and file name in the Link to File or URL box, or click Browse to find the file.

5. After entering or locating the file in its new location (or with its new name), click OK in the Edit Hyperlink dialog box. The dialog box closes and your hyperlink is corrected.

 TIP You will be prompted to save your document each time you attempt to edit your hyperlinks, which is a helpful hint: It's a good idea to save your document after making any changes.

After you place a hyperlink in your Word document, you may also want to change its appearance. Perhaps you don't like the look of a long path and file name. Maybe if you've pasted a section of a letter or spreadsheet, the section is taking up too much room. To reduce the hyperlink to a single word or short phrase, follow these steps:

1. Point to the hyperlink you wish to edit and click your right mouse button.
2. Choose Hyperlink from the pop-up menu.
3. From the submenu, choose Select Hyperlink. The hyperlink becomes highlighted.
4. Type the word or short phrase that you want to appear as your hyperlink.
5. Click away from the selected hyperlink or press one of your arrow keys to deselect it. Your hyperlink is now represented by the text you typed.

Figure 18.6 shows a renamed hyperlink.

Part
IV

Ch

18

FIG. 18.6
Select and rename your hyperlink to save space on-screen or create a more attractive or informative link.

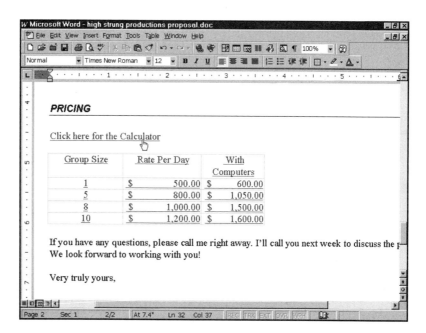

CHAPTER 19

Working with Other Office 97 Applications

Using the clipboard and Windows' object linking tools (OLE), you can insert sections of files created in Excel, PowerPoint, or Access, or you can embed these other Office 97 applications directly into your Word document. The Microsoft Binder enables you to combine files you create in Word, Excel, PowerPoint (or any Microsoft program) into one file for collating and printing a large presentation or proposal. By integrating these other programs (or simply the files created with them) you add dimension and power to your Word documents. ■

The Clipboard—the basics and more

Use the Clipboard to move and share sections of documents, spreadsheets, charts, and graphics. Understanding the powers and limitations of the Clipboard will save you from recreating objects that you could be sharing between applications and files.

Paste special

Embed pasted and inserted objects in the your Word document. Maintain the link between the source and target objects, and your target object will update each time a change is made to the source.

Binding it all together

Use the Microsoft Office Binder to collate your Word, Excel, and PowerPoint files. Create a great report or presentation by gathering the considerable power of your Office 97 applications.

Understanding the Clipboard

The Clipboard is a Windows feature, available in both Windows 3.x and Windows 95. Using your computer's memory, the Clipboard holds sections of documents, spreadsheets, graphics—any Windows application file—and allows you to move or duplicate these pieces in the same or another file. The following is a list of rules for using the Clipboard:

- You can Cut or Copy text, numbers, data, or graphics to the Clipboard. To insert the item in another location, you'll Paste it. The Clipboard works with any Windows application.

- If you need to move a selection from one place to another—between documents or within the same document—Cut it. Paste the selection in a new location.

- To share or duplicate a selection, Copy it. Copying leaves the original alone, and makes a duplicate for pasting elsewhere.

- The keyboard shortcuts for the Clipboard are Ctrl+X to Cut, Ctrl+C to Copy, and Ctrl+V to Paste. Clipboard commands are also found in the Edit menu and on the Standard toolbar.

- The contents of the Clipboard are temporary. Once you exit Windows, whatever you have on the Clipboard is flushed out of your computer's memory.

- The Clipboard only holds one selection at a time.

- While a selection is on the Clipboard, it can be Pasted as many times as you need it, in as many places as you need it.

CAUTION

Use Cut carefully. It's very easy to cut something with the intention of moving it to another file or location in your current document, and then accidentally lose the selection by exiting Windows or placing another selection on the Clipboard.

If you're not sure what you have on the Clipboard, a quick way to find out is to open a blank Word document, and press Ctrl+V. Close the document without saving after you view the Clipboard's contents. This method has some limitations because if the nature of the Clipboard's contents aren't compatible with Word's default text format, the content may not look like it did in its original location. An example of this is a section of an Excel spreadsheet appearing as a Table when pasted into a Word document.

Another way to view the contents of the Clipboard is to use The Clipboard Viewer. This Windows Accessory also enables you to edit and save the contents of the clipboard. To use this feature, follow these steps:

1. Click the Start button, and choose Programs from the Start menu.
2. Choose Accessories, and then Clipboard Viewer from Accessories submenu. The Clipboard Viewer window opens (see Figure 19.1).

FIG. 19.1

View, edit, and save the contents of the Clipboard with the Clipboard Viewer, found in Windows' Accessories.

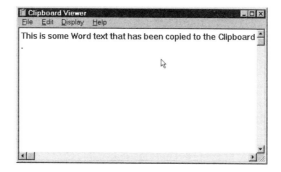

3. After viewing the contents of the clipboard, you can choose File, Exit to close the Clipboard Viewer program.

The Clipboard Viewer gives you some alternatives for looking at the Clipboard contents. From the Clipboard Viewer's Display menu, you can choose to view the selection in a variety of formats. The formats that are available from the menu will be dictated by the nature of the original Clipboard selection.

Figure 19.2 shows the Clipboard Viewer's display of a selected and copied section of an Excel spreadsheet. The Bitmap Display type was chosen so that the spreadsheet would appear as it did in the source file.

FIG. 19.2

Try different Clipboard Viewer Display formats to find one that best represents the original selection.

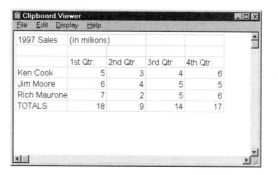

Part
IV

Ch
19

The Clipboard Viewer also allows you to delete the contents of the Clipboard. In the Clipboard Viewer window, choose Edit, Delete. You can also press Delete on your keyboard. A prompt asks you to confirm your intention to clear the contents of the Clipboard. Click Yes (see Figure 19.3).

N O T E Deleting the contents of the Clipboard can free your system's resources. If you receive low memory messages or your system seems sluggish, try clearing the Clipboard of any large selection that you previously cut or copied. As a safeguard against losing something you've cut, view the Clipboard's contents before deleting it. ■

FIG. 19.3
Click Yes to clear the
contents of the
Clipboard.

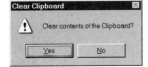

Using the Clipboard with Office 97 Applications

The Clipboard is the most powerful tool for sharing data between the Office 97 applications, and it's very simple to use. In the following sections of this chapter, you'll be using Word as the target location for selections from the other Office 97 applications.

To paste a section of an Excel spreadsheet into a Word document, follow these steps:

1. Open the Word document into which you want to paste a selection from an Excel spreadsheet.

2. Open Excel 97 by clicking the Start button and choosing Microsoft Excel from the Programs menu.

3. Open the Excel spreadsheet that you want to use with your Word document.

4. Select the portion—known as a *range* in Excel—of the spreadsheet that you want to paste into the Word document.

> Excel allows you to select non-contiguous sections by holding the Ctrl key as you click and drag through cells. However, when you paste the selections, they'll appear as one group of contiguous table cells in the Word document.

5. Choose Edit, Copy from the menu, or press Ctrl+C.

6. Switch back to your Word document by clicking the Microsoft Word button on the Taskbar.

> Another quick way to switch between open and running applications is to press Alt+Esc.

7. In the Word document, position your cursor where you want to place the spreadsheet section. Choose Edit, Paste or press Ctrl+V. The selection appears as a table in your Word document.

> To place the spreadsheet, you can also click the Paste button on the toolbar.

Follow the preceding instructions to move or duplicate any Office 97 content—PowerPoint slides and graphics, Excel charts, or Access data records—into a Word document.

Using Paste Special

Using the Paste command will insert the cut or copied selection into your document, and that's where the relationship between the source (where you got the selection) and the target (where you pasted it) ends.

To maintain a relationship between the source and the target, you use Paste Special. Maintaining the connection between the source and target enables you to update the target automatically when changes are made to the source. For example, if you have a section of an Excel spreadsheet that you want to use in a report you're composing in Word, Paste Special will allow you to change the numbers in the Excel file, and see the changes reflected in the Word document. This variation on the Paste command is also called *paste linking*.

To Copy and Paste Link your source and target files, perform these steps:

1. Open both your source and target files.
2. Using the Taskbar, switch to the source file, and select the portion of the file to be copied.
3. Choose Edit, Copy or press Ctrl+C.

 T I P Do not cut a selection that you're going to Paste Link. If you cut the selection, there won't be a source selection with which to link.

4. Switch to the target file, and position your cursor in the place where you want to insert the pasted selection.
5. Choose Edit, Paste Special. The Paste Special dialog box opens (see Figure 19.4).

Part
IV
Ch
19

FIG. 19.4
Paste Special
enables you to link
your source and
target files through
the pasted selection.

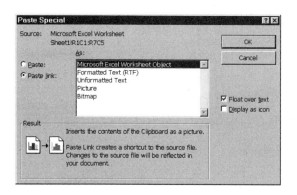

6. Click the Paste Link option button.
7. In the As box, choose the type of *object* that you want to paste. Word will offer a list of the most appropriate formats, detecting the application used to create the selection.

> **N O T E**   An *object* is an independent entity that exists in a document (or any user file). The Paste Link object maintains a connection to the application that created it. Choosing a non-object format from the As list will maintain a link to the original source content, but not to the application used to create the source. ▨

8. Set your options for how the linked selection will appear in your document:
   - *Float over Text.* Choose this option if you want to be able to drag and move the pasted object anywhere in the Word document. If you turn this option off, the object will be integrated into the document's text layer.
   - *Display as Icon.* Check this box to place a picture in your document that, when double-clicked, will open the pasted object. This can save room on your document page if the pasted selection is very large.

9. Click OK to Paste Link your selection into your Word document and close the dialog box.

To test your link, double-click the pasted selection. The application associated with the source document opens, as does the file from which the pasted selection came. You can then edit the source—in other words, change, add to, or delete the content of the selected section. When you switch back to your target file, the content of the pasted selection has changed as well.

Embedding an Object into a Word Document

Another method of embedding an object in your Word document is to insert, rather than paste, the object. This approach gives you two choices for embedding an object:

- ▨ Insert a new, blank section that you can build from within Word
- ▨ Insert a section of an existing, saved file

Either type of embedded object can appear as an icon, taking up less space in your Word document when it's not in use.

> **N O T E**   The process of embedding an object in your Word document uses a Windows feature known as Object Linking and Embedding, more commonly referred to as OLE (pronounced "olay"). This feature is at work when you insert an object or Paste Link an object into your Word document or any other Windows application file. ▨

To insert a new, blank embedded object, perform these steps:

1. Open your target document, and position your cursor where you want to insert the object.
2. Choose Insert, Object. The Object dialog box opens.
3. Click the Create New tab.
4. Choose from the Object Type list (see Figure 19.5). This list will contain objects representing all of the software applications loaded on your computer.

FIG. 19.5

Choose the type of object to embed in your document.

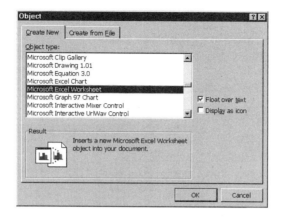

5. Turn your object's display options on or off:
   - Float over Text is on by default. This means that the object can be moved freely on top of the text layer. Turn this option off if you want the object to be integrated into the text layer with your paragraph text.
   - Click the Display as Icon check box if you want your embedded object to appear as an icon in your Word document.

6. Click OK. The blank object is embedded in your document in its own window. Figure 19.6 shows an object embedded as an icon in a Word document. Figure 19.7 shows an embedded object as part of the Word document.

N O T E If you choose Display as Icon, the embedded object will appear as an icon when inactive. When double-clicked (to activate the object) the object will appear in a separate, complete window on top of your Word document. Objects not displayed as icons will appear in a box within the Word document, and when activated (by double-clicking), the Word toolbar will change to display toolbars from the source application.

7. Enter your object's content. You have the full power of the source application at your disposal for editing, formatting, and printing the object.

TIP If you embed your object as an icon, choose File, Close and Return to (*Name of Source Document*) in the source object's application window to go back to the text layer of your Word document.

8. Save the document and its embedded objects by choosing File, Save.

When you use your Word document in the future, the embedded objects will open right along with it, just as you left them the last time you edited them and saved the Word file.

Part
IV
Ch
19

FIG. 19.6
This figure shows an embedded object in its own window.

Object icon

Enter your object's content

Object application window

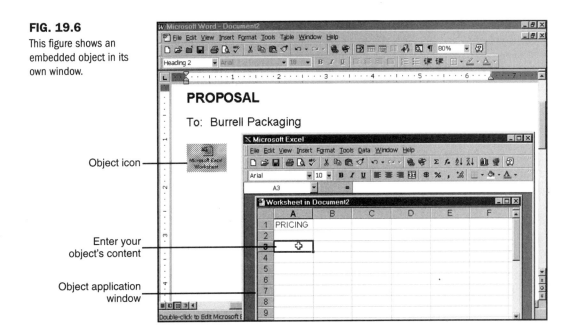

FIG. 19.7
This figure illustrates an embedded object integrated into the Word document.

Tools for the embedded object's application are part of the Word window

The embedded object

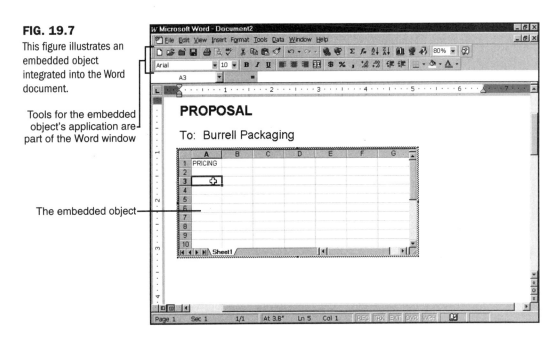

To embed a portion of an existing file in a Word document, follow these steps:

1. Open your target Word document and place your cursor where you want to insert the object.

2. Choose Insert, Object from the menu.

3. Click the Create from File tab in the Objects dialog box (see Figure 19.8).

FIG. 19.8
Use the Create from File tab to embed a section of an existing file in your Word document.

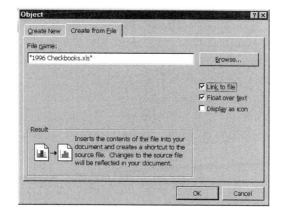

4. Type the exact path and file name for the file you want to embed. If you don't know the path and file name, click the Browse button. After finding your file in the Browse dialog box, click OK to return to the Objects dialog box.

5. Set your object's options:

   • *Link to File.* Click this check box if you want to create and maintain a connection between the source file and the target document.

   • *Float over Text.* This is on by default. Turn option off if you want the embedded object to be part of the text layer.

   • *Display as Icon.* Select this option if you want the embedded object to appear as an icon in your target document.

6. Click OK to insert the embedded file and close the dialog box.

When you embed an existing file, the file's content is automatically part of the Word document.

To edit the content of the embedded object, double-click the object to activate the application and its toolbars. Save your document after embedding the file, and after any changes to the embedded content.

Part
IV

Ch
19

Working with Scraps

Scraps are selections from your Office 97 files that are saved on the Windows 95 Desktop. Unlike the Clipboard and its transient content, scraps can be saved for as long as you need them. You can drag a scrap from the Desktop to your Word document (or any Office 97 file) whenever you want to, and the scrap remains on the desktop for repeated use.

To create a scrap, follow these steps:

1. Select a section of your document, spreadsheet, presentation, or database.
2. Click the Restore button in your active application window (if it's currently Maximized) or resize the window with your mouse so that an empty portion of your Desktop is visible outside the application window.
3. Drag the selection out of the application window, and on to the Desktop. Release the mouse. A scrap icon and description appear on the desktop.

Figure 19.9 shows a Scrap from an Excel spreadsheet that can be dragged into the open Word document.

FIG. 19.9
Drag a document selection to the Desktop to create a reusable scrap.

Scrap—

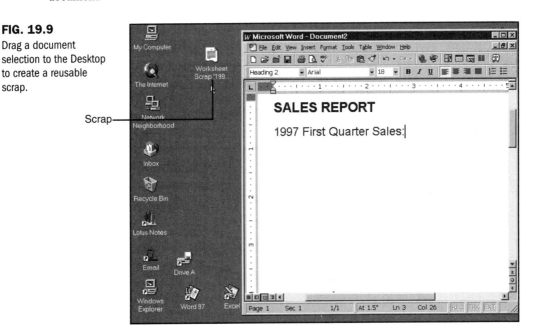

To use your scraps, drag the Desktop scrap icon into an open application window or to the target application file's Taskbar button. To perform a more precise placement of a scrap, right-click the scrap icon, and choose Copy. You can then click a specific spot in your target file, and choose Paste to insert the scrap's content.

Binding Office 97 Files

The Microsoft Office Binder enables you to group files created in Word, Excel, and PowerPoint (as well as other Microsoft products, such as Project) for the purpose of creating a proposal or report. To create a Binder for your Office 97 files, follow these steps:

1. From the Start button, choose Programs, Microsoft Binder. The Binder program starts, and a new, blank Binder screen opens (see Figure 19.10).

FIG. 19.10
Use the Microsoft Binder to group files created in Word, Excel, PowerPoint, or any other Microsoft application.

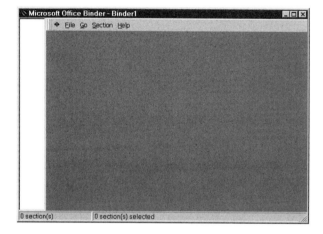

2. Open the Windows Explorer or My Computer and display the first file that you want to place in the binder.
3. Drag and drop the file from the Explorer or My Computer window into the Binder window's left pane.
4. As you add files, they appear in the left pane of the Binder window. When dragging and dropping additional files into the Binder window, be sure to place them in the order you want them bound. Figure 19.11 shows a series of files added to a Binder.

N O T E The application menu and tools for the file that you've added to the Binder will appear in the Binder window, enabling you to work on the file from within the Binder program. ▦

To use your Binder, you'll want to print your bound files. Each file added to the Binder has been added as a separate section. To print your entire Binder follow these steps:

1. Choose File, Print Binder from the Binder menu.
2. Select the All Visible Sections option.
3. Enter the Number of Copies to be printed.
4. Make sure the Collate option is turned on if you will be printing multiple copies.

Part
IV

Ch
19

FIG. 19.11

Drag your files from the Explorer or My Computer window into your Binder, placing them in the order you want them bound.

Files added to binder—

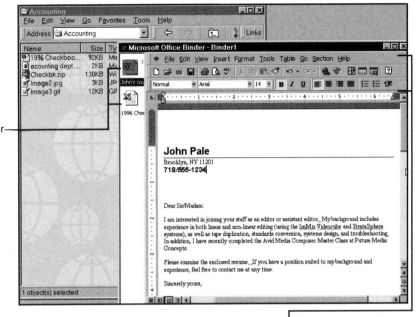

Word menu and toolbars displayed for selected section

5. Choose Cons<u>e</u>cutive from the Numbering Group to number the pages in the binder from beginning to end, spanning the sections. Choose Re<u>s</u>tart each Section if you want each section to be numbered independently.

6. Click OK.

If you need to change the order of your sections, you can drag the section icons, moving them up and down within the group of sections. You can also choose <u>S</u>ection, <u>R</u>earrange, and choose the section you wish to move. Click the Move Up or Move Down buttons, as necessary. Click OK to close the dialog box and put your order changes into effect.

The files you add to your Binder are copied to it, meaning that they also remain in their original locations on your local or network drive. If you save your Binder, you will be saving the files again, as part of the Binder file. This can take up a lot of drive space, so you may decide not to save your Binder files unless a great deal of work went into the binding process or if the files you bound were edited within the Binder and those changes are not part of the original files. To save your Binder file, perform these steps:

1. Choose <u>F</u>ile, <u>S</u>ave Binder in the Binder window.

2. Give the Binder a name and choose a drive and folder location for the file.

3. Click Save.

Office 97 Integration and Automation

Automating Word with Visual Basic for Applications

Microsoft has made its long-promised strategy a reality. Each of the Office 97 applications now supports Visual Basic for Applications (VBA). This enables average users and developers alike to create programs (procedures) within the applications. In Word, procedures can be created to automate frequently performed tasks. ■

Procedures—formerly known as macros

In earlier versions of Word, the term macros applied to any series of steps that you chose to record. Recording these steps made it easy to repeat them at any time, by pressing a keyboard shortcut or clicking a toolbar button. With Visual Basic for Applications (VBA), Word 97 enables the user to create macros, now known as procedures, in Visual Basic, a simple and powerful programming language.

Record, run, and edit

The three things you can do with a procedure are record (create) it, run (use) it, and if it fails or requires changes for any reason, edit it. This chapter will prepare you to create simple procedures and make changes to their function and content.

User ability

Create data entry boxes and user prompts to make your procedures more friendly for yourself and other users.

Understanding Procedures in Word 97

Deciding which word processing tasks warrant the creation of a procedure may be the hardest part of the whole VBA process. With all of Word 97's Auto features (AutoFormat, AutoText, AutoCorrect), many of the tasks that might have required a macro in the past (inserting an often-used paragraph, for example) are now handled by Word's standard features.

Yet, you may still want to create a procedure (macro) to perform tasks for which Word has an Auto feature, if only to customize when and how the task is executed. For example, you may want to create a standard letter closing for all office correspondence. Normally, you could create an AutoText entry for each person in the office, perhaps triggered by his or her initials. With a procedure, however, you can create the letter closing and add an automated user dialog box that prompts the typist for the letter author's name. This saves the creation of many separate AutoText entries, and eliminates people forgetting which AutoText abbreviation to use.

As you become familiar with Word's many powerful features, you'll find ways to integrate them into more elaborate procedures. In this chapter, you'll create a very basic sample procedure, running it, and then editing it's content and function.

Recording a Procedure

You begin the process of recording a procedure by planning the steps your procedure will perform. You should at least have the steps clear in your mind, if not on paper. Planning ahead will potentially save you hours of testing and editing time, especially with more complex procedures.

The procedure you create in this chapter involves inserting a disclaimer paragraph at the end of a hypothetical client proposal. Later, after running the basic procedure, you'll add data entry boxes to the procedure to enable the user to customize the content of the paragraph.

To create a procedure, you must first turn on the recorder. Follow these steps:

1. Open a new, blank document by clicking the New button on the toolbar, or choosing File, New from the menu and double-clicking the Blank Document icon in the General tab.

2. Choose Tools, Macro from the menu. Select Record New Macro from the submenu. This opens the Record Macro dialog box (see Figure 20.1).

3. Type a name for your macro. For this process, use the name **Disclaimer**.

TIP Macro names can be up to 80 characters long, but can contain no spaces or symbols.

4. Choose to run the macro from the keyboard or a toolbar by clicking the appropriate button:

   - *Toolbars*. If you assign your macro to the toolbar, you will drag the macro name to the toolbar of your choice. You can set the size and location of the button. Figure 20.2 shows the Customize dialog box.

- *Keyboard.* Press the keyboard shortcut that will trigger your macro. If the shortcut is already assigned to another function, Word will tell you, and you will be prompted to choose another one. Try to use a key combination that will be easy to remember, such as Alt+D for Disclaimer, as in our example. Figure 20.3 shows the Customize Keyboard dialog box.

FIG. 20.1
Enter a name for your macro and choose to assign it to the keyboard or toolbar.

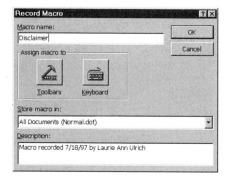

N O T E If you skip the Assign Macro section in the process of naming and recording your macro, you will be able to run your procedure later by choosing Tools, Macro, and then selecting the macro by name from the list. ■

FIG. 20.2
Choose a toolbar to which you'll add your button and drag the macro command to place it.

Drag the macro command name up to the toolbar

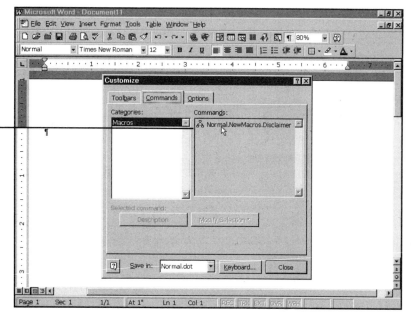

Part
V

Ch
20

FIG. 20.3
Use the Customize
Keyboard dialog box to
assign a keyboard
shortcut to your macro.

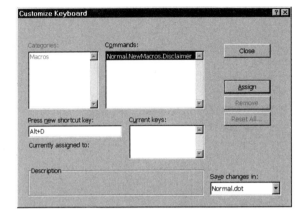

5. Click Close (or <u>A</u>ssign and then Close if you're assigning a keyboard shortcut) in the Customize dialog box. The macro is now recording. A small recording toolbar floats on your Word document.

 You can't use your mouse on the text layer of your document while the macro is recording, so click your formatting buttons or apply menu commands to format text and paragraphs before you begin typing the content.

6. Choose <u>F</u>ormat, <u>P</u>aragraph from the menu. In the Left and Right Indent boxes, enter a measurement of 1". Click OK.

7. Type the following text:

   Pricing quoted in this proposal is only valid for thirty (30) days from the date of the document as seen on page 1. Product availability from our suppliers can affect described delivery dates. We will make every effort to inform you of delivery delays and unforeseen changes in pricing as they occur. Notice will be given in writing, via fax.

   Figure 20.4 shows the typed paragraph, formatted as directed, with the floating toolbar on-screen.

8. Click the Stop button on the recording toolbar.

N O T E You can discard the document that contains the paragraph you created for this macro. The text was saved as part of the program, and the document serves no further purpose. ■

FIG. 20.4
Click the Stop button when you finish formatting and entering the content of your macro's paragraph.

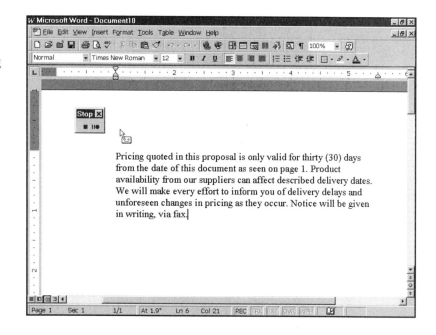

Running a Procedure

After you record your macro, you'll want to test it. To run your macro in a blank document for testing purposes, follow these steps:

1. Open a new, blank document.

2. Place your cursor in the document at the point where you want the macro to insert the paragraph.

3. If you chose to assign your macro to the toolbar, click the button you created. If you assigned it to the keyboard, click the shortcut you chose.

The macro runs, repeating the steps you performed while the recorder was running, in the order in which they were performed. In the example, you'll see your cursor move in 1" to the left, and then the text will appear, bound on the right by the 1" right indent you set.

Part
V

Ch
20

Viewing Your Visual Basic Content

Even if your macro ran perfectly, you'll want to examine the Visual Basic program that made it all happen. As you recorded the steps by performing your formatting and typing actions, lines of Visual Basic programming code were written and stored in the file you named when you named your macro.

To see your Visual Basic content, follow these steps:

1. Choose Tools, Macro from the menu.
2. Select Macros from the submenu, and select your macro by name from the list.
3. Click the Edit button. Your macro opens on-screen.

Figure 20.5 shows the Visual Basic window with your macro displayed.

FIG. 20.5
Read the lines of Visual Basic code created as you recorded the steps of your macro.

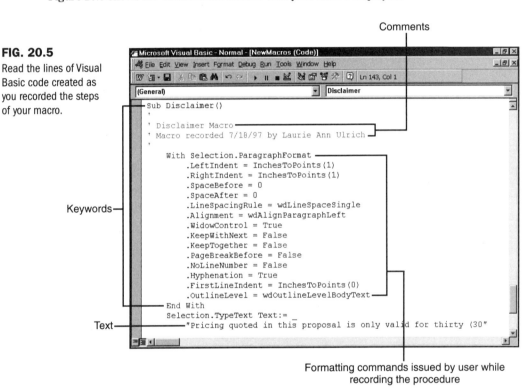

Comments

Keywords

Text

Formatting commands issued by user while recording the procedure

Each line of your procedure is called a *statement*. Those statements appear in several colors:

- The text you type while recording your macro (the disclaimer paragraph content) appears in black. Your formatting commands (the left and right indents) also appear in black.
- Comments (descriptive or instructional text) appear in green.
- Keywords (Visual Basic commands) appear in blue.

Editing a Procedure

For non-programmers and users unfamiliar with Visual Basic, editing a procedure can seem like a complex task. In this section, you will learn the basics for editing your VBA code.

Your procedure (macro) consists of four parts:

- *Headers and Footers*. Your procedure's header is either `Sub` or `Function`. The footer appears as `End Sub` (or `End Function`) and marks the end of the procedure. For macros like the disclaimer paragraph, the header will be `Sub`. You'll see `Function` headers on macros that perform calculations. The disclaimer macro's header appears in Figure 20.6.

FIG. 20.6

This figure illustrates the Disclaimer procedure's header, comments, and keywords.

```
Sub Disclaimer()
'
' Disclaimer Macro
' Macro recorded 7/18/97 by Laurie Ann Ulrich
'
```

- *Comments*. Comments are parenthetical remarks added by the user to clarify a given step in the procedure. Visual Basic doesn't act on a comment—the single quote (') that precedes it tells VB to ignore the text that follows it. It's a good idea to add comments to your procedure, especially if anyone else will be running and editing it.
- *Keywords*. Visual Basic commands appear in blue, and are part of the Visual Basic programming language. Keywords are the words that represent actions to Visual Basic. Figure 20.7 shows the keywords in the disclaimer procedure.
- *Text*. The text that you type during the recording of your macro becomes part of the Visual Basic program, preceded by a Visual Basic command. Figure 20.7 shows the text lines for the disclaimer procedure.

FIG. 20.7

Instructions to insert the text you typed while recording the macro become lines of programming code in your Visual Basic procedure.

```
Selection.TypeText Text:= _
    "Pricing quoted in this proposal is only valid for thirty (30"
Selection.TypeText Text:= _
    ") days from the date of this document as seen on page 1. Pro"
Selection.TypeText Text:= _
    "duct availability from our suppliers can affect described de"
Selection.TypeText Text:= _
    "livery dates. We will make every effort to inform you of del"
Selection.TypeText Text:= _
    "ivery delays and unforeseen changes in pricing as they occur"
Selection.TypeText Text:="  Notice will be given in writing, via fax."
```

The long underscores break lines of text into readable portions, although the lines print as continuous text when your macro is run

Using Input and Message Boxes

Input boxes and Message boxes involve your macro's user in the process of running the procedure. Input boxes ask for information that affects the content and functioning of the procedure. Message boxes let the user know what's happening behind the scenes while the procedure is running.

Adding Input boxes to your procedure enables your users to customize the content and outcome of the procedure. For example, in the disclaimer macro, it might be helpful to have a specific salesperson's name appear, along with his or her direct phone number, at the end of the disclaimer paragraph. Without an Input box to prompt the user for a name and phone number, however, the user would have to manually edit the last sentence after running the macro.

To add an Input box to the disclaimer procedure, follow these initial steps:

1. Open your macro for editing by choosing Tools, Macro, and then selecting Macros from the submenu. Select the Disclaimer macro and click the Edit button.

2. Select all the text between the Header `Sub Disclaimer()` and the Footer `End Sub`

3. Choose Edit, Copy from the menu. The selected content is now on the Clipboard.

4. Choose Insert, Procedure from the menu. The Add Procedure dialog box opens (see Figure 20.8).

FIG. 20.8

Copy and Paste the selected section of your procedure to create an Input box.

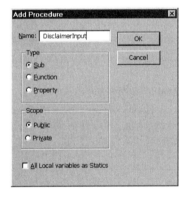

5. Type **DisclaimerInput** in the Name box. Click OK.

6. Choose Edit, Paste from the menu. This will paste the copied section into the procedure, creating a new *module*.

7. Place your cursor at the end of the line before the `End Sub` statement. Add a blank line between this last line and your `End Sub` statement by pressing Enter once.

8. Enter the `InputBox` commands and user prompts, as shown in the following. Be sure to type it exactly as it appears:

Selection.TypeParagraph

Selection.TypeText Text:="Call "

Selection.TypeText Text:=InputBox("Enter the salesrep's name:")

Selection.TypeText Text:=" at "

Selection.TypeText Text:= InputBox("Enter salesrep's phone number:")

Selection.TypeText Text:=" if you have any questions or concerns. "

Selection.TypeParagraph

N O T E The InputBox command will cause Visual Basic to open a dialog box for the macro user as soon as that step in the procedure is reached. The user will enter the requested information and click OK to continue the procedure. ■

Your new procedure now contains the Input box module, and will prompt you for information and add the new sentence at the end of the paragraph when you run the procedure. Figure 20.9 shows the Visual Basic content after adding the module.

FIG. 20.9

Your procedure now includes two InputBox commands and text for a sentence with the user's entries.

```
Selection.TypeText Text:= _
     " of delivery delays and unforeseen changes in pricing as the"
Selection.TypeText Text:= _
     "y occur. Notice will be given in writing, via fax."
Selection.TypeParagraph
Selection.TypeParagraph
Selection.TypeText Text:="Call "
Selection.TypeText Text:=InputBox("Enter the salesrep's name:")
Selection.TypeText Text:=" at "
Selection.TypeText Text:=InputBox("Enter salesrep's phone number:")
Selection.TypeText Text:="if you have any questions or concerns."
Selection.TypeParagraph
End Sub
```

InputBox commands

After the adding the Input box module, you will want to run your new procedure with Input module. To do so, follow these steps:

1. In the Visual Basic Editor window, choose File, Close and Return to Microsoft Word. Figure 20.10 shows a user Input box.

FIG. 20.10

Input boxes prompt the user to enter informa- tion that will become part of the procedure's final product.

Microsoft Word

Enter the salesrep's name:

OK

Cancel

Richard Maurone

2. To run your new procedure with the Input module, choose Tools, Macro from the menu.
3. Select Macros from the submenu. The Macros dialog box opens. Choose DisclaimerInput and click the Run button. You can also double-click your macro's name to run it.

Figure 20.11 shows the completed paragraph, as produced by the `DisclaimerInput` procedure.

The Disclaimer procedure is very simple, and the Input boxes that appear aren't going to con- fuse or alarm the users. However, in more elaborate procedures, it can be helpful to the user to offer messages at certain points during the running of the procedure. In the Disclaimer proce- dure, you could add a message box to inform the user that the procedure will be prompting them for the information about the sales representative. This can be accomplished with one simple line of Visual Basic code.

FIG. 20.11

The Disclaimer paragraph, including the added sentence and sales representative's name and phone number.

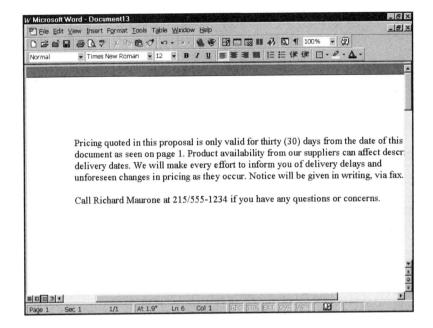

To add a message box, follow these steps:

1. Open the DisclaimerInput macro.

2. In the Visual Basic window, position your cursor at the end of the last line that reads `Selection.TypeParagraph`.

3. Press Enter.

4. On this new blank line, type the following:

   MsgBox "You will now be prompted to enter information about the salesrep."

5. Choose File, Close and Return to Microsoft Word from the menu.

6. Go to a blank document and test the DisclaimerInput macro.

Figure 20.12 shows the Message Box you added to the `DisclaimerInput` procedure as it appears when the macro is run.

FIG. 20.12

Message boxes let the user know what is happening while the macro is running. The more complex your macro is, the more message boxes you'll want to add to the procedure.

Index

Check out Que® Books on the World Wide Web
http://www.quecorp.com

As the biggest software release in computer history, Windows 95 continues to redefine the computer industry. Click here for the latest info on our Windows 95 books

Examine the latest releases in word processing, spreadsheets, operating systems, and suites

Find out about new additions to our site, new bestsellers and hot topics

Make computing quick and easy with these products designed exclusively for new and casual users

The Internet, The World Wide Web, CompuServe®, America Online®, Prodigy® —it's a world of ever-changing information. Don't get left behind!

In-depth information on high-end topics: find the best reference books for databases, programming, networking, and client/server technologies

Stay on the cutting edge of Macintosh® technologies and visual communications

A recent addition to Que, Ziff-Davis Press publishes the highly-successful *How It Works* and *How to Use* series of books, as well as *PC Learning Labs Teaches* and *PC Magazine* series of book/disc packages

Find out which titles are making headlines

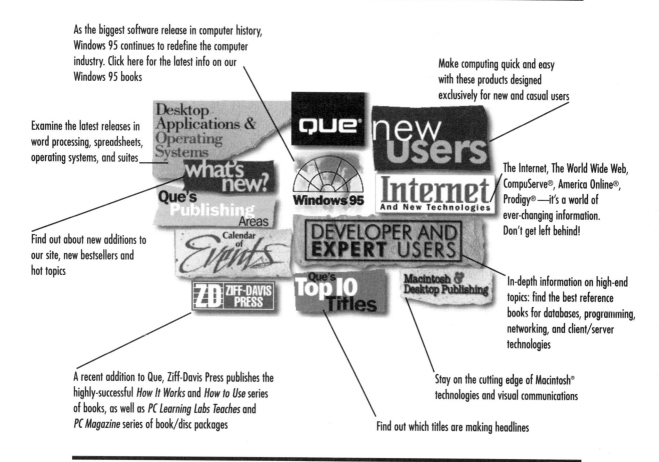

With 6 separate publishing groups, Que develops products for many specific market segments and areas of computer technology. Explore our Web Site and you'll find information on best-selling titles, newly published titles, upcoming products, authors, and much more.

- Stay informed on the latest industry trends and products available
- Visit our online bookstore for the latest information and editions
- Download software from Que's library of the best shareware and freeware

Complete and Return this Card
for a *FREE* Computer Book Catalog

Thank you for purchasing this book! You have purchased a superior computer book written expressly for your needs. To continue to provide the kind of up-to-date, pertinent coverage you've come to expect from us, we need to hear from you. Please take a minute to complete and return this self-addressed, postage-paid form. In return, we'll send you a free catalog of all our computer books on topics ranging from word processing to programming and the internet.

Mr. ☐   Mrs. ☐   Ms. ☐   Dr. ☐

Name (first) ☐☐☐☐☐☐☐☐☐☐☐☐   (M.I.) ☐   (last) ☐☐☐☐☐☐☐☐☐☐☐☐☐☐☐☐☐☐

Address ☐☐☐☐☐☐☐☐☐☐☐☐☐☐☐☐☐☐☐☐☐☐☐☐☐☐☐☐☐☐☐☐☐

☐☐☐☐☐☐☐☐☐☐☐☐☐☐☐☐☐☐☐☐☐☐☐☐☐☐☐☐☐☐☐☐☐

City ☐☐☐☐☐☐☐☐☐☐☐☐☐☐☐☐☐☐   State ☐☐   Zip ☐☐☐☐☐ ☐☐☐☐

Phone ☐☐☐ ☐☐☐ ☐☐☐☐   Fax ☐☐☐ ☐☐☐ ☐☐☐☐

Company Name ☐☐☐☐☐☐☐☐☐☐☐☐☐☐☐☐☐☐☐☐☐☐☐☐☐☐☐

E-mail address ☐☐☐☐☐☐☐☐☐☐☐☐☐☐☐☐☐☐☐☐☐☐☐☐☐☐☐☐☐☐

1. Please check at least (3) influencing factors for purchasing this book.

Front or back cover information on book .... ☐
Special approach to the content .... ☐
Completeness of content.. ☐
Author's reputation .... ☐
Publisher's reputation .... ☐
Book cover design or layout .... ☐
Index or table of contents of book .... ☐
Price of book.. ☐
Special effects, graphics, illustrations .... ☐
Other (Please specify): _____ ☐

2. How did you first learn about this book?

Saw in Macmillan Computer Publishing catalog .... ☐
Recommended by store personnel .... ☐
Saw the book on bookshelf at store .... ☐
Recommended by a friend .... ☐
Received advertisement in the mail .... ☐
Saw an advertisement in: _____ ☐
Read book review in: _____ ☐
Other (Please specify): _____ ☐

3. How many computer books have you purchased in the last six months?

This book only .... ☐   3 to 5 books .... ☐
2 books................. ☐   More than 5 .... ☐

4. Where did you purchase this book?

Bookstore .... ☐
Computer Store .... ☐
Consumer Electronics Store .... ☐
Department Store .... ☐
Office Club .... ☐
Warehouse Club .... ☐
Mail Order .... ☐
Direct from Publisher .... ☐
Internet site .... ☐
Other (Please specify): _____ ☐

5. How long have you been using a computer?

☐ Less than 6 months   ☐ 6 months to a year
☐ 1 to 3 years   ☐ More than 3 years

6. What is your level of experience with personal computers and with the subject of this book?

	With PCs	With subject of book
New	☐	.... ☐
Casual	☐	.... ☐
Accomplished	☐	.... ☐
Expert	☐	.... ☐

Source Code ISBN: 0-7897-1441-8

7. Which of the following best describes your job title?

- Administrative Assistant ☐
- Coordinator ☐
- Manager/Supervisor ☐
- Director ☐
- Vice President ☐
- President/CEO/COO ☐
- Lawyer/Doctor/Medical Professional ☐
- Teacher/Educator/Trainer ☐
- Engineer/Technician ☐
- Consultant ☐
- Not employed/Student/Retired ☐
- Other (Please specify): _____ ☐

8. Which of the following best describes the area of the company your job title falls under?

- Accounting ☐
- Engineering ☐
- Manufacturing ☐
- Operations ☐
- Marketing ☐
- Sales ☐
- Other (Please specify): _____ ☐

9. What is your age?

- Under 20 ☐
- 21-29 ☐
- 30-39 ☐
- 40-49 ☐
- 50-59 ☐
- 60-over ☐

10. Are you:

- Male ☐
- Female ☐

11. Which computer publications do you read regularly? (Please list)

_____
_____
_____
_____
_____
_____
_____
_____
_____
_____

Comments: _____
_____
_____

Fold here and scotch-tape to mail.

MACMILLAN COMPUTER PUBLISHING USA

A VIACOM COMPANY

Technical ---- Support:

If you need assistance with the information in this book or with a CD/Disk accompanying the book, please access the Knowledge Base on our Web site at **http://www.superlibrary.com/general/support**. Our most Frequently Asked Questions are answered there. If you do not find the answer to your questions on our Web site, you may contact Macmillan Technical Support **(317) 581-3833** or e-mail us at **support@mcp.com**.